THE BEST OF ALL THINGS
GOLF

*An Exploration of the Best Travel,
Courses, Architects, Players, Books,
Movies, & Hobbies*

JACK M. HAMMEL

All photographs in this book are by the author, Jack M. Hammel, or his family members.

© 2023 Jack M. Hammel

All rights reserved. No part of this publication may be reproduced, distributed, or transmitted in any form or by any means, including photocopying, recording, or other electronic or mechanical methods, without the prior written permission of the publisher, except in the case of brief quotations embodied in critical reviews and certain other non-commercial uses permitted by copyright law.

ISBN: 979-8-35092-863-1

*To my wife, Kathy,
whose daily expressions of the virtues
of humility, kindness, laughter, love, and faith
serve as a constant inspiration
and a window through which
to see the meaning of life.*

CONTENTS

Preface 1

CHAPTER I Links to The Links of Scotland & Ireland, and a
Day in the Park(lands) 4

CHAPTER II Golf in the Major Regions of the USA 79

CHAPTER III The Best Courses (Ranking of the Top 100 Courses Played
* Plus Architect & 5 Star Scale Rating) 148

CHAPTER IV The Best Golf Architects (Top 10) 153

CHAPTER V The Best Golfers (And the Greatest of Them All) 159

CHAPTER VI The Best Golf Books (Top 50) 176

CHAPTER VII The Best Golf Movies 187

CHAPTER VIII Playing Hickory Golf 190

CHAPTER IX The Ultimate Home Golf Retreat – Collecting Golf
Antiques, Reproductions & Other Decor 194

CHAPTER X And for Dessert - Future Golf Trips & Lessons Learned 211

APPENDIX I List of All Courses Played by Location According to
Star Rating (in alphabetical order) Plus Architect 226

APPENDIX II A Par 72 Dream Course Consisting of the Best 18 Holes
From the Best Courses Played List 235

APPENDIX III A Par 27 Dream Short Course Consisting of the 9 Best Par-3s
From the Best Courses Played List 236

APPENDIX IV The Hidden Gems List 237

Acknowledgments 239

About the Author 240

PREFACE

Royal Troon Par-3 8th "Postage Stamp" Hole

While I very much enjoy playing the game of golf, I have, over the past 25 years or so, developed an almost equal "interest" (a more euphemistic term than "addiction") in other facets of the sport. It began with Golf Channel marathons and recording virtually every professional tournament. (Watching live risks losing your mind from the seemingly endless torture of repeated commercials about golf equipment, retirement investing, cholesterol reduction, insurance, and erectile dysfunction.) This led to a desire to read magazines, and then books (over 1,000 to date!) about golf instruction and history, as well as those detailing the relative merits of courses, architects and players, along with numerous golf novels. And, of course, the golf-obsessed individual winds up watching every golf movie ever made - at least twice - and several up to a dozen times. Next stop, vacations that include an opportunity to play golf once or twice, followed by some golf-specific travel, both at home and abroad (approximately 250 courses thus far). Then came the need for a special room in the house with a golf atmosphere consisting of paintings, prints, books, antique balls and tees, hickory shafted clubs, statuary, waste baskets, clocks, etc. Upon moving into our retirement village home, the golf room turned into golf *rooms*, including the guest bathroom and the golf cart section of the garage, which was transformed into an old-school locker room/museum. This led to the natural conclusion that the backyard would seem out of place without a short pitching hole, complete with a formal tee box area. And then came the discovery of, and participation in, a Hickory golf society, which not only holds tournaments but also involves players wearing retro attire such as plus fours, dress shirts, ties, and flat caps. There's more, but hopefully you get the picture that my passion for the game includes not only many rounds of golf, but also a well-rounded interest in everything it offers off the course.

This books aims to introduce the reader to some possibly new areas of golf interest or to assist in expanding existing ones. It will save you time by furnishing you with, if you will, a form of golf "Cliffs Notes." By reading a single book, you will obtain the knowledge necessary to participate intelligently in discussions and debates about the greatest golf travel, courses, architects, players, books, and movies. The course reviews and rankings can inform and facilitate the selection of your "bucket list" of golf courses. They will also assist you in planning your travel to the great linkslands and beyond. In addition, you will learn how easy it is to decorate your home inexpensively with golf collectibles, while also getting a quick primer on hickory golf. And, finally, you can join me in the 19th hole grill room of your choice for a pint. Here, we will discuss unfinished golf travel business and how lessons learned in golf can keep us in the fairway of life. But, first, I will share with you a brief introduction to my golf game (and promise to say little more on the subject thereafter) so that some of the commentary and opinions, particularly concerning the referenced courses played and favored, might have a little context.

I would describe myself as a good, but by no means great, golfer. When I was 40, I began to focus more seriously on the game, regularly playing/practicing at least once a week. At that time, I carried a handicap of around 20. Within 10 years, following an extra day of play per week, it dropped to single digit, where it has remained without interruption for 15 years, bottoming out at a 4, but more typically in the 5-8 range. One of my highlights as a player includes shooting a 72 (4 under par 31 on the back nine) at the famous King's Course at Gleneagles in Scotland. This score was facilitated by an eagle, par, hole in one, par, birdie on the final five holes - achieved after 54 sleepless hours due to a wide-eyed overnight flight, then purposefully staying awake after arrival until late in the evening in an attempt to conform sleep hours to the time zone change, only to be rewarded with a good old fashioned case of exhausted insomnia!

I won the gross score 36 hole club championship at each of our retirement community's two courses in the same year, strongly aided by our three lowest handicappers being away on vacation. However, my proudest moment in golf came a few post-pandemic lockdown years later when the championship was held as a single, two-day, 36 hole tournament played over both courses. The field consisted of approximately 80 men aged 55 or older, including 16 individuals carrying a single digit course handicap (a few at scratch). I finished third among the gross scores, shooting eight over par for the 36 holes, one stroke behind the second-place finisher, and tied the score of the defending champion (and ultimate winner) on the second day of play (but, alas, it was not enough to catch up with his brilliant 68 on the first day). Aside from the satisfaction of playing well against a strong field, I was grateful to bounce back from an abysmal finish in the final group of the previous year's championship, when an off-and-on battle with the yips (involuntary jerking of the right hand just before impact) returned with a vengeance - the curse of being told too often that one is a great putter! Over the years, I had tried several "fixes" for the yips, and they would work for a while only to return without warning. Then, shortly before the above-referenced third-place championship finish, I adopted a method that makes it almost physically impossible to yip, and I have not had even a hint of one since. So, what is the method? To find out, I invite you to read on. If you are a golf addict, I suspect you will!

CHAPTER I

Links to The Links of Scotland & Ireland, and a Day in the Park(lands)

Doonbeg Par-4 15th Hole£

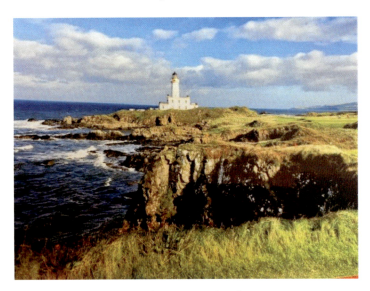

Turnberry Par-3 9th Hole

SCOTLAND

THE BEST OF ALL THINGS GOLF

IRELAND

1. Corballis
2. The Island
3. Portmarnock
4. Portmarnock Hotel
5. The K Club
6. Druids Glen
7. Old Head
8. Dooks
9. Tralee
10. Ballybunion (Old & New)
11. Doonbeg
12. Lahinch
13. Adare (Manor)
14. Adare (Club)
15. Dromoland
16. Ashford Castle
17. Carne
18. Ennsicrone
19. Sligo
20. Strandhill
21. Donegal
22. Rosapenna (Sandy Hills, Tom Morris & St. Pat.)
23. Port Salon
24. Port Stewart
25. Royal Port Rush
26. Ardglass
27. Royal County Dn.

This chapter focuses on my introduction to, and ultimate immersion in, the fascinating world of "links" courses in Scotland and Ireland. These feature nonarable sandy topsoil, a virtual absence of trees, windswept undulations, ridges and dunes, and meandering burns (streams) on ocean-receded coastal land (including seaside cliff courses even though, in some cases, these do not, technically, share all the attributes of true "links"). However, parkland (i.e., inland) courses should not be anathema when traveling to these countries. Mere USA-style "transplants," no, but parkland courses with distinctive Scottish and Irish characters can expand the golf palate and provide lasting memories. For example, when was the last time you played an American course that included a centuries-old castle, abbey ruin, or quaint hundreds-of-years-old village in full view? The discerning golf traveler can find this form of magnificence within a rainbow's distance from some of the best links courses in the area. Moreover, the accommodations and/or dining facilities associated with these inland courses are often themselves former castles and manor houses. Here, one can relax amid antique furnishings and admire the rich paneled wood and rock walls laced with historical paintings and prints, armor, and other artifacts depicting the local culture and history. As such, both the golf and the après golf can be fully embraceable experiences in non-links settings.

In short, you are missing essential elements of these golf islands if you bounce from one links course to the next and shun the inland layouts out of a myopic sense of wanting to be a "traditionalist." While the focus can and should be the links that are so unique and abundant in this part of the world, room should be reserved for a parkland course or two when visiting the auld sod.

So, hop aboard; it's time to travel to the home of golf!

TRIP 1 –
St. Andrews Links (Old Course) - (May 1982)

In 1981/1982 I spent my second year of law school studying abroad at the University of Notre Dame's facility in the Mayfair District of London. One of my classmates had done some homework and ascertained that a tee time could be secured at the Old Course at St. Andrews for a student rate of $20. Yes. $20! He proposed a fast and furious weekend trip to take advantage of this opportunity.

It didn't take much prodding to convince me and another classmate to go for the green. The getaway was not without its trials and tribulations, but the sojourn to golf's Mecca was undoubtedly worth it as it planted the seed of a love affair with links golf that actually would not break the ground's surface until 30 years later. Fortunately, I kept an informal journal of that year abroad; so here is an extract reflecting that unforgettable weekend:

"Up at 6:30 AM for the big St. Andrews weekend. Paul, Haig and I picked up a Mini Metro at the rental car joint and headed out. None of us had ever driven on the other side of the road before; so things were a bit hairy at first. (I couldn't drive because I left my license at home in the USA.) After a while, we got used to the roundabouts, which are big circles with cars coming in from all directions. Once you are in, you have the right-of-way. We made it to York at about noon and had a nice pub lunch followed by a quick look at the cathedral and medieval walls. The sign system is the worst I've ever seen – or should I say: "Didn't see?" We spent two hours trying to get through three cities as there were no by-passes. We spent the night in Edinburgh in the same little B&B where I'd stayed during a vacation break while studying abroad in 1978. Got up early Saturday morning for what was to be one of the best days of my life. Headed for the home stretch to St. Andrews amid beautiful sunshine and scenery. Our hotel was two blocks from the Old Course. Walked to the Starter's hut to ensure our 3:28 PM tee time was still OK. Looked great to see my name posted on the board adjacent to the Royal and Ancient clubhouse. We walked around the university town built of solid, homogenous stone. It is quaint, with the cathedral and castle ruins perched on cliffs with the raging sea below. We ate at an old pub named "The Niblick" with rock walls and antique furnishings. (Today the "Golf Inn" at One Golf Place.) Then we went back to the Starter's hut to pick up our brand new rental clubs. Practiced a little before the warmth and sunshine turned to frigid, windy, and overcast conditions. We retreated indoors to order some hot chocolate and scones. We returned and teed off in triple layers and ski caps in the thick of cold, howling winds and hail. We stood 10 feet apart and still couldn't hear each other, even when yelling! It didn't take long before we lost a couple of balls in the bright yellow, thorny gorse plants. We quickly realized why links golf can be particularly difficult. But, Irish luck was with us as the weather broke on the 6th hole, becoming sunny and relatively warm, and staying that way, for the most part, for the balance of the round. My big thrill was sinking a 35-foot downhill putt that snaked its way among several large moguls. Haig and I were tied as we stepped up to the final tee. With the slowly setting sun beaming against the R&A clubhouse, and the Swilcan bridge in the foreground, it felt like we were on television playing in the British Open. That night, we had a big steak dinner (the first one in eight months). Sunday, we drove back to London immersed in a terrific storm, but made it safe and sound."

And, so, I received my links golf baptism. While I loved the "Auld Grey Toon," and the sense of history that oozed from the hallowed ground of its Old Course, I can't say that my introduction to links golf, from a pure playing perspective, was love at first sight. It's not like I couldn't see the forest for the trees. There was no forest, and there were no trees! Growing up, when I occasionally played the game, I was used to Ohio's warm summer weather, relatively pristine course conditions, and "fair", wooded layouts. Random pot bunkers in the middle of fairways? Other, revetted (stacked sod) bunkers so large and deep they look like the remnants of a B-52 Bomber drop? A one-lane road named Granny's Wynd bisecting the first and eighteenth fairways? Massive, undulating double greens? All so foreign.

Amazement, but not love, at first sight. I later learned this was a first impression shared by many of the most outstanding American professionals going back over a century. Tom Watson (five-time British Open (aka "Open") champion, but never at St. Andrews) had this to say about his first impression of the Old Course: "... one of strange ambiguousness. I didn't like it, nor for that matter, did I hate it." In 1946, Sam Snead decided to play in the Open at St. Andrews. He was looking out the window of the train as it was nearing the train station that was then located near the Old Course. He asked the fellow next to him the name of the "abandoned golf course." The startled gentleman sternly informed him that the course was, indeed, St. Andrews! Snead would soon compete on that "unkempt" course for the Open's claret jug (and win). This was his first and last appearance at the Open during his prime. He complained that the $600 prize money didn't even begin to cover his travel expenses. The first time a young (and, at that time, temperamental) Bobby Jones played St.

Andrews, in the 1921 Open, he became so frustrated with the unbridled nature of the course that he tore up his card and stomped off in frustration. Yet, several decades later - after having won both the Open and the British Amateur there - he made the following comment at a ceremony where he was only the second American to be named an honorary citizen of the city (Ben Franklin was the first and Jack Nicklaus became the third in 2022): "I could take out of my life everything except my experiences at St. Andrews and I would still have a rich, full life." No wonder the Scots called Jones "Our Bobby." This Bobby is even more cherished among the Scots than "Greyfriars Bobby," a Skye Terrier dog revered for standing guard by the grave of his owner for 14 years before he, too, died. (A popular statue/fountain commemorating Greyfriars Bobby is located near the George IV Bridge and the National Museum of Scotland in Edinburgh, as is a pub named after him.)

Famed golf course architect Alister MacKenzie emphasized that a good golf course often needs to grow on one like a good painting, music, etc. So true for me as it pertains to the Old Course at St Andrews. Many years later, having played dozens of great links courses, I came to fully appreciate the numerous seminal features of this layout, and the singular town hugging it tightly and affectionately like a newborn child. I also better understood that courses shaped mainly by nature, not bulldozers, will not always be fair. But, they do better reflect the spirit and conditions that influenced those who invented the game. George Duncan, winner of the 1920 Open, perhaps summed up the Old Course best when he said: "St. Andrews has got character and features that you find nowhere else. You can play a damned good shot and find the ball in a damned bad place. That is the real game of golf." (And probably why match play and stableford have been the favored formats on links courses over the centuries. Under match play rules the player plays directly against the opponent in a head-to-head match, rather than comparing total strokes played at the end of the round, as is done in medal play. The player wins a hole by completing it in the least number of strokes, and wins the match when winning by more holes than remain to be played. So, for example, a person who is up by three holes, with two left to play, would be the winner of the match. In stableford scoring, the objective is to get the most points, rather than the lowest score. One point is earned for a bogey, two for a par, three for a birdie, four for an eagle and five for an albatross. Double-bogies and worse get zero points. In short, these two formats allow the classic round-wrecking "blow-up" hole(s) experienced in medal play to be tossed and forgotten. They allow you to forget the total score, and remember the total game!)

TRIP 2 –

Ashford Castle/Adare Golf Club (Manor Resort Course)/Adare Manor Golf Club (Abbey Course)/Ballybunion Golf Club (May 2013)

The year 2013 was a time for celebration. I retired from my long-term role as In-House Legal Counsel for the Archdiocese of San Francisco. After 18 years living in the South Bay, we moved into our newly built North Bay home in the Sonoma Valley wine country village of Oakmont. Our daughter, Michelle, graduated from college. And, in May, my wife, Kathy, and I (and Michelle as a graduation gift) departed for Ireland. It was not a golf trip per se (I didn't bring my clubs, and Ballybunion was the only scheduled course) but, as things turned out, I weaved in some nice parkland golf experiences.

We landed at the Shannon airport and were met by our prearranged driver, Tommy Walsh. (By the end of the trip he was like family and, in subsequent years, we referred him to other family and friends who adopted him as one of their own. Warning. As a former trucker, Tommy has a lead foot!) We like to think of our homes as castles in the figurative sense. But, for a few days, our home was a castle in the literal form. Tommy dropped us off at Ashford Castle, the former residence of the Guinness (beer) family. During his first term as President, Ronald Reagan stayed here on a visit to his family's land of origin. Having mostly slept on overnight trains and 2-star pensions when traveling during my studies abroad in college and law school, this castle stay was more than a night and day difference. Keep in mind, however, that luxury hotels in Great Britain and Ireland are frequently half the price of those in the USA. So don't rule out a splurge here and there when making your travel plans. The castle is located a short walk from the tiny village of Cong in County Mayo. It was here that the slightly campy but endearing John Wayne/Maureen O'Hara movie "The Quiet Man" was filmed. And, for goodness sake, **Ashford Castle** even has a nine hole golf course designed by Eddie Hackett. It's nice, but not a show-stopper. Nevertheless, the views of the castle, Lough (lake) Corrib, and a shamrock-shaped bunker from various vantage points enhance its appeal.

After a couple of splendid day trips to Croagh Patrick (as in the holy mountain of Ireland's patron saint) and the lovely town of Westport, it was time for Tommy (actually Tommy's daughter, Karen, who subbed that day and drove quite a bit slower) to take us to the popular little village of Adare in County Limerick. But, not before stops at the lively city of Galway, the Burren (a vast, treeless, cryptic-looking fissured base of glacial-era limestone), a couple of fishing villages, castles in ruin, and the Cliffs of Moher.

Adare is frequently described as Ireland's prettiest village. Competition for that title is keen, but Adare certainly is up there with its beautifully maintained thatched-roof homes and shops. We avoided a letdown after our digs in a castle by staying at the Adare Manor resort. While not as expansive as Ashford Castle, it certainly shares its "rustic" elegance. And the rooms are enormous. Our bathroom alone, with its huge leaded glass panel windows, was as big as a standard hotel room in the USA. **Adare Manor** also has its own golf course, an 18 hole championship length design by Robert Trent Jones Sr. Tom Fazio recently gave it a significant facelift as part of a multi-million dollar makeover of both the Manor and course. It will host the 2027 Ryder Cup. The girls encouraged me to play it while they walked to the village to shop and visit a quaint tea house. It was delightful, particularly the several holes that play within view of the centuries-old ruins of a Franciscan friary and Desmond Castle, and the par-5 dog leg 18th hole that finishes with a shot over the Maigue river to a green adjacent to the Manor. I played the course before the revisions were made. I am told that it is now so meticulously pristine that some promoters refer to it as the "Augusta of Ireland." I suspect that is a bit of a stretch, but I wouldn't mind finding out. (That is, if I was invited to play a complimentary round in a Pro-Am, since the cost to play has doubled.)

Adare proved to be an excellent base camp for several memorable day trips. Sandwiched between these outings was yet another parkland course surprise. I mentioned the abbey and castle ruins next to the Manor's resort course. However, a second course (somewhat confusingly named "**Adare Manor Golf Club**") actually winds its way through these ruins. I assumed it would be very costly and difficult to get on. In fact, I walked right up to the pro shop, paid my $50, and was informed that the first tee was mine. The designer? Eddie Hackett strikes again! It was an incredibly unique experience and terrific fun.

And now, it was almost time for Ballybunion. But first, a horseback riding adventure! Michelle had always been fond of animals, but was particularly attracted to horses. As such, she attended a couple of pony camps during summers as a preteen. So, a guided horseback ride through the bucolic countryside to a ruined castle was at the top of her list during our stay at Adare. Her mother wasn't feeling particularly well and opted to get some rest. That left me as Michelle's riding partner. At the stable we were given a quick lesson on the Irish riding style. If I recall correctly, horses are fitted with a smaller, less comfortable saddle than those used in the USA, and the rider is required to keep time with the horse's three-beat gait canter by having their hips follow the up and down motion of the horse's back in quick succession. In short, it involved a lot of work and pain for an aging dad, so I fudged when the guide wasn't looking! Michelle thoroughly enjoyed the several-hour experience and was no worse for the wear. I, however, crawled out of bed the next day with every joint and muscle from the waist down crying in agony. But Ballybunion beckoned.

The exhilaration felt upon seeing County Kerry's renowned **Ballybunion** course, set amid the gigantic dunes and splashing ocean waves (along with the double dose of Advil I'd taken), pushed my thoughts of pain aside. Soon after checking in at the modern clubhouse, it was time to tee off. I was so amped that I didn't even notice the bone-chilling high winds. As for the girls, after taking a few snapshots, they leaped into the car for refuge from the elements and were on their way for some sightseeing, thinking their husband/father was out of his mind to pay hundreds of dollars for this experience.

I was introduced to my Junior level caddie, a local student who admittedly had spent much more time in life on the soccer fields than playing the game of golf. He was a very nice young man but, by the end of the round, his caddie "skills" made me think "Mr. Magoo." I managed to stay in the fairway most of the day. However, on the half dozen occasions when my ball did stray into the tall, wispy fescue, Mr. Magoo couldn't find it. Fortunately, I did. His lack of visual acuity and/or course knowledge also extended to green reading, as it was quite a bit off the mark. None of this detracted from a most rewarding first exposure to Irish links golf. The uniqueness begins on the first hole with an old graveyard on the right, ready to find a permanent resting place for sliced tee shots, without the need to hire a hearse. I was also fond of the visually seductive and relatively short, par-3 8th hole. However, beware, as it contains subtle features that can severely punish a shot that does not land in the proper place on or about the green. The most famous hole is the par-4 11th, with its commanding views of the rugged coastline. Its combined length and exposure to the harsh sea winds present quite a challenge. And there is the thinking man's par-5 16th hole. The tee shot requires a long carry over the thick grass when the wind is up. Then one must decide whether to lay up on the second shot or attempt to hit it through a narrow chute that leads to the green below. My favorite hole, however, is the par-4 17th. The dogleg begins from an elevated tee and works its way down to sea level. After negotiating the colossal dune on the left side of the fairway off the tee, one faces an approach shot with a grass bunker guarding the front of the green and an amphitheater-like dune area behind it.

Some view Ballybunion as the best course in Ireland. I would later visit others that, according to my rating factors, surpass it. However, despite its highly demanding nature, there is no denying that it is a special place. Renowned golf writer Herbert Warren Wind felt that it was the finest seaside course he'd ever seen. Tom Watson's sentiments were unequivocal: "Nobody can call themselves a golfer until they have played at Ballybunion; you would think the game originated there."

The following day Tommy dropped us off in Limerick, where we boarded the train for an enjoyable day trip to Dublin. The next day we found ourselves on a day trip to Killarney. Yes, it was a little touristy, but we embraced the tidy town, its fine cathedral, and the carriage ride through the park to the castle. Watching our recent college graduate revert to the ways of carefree children, skipping her way among the gigantic and numerous rhododendrons in full bloom was, alone, worth the excursion.

Tommy drove us to the airport in the morning, and after an emotional goodbye, we boarded our plane for home. But, I knew that I would be back someday.

TRIP 3 –

Royal Troon/Prestwick GC/Turnberry/North Berwick GC/Royal Dornoch/ Castle Stuart GC/Cruden Bay GC/Kingsbarns GL/Elie GC/St. Andrews Links (New Course) - (October 2017)

October of 2017 was my first trip abroad where the primary purpose was golf. It was also my first (and last) trip where I utilized the services of a professional golf tour company. It's not that these companies are a bad choice, particularly if you are planning a trip for a large group of players (e.g., more than four). It's just that I came to learn that it is considerably cheaper, and not very difficult, to simply make the travel, lodging, and course tee times myself via the internet. Moreover, while a select few tour companies (and elite hotels) have guaranteed tee time arrangements (some requiring a minimum of four players) with limited access courses such as St. Andrews and Muirfield, many others can not make a guarantee at the time you book through them. What they do is facilitate the process of applying for a tee time in advance and, if unsuccessful, enter you in the daily ballot for a few reserved spots/cancellations after your arrival. The company I used said they could not guarantee a tee time at St. Andrews, but had never failed to ultimately get someone on. I guess my friend Denis and I turned out to be their first! In fairness, we did not pursue their suggested doomsday option on our final day - getting in line at three in the morning to wait for any same-day, single golfer, walk-on openings that might arise sometime during the day. Nevertheless, we enjoyed having St. Andrews as a base for the final leg of our trip. As noted earlier, I was fortunate to have played the Old Course during my college years (albeit as a novice). And Denis was a go-with-the-flow individual who was happy just to play in Scotland - surprisingly for the first time, even though he hails from the nearby golfing island of Ireland.

I met Denis when we were paired together at my home course a couple of years before our trip to Scotland. His kids wound up settling in the USA, so he and his wife split their time between Ireland and the states. Despite the fact that he is highly intelligent and witty, I soon labeled him "The Absent-Minded Professor" given his penchant for being late, misplacing things, misremembering dates and times, etc. We learned that while we shared a common Irish heritage, we were often on opposite sides of political/social issues (e.g., Republican platform versus Democrat). Yet, unlike the increasingly polarized and tribal society we find ourselves in, Denis and I enjoy a respectful give and take on a variety of subjects and frequently find common ground. So, I did not hesitate when he asked if he might join me on my golf journey to Scotland.

I arrived at the Glasgow airport, where Denis awaited with his Volvo station wagon that he had brought with him on the ferry from Ireland. Soon thereafter, we arrived at our first stop, Troon, located on Scotland's southwest coast. The Marine Troon Hotel is next to the **Royal Troon** clubhouse, and my large room came with a French door window leading to a balcony that offered an incredible view overlooking the 18th green. After a leisurely dinner in the hotel, I was pleasantly surprised to immediately fall asleep and wake up, well rested, eight hours later. After checking in at the pro shop, I took a delightful stroll through the museum-like clubhouse. Then, it was time to play this James Braid design.

True to form, the weather was overcast and windy, but the excitement kept the body warm. My first impression was the course was a bit bland insofar as it did not have the massive dunescapes that I'd experienced at Ballybunion. But, worse was the fact that it seemed so unfair as there were random pot bunkers all over the fairways. Additionally, I soon learned that landing the ball on the green with a "perfect" shot was seldom rewarded as it would be in the USA. The first seven holes are downwind. This circumstance, along with the tightly mowed fairways, often sent balls landing on or about the green well off the back. So, I spent a good part of the round trying to maneuver the frequently required low and roll links style of play.

Everyone faces the famous short, par-3 "Postage Stamp" 8th hole with a combined sense of exhilaration and fear. It has an elevated tee overlooking a gully. The narrow green, set against a large sandhill, is well protected by several cavernous, steep-faced bunkers. The difficulty is heightened when the winds are up, which typically is the case. Fortunately, at this point, my club choice and trajectory adjustments paid off as I managed an easy tap-in par on this often round wrecking hole. (In 1997, Tiger Woods' brilliant 64 in the third round of the Open had him in contention in the final round - until he recorded a 6 on the Postage Stamp hole. Another contestant in that same tournament missed the cut after obtaining a 10 on it. But these scores can't quite compare to the 15 taken by a German amateur attempting to qualify for the 1950 Open!)

The back nine plays extra long with its severe headwinds. While not my favorite from an aesthetics point of view, it was a thrill to play a course so steeped in history. Just 15 minutes down the road, an even more historic venue greeted us the following day.

Prestwick Golf Club doesn't have the designation "Royal," but we felt like golf royalty there. The relatively small clubhouse is classic "old school," and the staff was extremely welcoming and kind. The course, designed by Old Tom Morris, is lovingly quirky though not long enough to host the Open anymore. However, it hosted 24 of them (including the first twelve) between 1860 and 1925, second only to the Old Course at St. Andrews. All the holes have a certain charm, but several have a uniqueness about them that lets you know you are not in Kansas anymore! A couple of the most famous include the par-3 5th hole ("Himalayas"), hit blindly from the tee over a huge sandhill, and the par-4 17th ("Alps"), which requires another blind approach shot over a large hill, with the vast "Sahara" bunker waiting on the other side, fronting the punch bowl green. Ironically, the biggest adrenaline rush came *after* the round in the locker room, where we spent 30 minutes looking for the Absent-Minded Professor's car keys!

Next stop, **Turnberry** (technically "Trump Turnberry Resort"). Once again, just a short drive from the previous course. And, in between rounds, one can admire the beautiful villages of Ayrshire (the land of Scotland's national poet Robert Burns) and Culzean Castle (which General Eisenhower used as his headquarters prior to the Normandy invasion and where the top floor was later reserved for his lifetime use). Say what you will about his politics/personality; after assuming ownership of Turnberry Donald Trump commissioned some magnificent revisions in 2016. These were made to an already fine Open venue - most famous for the 1977 "Dual in the Sun," won by Tom Watson over Jack Nicklaus, and the sad 2009 playoff loss by Watson (at age 59!) to Stewart Cink. We ran into a steady mixture of cold, wind and rain, and I had my worst score of the trip. Still, I thoroughly enjoyed the round. The course has a little bit of everything, from fairway valleys amid dunes to shots over the ocean to an ubiquitous lighthouse. The clear favorite is the remodeled par-3 ninth hole (formerly a par-4). The shot plays over the rocky coast to a green adjacent to the lighthouse. While the hotel is a bit over-the-top, it commands an extremely majestic position above the course. It is quite comfortable and convenient, albeit pricey.

Edinburgh, with its majestic castle standing guard atop its own Rock of Gibraltar, served as the perfect location for a sightseeing rest day. We stayed at The Royal Scots Club, housed in a small, stately, and reasonably priced Georgian building across from a park and just a short walk to the city center attractions.

The next morning, we took a peaceful 25-mile coastal drive east to **North Berwick** to play its outstanding West Course, designed primarily by David Strath. There is more than a hint of St. Andrews about the place as the 18th hole plays along a row of residences and hotels, and the old clubhouse abuts the shore and quaint city. Like Prestwick, North Berwick Golf Club has a number of unique holes, including the most copied one in golf - the par-3 15th "Redan" (named after a Russian earthwork fortification erected during the Crimean War). Another, virtual one-of-a-kind, hole is the par-4 13th (the "Pit"), where the fairway plays along an old stone wall which then immediately fronts a sunken green, behind which is a large sandhill and the sea. And then there is the par-4 16th hole, which essentially consists of two greens separated by a deep swale. North Berwick is an extraordinarily distinctive and fun course. The next day it was time to head for Dornoch in the far north Scottish Highlands.

Given that this was the longest drive of our trip, we made a couple of nice leg-stretching stops. First, we explored the impressive ruins of Urquhart Castle, which overlooks Loch Ness - home of its shy monster, "Nessie." We then visited the excellent museum at the Culloden Battlefield (where the British defeated Bonnie Prince Charlie and his Scottish Highlanders in 1746 - the recreation of which you may have witnessed on the popular television series "Outlander"). An hour or so later, we entered the lovely little village of Dornoch, home of **Royal Dornoch Golf Club** and the birthplace of famed course architect Donald Ross. After an apprenticeship at St. Andrews under Old Tom Morris, Ross served as head greenskeeper here before moving to the United States.

We checked in at the Royal Dornoch Hotel, which sits resplendently above the first tee. While Dornoch is relatively remote, it has, over the past few decades, rightly earned its classification as a must-play Scottish links venue.

And, in fact, after finishing several rounds there, Tom Watson said: "The most fun I ever had playing golf." Here, Old Tom Morris once again left his mark of great course design. Royal Dornoch sits on a plateau, offering a commanding panorama of land and sea. The layout takes full advantage of these in a most natural way. The surrounding hills and barriers are saturated with spiky gorse plants that bloom in brilliant yellow when in season (unfortunately, not much during our stay). Proper shot angles and accuracy are critical as there are many elevated undulating greens with steep drop offs. The most famous hole, the par-4 14th ("Foxy") was considered by Harry Vardon to be "the most natural" par-4 in golf. Surprisingly, it is bunkerless yet quite challenging due to its length and wide, narrow, elevated green.

The next day, we played a relative newcomer, **Castle Stuart,** a Gil Hanse design built in 2009 but already a four-time host of the Scottish Open. It boasts a very modern-style clubhouse with splendid views. Fairways are ample in width. The par-3s are the stars (three hugging the Moray Firth and another aiming straight through the hills, with Castle Stuart in the background). The par-5 18th is one of the best finishing holes in golf, a dogleg facing the clubhouse from the tee and then turning right toward a green perched on a little peninsula overlooking the estuary. For those looking to play a well-conditioned links course in a not overly penal setting (minimizing your chances of losing those quality balls you brought), with a variety of well-laid-out holes offering beautiful views, Castle Stuart will fit the bill.

We then loaded our clubs and headed east for a round at **Cruden Bay Golf Club,** one of the true icons of golf, not only in Scotland, but the world. Like Royal Dornoch, it took some time for Cruden Bay to be "discovered" by golfers outside of Great Britain. But, today, it has obtained near cult status among serious students of golf history and natural architecture, as well as those simply wanting to play something truly unique and fun. However, given that many serious golfers are still unfamiliar with Cruden Bay, it deserves classification as a large jewel in the crown of Hidden Gems. Once again, Tom Morris gets the credit for the initial layout, though Tom Simpson made a number of revisions in 1926. The course meanders through giant dunes, crosses burns, and offers some spectacular views of the bay (and Slain's Castle - the inspiration for Stoker's "Dracula"). There are a couple of reachable par-4s, several blind shots, and a few sunken greens. My only complaint (which I later learned I shared with noted golf architect Tom Doak) is that they have allowed thick rough to intrude on the play in order to add more challenges. Hopefully, they have reconsidered that approach. If a fair amount of quirkiness is not your cup of tea, steer clear. But, if you enjoy playing a "different" course, such as North Berwick, then Cruden Bay will not disappoint. As for our lodging, the nearby historic Kilmarnock Arms Hotel was modest, tasteful and cozy. The pub-style restaurant offers a meat medley dinner option to die for while you stay warm by the rock-walled fireplace.

Our final destination was the incomparable golf town of St. Andrews, located 30 miles northeast of Edinburgh. En route, we paid a quick visit to Glamis Castle, one of the settings for Shakespeare's Macbeth. The Best Western Scores Hotel served as our headquarters. (I understand it recently changed ownership, with significant renovations undertaken.) It proved to be an excellent choice. My room overlooked the long beach strand behind the Royal and Ancient Clubhouse. You know, the one featured in the film "Chariots of Fire," where a couple of dozen British Olympic hopefuls can be seen running through the lapping water's edge in what appears to be their underwear while reverberating Vangelis music blares away. We dined at the historic Jigger Inn, next to the Old Course's famous "Road Hole." (A Jigger was a low lofted hickory shafted club primarily used for low approach and chip shots.) The Inn once served as the small lodge of the station master of the former St. Andrews Links railway station. Pub grub and ales are the mainstay of this lively little 19th on the 17th.

Failing to win the ballot for spots on the Old Course, we played the Old Tom Morris-designed **Elie** (aka "The Golf House Club"), where the celebrated golfer/designer James Braid grew up and honed his skills and later made some revisions to the course. The club installed a practical and enchanting feature to deal with the fact that the shot from the tee on the first hole is a blind one. They placed a World War II periscope in the pro shop! Once the Starter gives the thumbs up, you are ready to ship off to play a distinctive layout next to the village and the sea. If you have an affinity for par-4s, you will encounter no less than 16 of them! I did have one strange experience here. While I was changing in the locker room an elderly, mustached gentleman stepped in. He was wearing an impeccable tweed jacket and matching plus fours. It was like stepping back in time. I said that I loved his outfit, and he merely scoffed. I thought maybe he misunderstood me and/or my seriousness, so I repeated the comment. Once again, he gave the same curt response. I felt terrible that I obviously offended him. The next day, I received solace from the Starter at Kingsbarns who, after sharing my experience, said that I did nothing wrong. Rather, he noted, some of the blue bloods at Elie take themselves just a bit too seriously.

Kingsbarns Golf Links (we struck out again on the Old Course ballot), designed by Kyle Philips in 2000, is at or near the top of the favorites list of most Americans who come to Scotland to play links golf. This is no surprise insofar as it (like Castle Stuart) is pretty wide open and in mint condition, with marine views on every hole. The varied terrain, with restrained dunescapes and ridges, was virtually all manufactured over former flat farmland. However, unlike many courses in the USA, the transformation is not patently obvious or overdone (as in the thousand- bunkered Whistling Straits). There are many very good holes though, in my opinion, none that are awesome. My favorites are the par-5 12th dogleg left hugging the coastline and the par-4 18th, where a centuries- old water conduit and bridge were uncovered during construction and preserved next to a steep embankment in front of the green. The clubhouse is warm and inviting, tastefully combining traditional decor with modern amenities.

In the land of Angus beef and Haggis, we were pleasantly surprised to locate a genuine Italian restaurant named "Little Italy" in the heart of St. Andrews. It's popular with locals, students, and visitors alike. So, be sure to get a reservation.

Yet again, we were unsuccessful with the Old Course ballot. Denis was so enamored with Kingsbarns that he returned for another crack at it. As for me, I was perfectly content to play the **St. Andrews Links New Course**. (Actually, the course is not all that "new" in that it was designed by Old Tom in 1895.) Just as Pacific Grove golf course is affectionately referred to as the "Poor Man's Pebble Beach," the same might be said of the New Course vis-a-vis the Old Course. Aside from sharing the same designer, they also enjoy many of the same features and views. Afterward, with the sun setting and only a few players still on the Old Course, I walked a few holes and paid particular attention to the Road Hole. I hit imaginary shots from various angles in and about the notorious bunker, road, and sloped green to better understand why this is one of golf's most famous and feared holes. After a casual dinner at Hams Hame's cellar pub and grill, it was time to get a final night's rest at the Scores before an early morning departure for home.

Speaking of home, I was very fortunate to have one to return to. While in Scotland, I learned that the then-worst fire in California history had begun leveling huge swaths of residential areas in Sonoma County, which caused many thousands, including my wife and some of her relatives, to evacuate. The fire came within a long par-5 length of reaching our retirement village, but it was saved by the heroic efforts of an army of firefighters who successfully drew a line in the sand. Eerily, the drought-plagued area would experience a virtual repeat two years later. Ironically, prior to these fires there had not been a significant one in the area in over fifty years. As Eric Clapton sang: "Let it rain."

TRIP 4 –

The K Club/Druids Glen/Portmarnock GC/Old Head Links/Dooks GL/ Tralee GL/Ballybunion GC (Old & Cashen)/Doonbeg/Lahinch GC/ Enniscrone GC/County Sligo GC/StrandHill GC/Portstewart/Royal Portrush/Royal County Down GC/Ardglass GC (May 2019)

Having had a nice dose of Scottish golf in 2017, Denis convinced me that his homeland of Ireland was entitled to equal time. In fact, we gave it more than proportionate time, and in a manner that would have made Admiral Magellan proud - we circumnavigated the entire island, albeit by land, over the space of three weeks. I planned and booked all aspects of the trip myself rather than going the tour company route. It was a seamless process.

We selected the month of May for the trip in the hope that it would offer some relatively reasonable weather. Save for an inauspicious start, this generally proved to be the case. After landing in Dublin via my direct flight from San Francisco (I always try to fly direct to Europe to avoid the dreaded connection nightmares often experienced in the USA.) I took a taxi to the nearby quaint town of Celbridge (birthplace of Arthur Guinness). The historic and moderately priced Celbridge Manor Hotel proved to be an excellent locale for the first leg of our journey. Denis arrived the next day with his moderately sized Hymer motorhome, which would serve as our mode of transportation and his frequent residence (while I roughed it in the hotels).

We began our golf trip at **The K Club**. This Arnold Palmer parkland design was the venue of the 2006 Ryder Cup - where the Europeans thrashed team USA 18 1/2 - 9 1/2. The weather was cold and rainy, causing the course to play extra long. I was underwhelmed. There are a few nice holes along the Liffey River, but the over-reliance on manufactured ponds, streams and lakes (including one with a large spewing fountain on the final hole) and water in general (in play on 14 holes) had me wondering whether I was in Ireland or Florida.

The next day's play at **Druids Glen**, another inland course, left me overwhelmed. It was not because the weather or my game improved compared to that at the K Club (both were equally poor). Rather, for me, it was because this Pat Ruddy design has a nice "Irish-American" golf vibe (save for the tacky last hole with water cascading from fake ponds and a stream). The club opened in 1995 and, a year later, began a string of four straight years as host of the Irish Open. There are many terrific historical photos of the tournament in the stately old manor-turned clubhouse, which includes a mellow grill room. I absolutely loved the par-3s here. The one on the second hole has several features inspired by the Road Hole at the Old Course at St. Andrews. The 8th and 12th holes had the soothing look and feel of the 16th and 12th at Augusta National. And, like that famed course during Masters week, verdancy and bloomage were at their peak. A great sense of blissfulness was felt walking over the ancient-looking arched stone bridges that span the gently flowing streams. It is a perfect blend of nature, sport and fun. In 2022 Druids Glen closed its course and lodging for renovations and is scheduled to reopen in 2023. It will be interesting to see the changes.

Taking a break from golf, we spent a day sightseeing, including a walk around the grounds of often photographed Powerscourt Estate and Powerscourt Falls (the tallest in Ireland).

Now it was time to start the links portion of the Irish golf show, and we did so at the fabled **Portmarnock Golf Club** outside of Dublin. Because of its rich history, it is frequently referred to as the "St. Andrews of Ireland." Founded in 1894, the club has hosted more professional tournaments than any other in

Ireland, including the first of many Irish Opens. In 1960, Arnold Palmer teamed with Sam Snead here to win the Canada Cup (later named the World Cup). Eddie Hackett served as the club's professional from 1939-1950. No one would suggest that Portmarnock has Ireland's most spectacular course landscape (only the smallest of dunes and minimal elevation changes) or commanding views (though the 15th hole by the sea has both and was one of Arnold Palmer's favorite par-3s in the world). The course is a demanding test of golf skill, particularly if the wind is up as is customary (in spades on the first several holes the day we played). Many golfers appreciate its "fairness" since what you see from the tee box is pretty much what you get on the holes. Just don't get into the deep pot bunkers, or what you'll get is a triple bogey!

The next day, we headed south toward Old Head. Our first stop was a short drive in and around the beautiful and vibrant town of Kilkenny, with its well-preserved 12th-century castle dominating the scene. We then entered County Tipperary. Here, Denis introduced me to some local friends who provided an enthusiastic guided tour of the semi-intact Holy Cross Abbey, founded in 1168. It is said that Queen Isabella, the widow of King John, brought to Ireland a fragment of the True Cross and bestowed it upon the Cistercian Friars at their abbey, which then assumed the name of the relic. Nearby, we had the opportunity to see the imposing Rock of Cashel. It is believed that St. Patrick's conversion of the pagan King of Munster took place here in the 5th century. The castle fortress remained the seat of the Munster Kings for over 600 years before the King of Munster donated it to the Church.

Shortly before nightfall, we reached our hotel, WatersEdge, in Cobh, a picturesque port town just outside Cork (and the last stop before the Titanic's fateful journey to America). This was one of the few times that my penchant for very advanced planning did not pay off. I almost always book directly with the desired hotel and request a quiet room with a view. In nearly every case that request is honored. I am frequently upgraded. On this occasion, Denis decided at the last minute to take a break from Chez Motorhome and spend the night in the hotel. He was able to secure the last available room. We met for dinner a few minutes later. He remarked that he had a lovely room overlooking the tranquil harbor. I, on the other hand, was placed in a street-side chamber, and the white noise from my phone did little to dissipate the din of the traffic.

In the morning Denis was fit as an Irish fiddle, while I ate my "bacon" (aka ham) and eggs with one eye open. Chalk one up for the Absent-Minded Professor! But, there was no time for sulking. We hopped into the motorhome and soon passed through the beautiful fishing village of Kinsale and checked in at the pro shop at **Old Head Links**. This course rests on what is arguably the world's most spectacular golf setting, a steep, rocky little peninsula hundreds of feet above the exploding ocean waves. Unfortunately, the price to play the course is also mighty steep, even though the layout itself is only somewhat above average. There is a certain forced and incongruous nature about it. This is due, in part, to the promontory's limited real estate. There surely are a few exceptions, such as the par-4 4th hole, which plays along the cliff's edge toward a classic black and white stripe lighthouse, and the par-5 12th, a dramatic dogleg over and around the towering vertical crags. While the collective merit of the individual holes is a source of debate among experts and novices of golf course architecture, all agree that the scenery is fantastic. As such, it is probably worth playing once but, if coaxed to play again, I would vote to skip it and, instead, visit the Cliffs of Moher for similar, but inexpensive, views.

Our next scheduled stop was Tralee, but Denis was tired from the combined golf, driving, and his daily 5-7k runs. He called ahead, and the hotel, with typical Irish flexibility and kindness, said it would be no problem delaying our arrival until the following evening. Denis then did a quick search on his phone and secured an "interesting" roadside country lodge about halfway to our destination. Upon arrival, he asked the manager if it would be alright if he parked and hooked up the motorhome in their parking lot. And, of course, the response was: "No problem." If subsequent events caused the manager to regret that decision, he didn't let on. Instead, he offered some utility room items to help us after the Absent-Minded Professor backed into a lengthy string of overhanging party lights that became hopelessly entangled on the motorhome's roof apparati. The Keystone Cops rigged two brooms together with duct tape and climbed, probed, and pried for over half an hour before the vehicle was freed.

We worked our way northwest to play **Dooks Golf Links**, entitled to placement in the "Hidden Gem" category (though its notoriety has increased in very recent years). We wound up getting paired with the Captain of the club and another member. And, to our pleasant surprise, he instructed the pro shop attendant to comp our rounds. As is the Irish custom, we arranged a modest match play bet. Dooks is a very solid, enjoyable course and should not be missed if in the area. The setting is beautiful, on the edge of Dingle Bay, with marvelous views of the Reeks mountain range. There are modest dunes, heather, gorse, and even some trees thrown in. It includes a nice variety of holes, in good condition, with pleasantly contoured greens. I can not recall any weak ones. The par-3 4th and 8th holes, and the par-4 12th, offer perhaps the best combination of layout and views. As for the match? We were on the cusp of a one-up $20 victory on the final hole. The Absent-Minded Professor then showed admirable sportsmanship by conceding a tricky downhill curling 12-foot putt to our generous hosts, which resulted in a tie.

After a drink in the intimate bar and grill room, we headed for Tralee and checked in at the downtown Park Georgian Hotel. The following morning, we played **Tralee Golf Links**, designed by Arnold Palmer in 1984. I had high expectations, but the course did not meet the criteria for best courses outlined in Chapter III. The setting, including the beach where "Ryan's Daughter" was filmed and some enormous dunes, is pretty. However, I found many of the holes (save for the par-3 3rd and short par-4 15th) to be awkward, difficult (too many all-or-nothing shots), and tough to walk (constant elevation changes). To borrow a corny phrase used by some art critics: "It just didn't speak to me."

The next day was earmarked for rest. So, we spent the day driving around the Dingle Peninsula (where only recently Denis had run in a grueling full marathon that was beyond my comprehension). Dingle town is colorful and well-situated. A short drive from there, we stopped to visit a couple of original Irish Famine cottages and then passed sheep-filled glens and panoramas of the multi-hued bay water. Our last stop was the 1,000-1,500-year-old Fahan Beehive Huts made of dry stacked stones. Their exact origin is uncertain, though likely they once were lived in by hermit monks and later used as stables and storage facilities by shepherds and farmers. Gaelic (Irish) is heavily spoken in this region.

In Ireland, the schools require 12 years of study in the language, but few outside of several Gaelic-speaking enclaves ever master or use it (though signs are in both English and Gaelic to keep the heritage at the forefront). As such, I was most impressed when I heard Denis speaking the tongue fluently with the museum's director, sharing the story of how he and some hiker friends had trespassed the property 40 years prior - forced to shelter themselves for the night in one of the huts during the area's most violent storm in a decade.

We returned to Tralee for an authentic Italian dinner at the Il Pomo Doro restaurant, and the following morning I took a short walk to attend Mass at the impressive St. John's Church before we departed for Ballybunion. On the way, we stopped to visit the ruins of Ardfert Friary, home of St. Brendan the Navigator. Once in Ballybunion, the 19th Lodge, directly across the street from the course, offered a convenient, pleasant and friendly place to stay. We enjoyed an outstanding dinner at the elegant Stroller's Bistro, also just a stone's throw away. The following day, it was time for a **Ballybunion** golf reunion.

Decades ago, many Irish purchased lifetime memberships (with little or no subsequent annual dues) at the best golf clubs on the island for a pittance. This was made possible by charging significant green fees to Yanks and other links golf fanatics from around the world. It was a win-win arrangement - subsidized golf and reserved tee times for the locals, and access to exclusive clubs and courses by the visitors. Denis took advantage of this opportunity, so I played as a member's guest at Ballybunion's Old Course (where I'd played in 2013) and its newer, Cashen Course.

First, we played the **Cashen**. After the first few attractive and relatively easy holes, I thought I was in heaven. The multiple dunes and elevated views were even more dramatic than on the Old Course. However, by the end of the round, I was a whipped dog as the layout proved to be typical Robert Trent Jones Sr. - extremely difficult. Approach shots to the small, severely contoured greens were particularly toxic as Jones often failed to provide the standard links run-up option. Not helpful in howling winds. The tight fairways and thick, high rough in the steep hills and abysses made many rescue shots nearly impossible. I felt that if only they could expand, reroute, and reshape parts of the course and expand the greens, it could be an absolute jewel. And, so, I was overjoyed when I learned that in July of 2023, the club membership voted to adopt a plan of action along these lines - under the tutelage of Tom Watson. The first phase of the work is expected to commence in November 2023. Having two grand courses will result in even greater fame for the club *and* significantly boost to the local economy, as Ballybunion will become more of a golf destination rather than a golf rest stop.

After finishing our round on Cashen, we headed over to play the **Old Course**. Things had changed little since my prior round there in 2013. As such, I will not repeat my impressions. The previous night's experience at Stollers Bistro was so good that we did it again that evening.

Our next stop, at **Doonbeg**, proved to be one of the biggest highlights of the trip for many reasons. The lodging has an aura of understated country elegance rather than the overly gilded atmosphere familiar at other Trump properties. The main lodge, restaurant, and clubhouse look like a homey castle that has been around for centuries. The dune-filled course is lush, overlooking an expansive crescent-shaped bay, and easily walkable. Fairways are generous, and the greens have natural and reasonable undulations. Every hole was a pleasure to play amid perfect weather. The layout is unfairly criticized for having a few fairways that cross others, some tee shots that require hitting over a green on a different hole, and/or occasional lengthy walks from the green to the next tee box. However, this was not the fault of the designer, Greg Norman. Rather, he merely adapted as well as he could to the significant environmental restrictions heaped on him. Favorite holes include the par-5 first hole, with a massive amphitheater-like dune overlooking the green, the panoramic par-4 6th, the ocean-hugging par-3 9th and 14th holes and the par-4 dogleg right 15th, with views of the Atlantic and lodge in the distance, along with a green virtually surrounded by more towering dunes.

Just 20 minutes away, **Lahinch Golf Club** provided the following day's excitement. While not quite the oldest course in Ireland, it is, nevertheless, its grand dame - full of raw beauty, challenge, and quirky charm. The usual great course architect suspects (Old Tom Morris and Alister MacKenzie) were primarily responsible for its design. (Martin Hawtree did some notable restoration and a few revisions that were completed in 2003.) One can easily see this when playing blind shots over the lofty dunes on the iconic par-5 4th hole ("Klondyke") and the par-3 5th ("Dell") and eyeing the fine array of unconventional greens and bunkers. I am also fond of the par-4 9th hole, which works its way up to a narrow green cut into the hillside, and the driveable par-4 13th, with a three-tiered green guarded by a large adjacent pit. A caddie is required here, and we had a knowledgeable one. On one heavily contoured green I had a 60-foot putt, and he pointed to a precise spot for me to aim at. Sure enough, after what seemed like a dozen seconds, the ball dropped in the cup! (I immediately handed him a $20 bonus for enabling such a thrill - which also happened to tie my tooth-and-nail match with Denis.)

After a robust breakfast in Doonbeg's main dining room overlooking the Atlantic, we continued our trek north, stopping at the Marian Shrine at Knock. In 1979, the future St. John Paul II held Mass before a crowd of 450,000 to commemorate the centenary of the apparition that took place there.

As the sun set, we pulled into the driveway of Denis' home in Sligo (more precisely, Rosses Point, a harbor village just outside Sligo town). It was here that poet-dramatist William Butler Yeats spent many summers with relatives. He asked for burial in the nearby village of Drumcliffe, beneath his beloved Benbulben Mountain. Rosses Point would serve as our refuge for the next several days. This came at an opportune time as the stinky socks piled up in Denis' motorhome cried out for a bath! Before retiring for the evening, we had a pleasant dinner at the celebrated Austies pub overlooking the harbor.

Denis tended to errands in Sligo the following day while I sauntered along its lovely riverside, lined with many shops and restaurants. I also paid a visit to its impressive and omnipresent cathedral on a hill. We joined up for a nice dinner at the historic Hargadon Bros pub and restaurant.

Golf resumed the next day at **Enniscrone Golf Club**. This course definitely deserves to be included as a "Hidden Gem," (though, like Dooks, the cat is now pretty much out of the bag). Enormous dunes abound, and a resident fox serves as a docent on a number of holes. The course (with five par-5s) is challenging but also fair, attractive and fun. The first hole, a par-5 dogleg right to a green overlooked by large dunes, sets the tone. Other standout holes, accentuated by the dunes, rolling fairways, descents and ascents and/or beach strands, include the par-4 12th and 13th holes and the par-5s at the 14th and 16th. It was a blustery day, and afterward, while having lunch in the clubhouse, I asked Denis and his friend Eamon whether the wind had left them feeling unsteady on their feet. They answered in the negative. (Later that night, I realized I actually was suffering from one of my occasional bouts of vertigo!)

Our next golf appointment was at **Strandhill Golf Club**. Still reeling from vertigo, I asked "Pedal to the Metal" Denis to take the turns with his sporty BMW on four wheels instead of two. Strandhill certainly has a pretty setting, with Knocknarae Mountain, Culleennamore Strand, and Strandhill Beach serving as backdrops. However, the fact that the only holes that I can recall with particular affection - the par-4 4th hole along the seashore with an approach to a dramatically raised green, the downhill par-4 13th that passes through a narrow corridor of dunes to a hollow green, and the par-3 14th hole with a green situated nicely inside some lower dunes - suggests that either the layout and conditions of the overall course were unremarkable or my case of vertigo had frayed my senses.

We walked a few holes at County Sligo Golf Club the following day, spectating at the Irish Amateur tournament. (Like Ballybunion, Denis wisely purchased a lifetime membership here, for a low fee, many years ago.) We had another fine dinner in Sligo town, accompanied by entertaining storyteller Eamon, at Bistro Bianconi.

When I woke up in the morning, the vertigo had finally dissipated. So I was raring to go when we teed off on **County Sligo's** scenic, albeit difficult, Harry Colt design. It frequently hosts major Irish tournaments, yet is not as well known as the other top-tier courses in Ireland due to its relative remoteness. But, it always shows up near the top of the rankings. My favorite hole is the uphill par-3 9th, with its dry stack rock wall adjacent to the green, revetted bunkers fronting it, and gigantic Benbulben Mountain dominating the background. The par-4 17th is a beautiful hole along the coast with a high dune backdrop to the green. However, it is almost impossible to reach in two, so bogey is a moral victory. The par-4 18th is a solid finishing hole that offers the opportunity to counter the 17th with a birdie.

We departed the following morning for Northern Ireland, the final swing of what Eamon called Denis and my "Golf Odyssey." The Bushmills Inn (originally a Coaching Inn in the 1600s) was the perfect choice of accommodation on the Causeway Coast. It afforded a convenient walk to the village of Bushmills (and its excellent distillery tour) and was a short drive away from our scheduled courses. The Inn's restaurant and bar have an atmosphere of warm, well-appointed historicity. The food is excellent.

The next day, we reported for golf duty at **Royal Portrush**. Excitement was in the air as the club would host the British Open in a few months. The pro shop was overflowing with Open logoed golf apparel and souvenirs. Grandstands had sprouted up everywhere. We were required to carry little artificial turf mats for use on fairway shots in order to preserve their immaculate condition for the tournament. This Harry Colt design (which previously hosted the only Open outside of Scotland and England in 1951) has, with its revived Open prestige, steadily climbed even further up the ranking charts in recent years. Overlooking a vast coastline with the clifftop ruins of Dunluce castle in the distance and having its fair share of generous-size dunes, it is a natural setting for traditional links golf.

Royal Portrush is demanding in nature, with precarious greens and tall, thick fescue often providing the carry from tees and hugging the fairways. As such, I found myself attracted to several less arduous but still clever holes (3, 5 and 12) rather than a couple of the more famous ones (4 and 16).

Later that evening, heading down the hallway to the Bushmills Inn restaurant, I had to ask myself whether I was experiencing an optical illusion. An unassuming but familiar-looking man was standing alone, admiring a painting (or perhaps hoping to avoid the gaze of golf groupies while waiting for a friend or family member to join him). I quickly realized that it was, indeed, Tom Watson in the flesh. I hesitated whether to acknowledge him or to keep on moving. I decided on the former, but with respectful reserve. I quietly said: "Tom?" He said: "Yes," followed by his familiar tightening of the lips into a soft, almost bashful grin. I briefly introduced myself and mentioned the golf journey I was on, with specific reference to Enniscrone. I asked if he'd played it as I was interested in his impressions. To my surprise, he said he had not. He then inquired, in that playfully demanding way of his: "Well, did ya like it?" I assured him I did and encouraged him to play it if he had time. We then exchanged our mutual pleasure in meeting one another, and I left him to his painting. My only regret was that I failed to mention that I believe he has golf's finest-looking swing. So rhythmic and repeatable. Perhaps he has heard it before. But, with the names of several historically great swingers of the golf club more frequently given this epithet, I'm sure he would have been proud to hear it again.

The next day we played another fine course, **Portstewart Golf Club**. There is no waiting to be impressed here, as the first hole is one of the most imposing openers in golf. With a tee box overlooking the Atlantic and perched high above the fairway below, this par-4 doglegs right to a green at the foot of enormous dunes. Many other fine holes meander through, around, and to numerous large dunes, such as the par-4 2nd, 5th and 8th holes. I was not a fan of holes 10 and 11 insofar as the fairways tilt hard from right to left and, even with an "ideal" shot to the far right of the fairway, the ball rolls all the way down to the far left with a bevy of dangerous bunkers waiting to swallow it. In any event, if playing Royal Portrush or the fine courses at Rosapenna, do not drive by Portstewart. Play it!

In the morning, we drove down through the magnificent Glens of Antrim, then back to the coast to the beautifully situated little village of Glenarm. This was a very emotional stop for me. The village was home to my great-grandfather, Henry Hamill, before he and his brother said goodbye forever to their family and emigrated to America circa 1870. It was surreal walking the streets where these Hamills once did the same. Amazingly, they managed to survive the great famine, as well as a cholera epidemic that broke out in a still extant tavern, wiping out a significant number of the village's population.

Further south, the Dufferin Coaching Inn in the small village of Killyleagh offered agreeable lodging with a restaurant next door. A double turreted castle sits at the top of the village's short main street, and a small harbor at its bottom. This served as our springboard to an epic round at **Royal County Down**. One of the Americans with whom we were paired summed up the course perfectly. Borrowing from the title of a famous baseball film, he said the place was a "Field of Dreams." But, it was not just the course. Rather, the impeccably maintained dunescaped, gorse-accented links, with its treacherous but magnificent beardies bunkers, was complimented perfectly by the dignified clubhouse, the nearby historic Slieve Donard Hotel, the towering Mountains of Mourne, and the waters of Dundrum Bay. All combine to form a jaw-dropping, transcendent image.

Old Tom Morris, and later Harry Vardon and Harry Colt, combined their design skills to form this splendid, picturesque layout. The front nine is widely considered the best that golf offers anywhere in the world. At the top of the list of great holes is the par-4 9th hole, so often seen in famous course photography. It captures all of the above-referenced features. While the back nine can not quite match the front, it does have a magnificent stretch from holes 10-14.

Yes, the course has several blind tee shots (with white rocks indicating the line of direction) that might irk the modern golfer seeking complete "justice," but leveling the obstructions would level the historical, natural mystique of the place. Yes, the bunkers are among the most difficult in the world. The solution? Stay out of them. (I managed to dodge every one of them and wound up shooting my lowest score on the trip.)

After a light lunch in the clubhouse we hopped into our golf chariot and headed off to play at **Ardglass Golf Club**, located in County Down, the most pleasant discovery of the trip. Ardglass is off the radar of even some of the most seasoned foreign golf travelers. But the secret is closer to becoming semi-secret, with continued investment to enhance course conditions. Nowhere else can you check in at the oldest clubhouse in Ireland (a medieval castle) and step to an elevated first tee with ancient cannons standing guard. The par-4 first hole moves upward, hugging the jagged coastal cliffs to a green tucked into the rocks. The second, a par-3, is similar, requiring a carry over the edge of the cliffs from the tee. The par-5 11th and par-3 12th are nicely situated along the sea's edge. Some criticize the middle holes as lacking inspiration. However, I found their relative simplicity to be endearing, set as they were among vegetation of varied colors in full bloom and playing around an old white stone cottage. The final hole flows downhill, with the castle serving as the backcloth.

Alas, we set off for the Dublin airport early the following day as it was time to return to the nua sod.

TRIP 5 –

Gleneagles GC (King's and Queen's Courses)/Carnoustie GL/ Panmure GC/ Musselburgh Links/North Berwick (The Glen Club)/Machrihanish GC/ Machrihanish Dunes GC/The Island Club (April/May 2022)

There were, of course, more critical disruptions in life caused by the COVID pandemic, which broke out in early 2020, than the suspension of, and/or severe restrictions placed on, leisure travel. Nevertheless, the frustrations and complications were real. As things eased up a bit, the confluence of rescheduled old plans by some, with the pent-up new plans of others, created quite a logjam relative to securing golf tee times. This held true even with regard to low-season travel to both the great courses at home (e.g., Bandon Dunes) and abroad (e.g., St. Andrews and Muirfield). With a certain hesitancy, I decided to move forward with travel to Scotland and Ireland in the early spring of 2022. Once again, I intended to play the various courses with my trusty sidekick, Denis. However, only a short time before our scheduled departure, he had to pull out. I was determined to proceed alone. But, a little more than a week before embarking, my wife, Kathy, came to the rescue and said she would like to join me!

At the time, Great Britain and Ireland faced a resurgence in various COVID strains. So, we masked up and departed with a certain degree of fatalism. (While the USA continued to require passengers from abroad to pass a COVID test as a condition for boarding planes to its country, Great Britain and Ireland had eliminated this precondition for Americans traveling to their countries.)

We landed in Edinburgh and hired a taxi to take us north one hour to our first destination - the magnificent parkland courses at Gleneagles. We passed on the expense of staying at the Gleneagles Resort, opting for far cheaper yet intimate and well-appointed accommodations at nearby Cairn Lodge, complete with a turreted entrance. The staff were incredibly cordial and helpful in every way.

Upon waking up the following day (or, as noted in the Preface to this book, not waking up since I never fell asleep), I took a short taxi ride to play the James Braid-designed **King's Course at Gleneagles**. This was the beginning of a series of ironies. Not only did I manage to play well that day despite suffering from severe sleep deprivation, but I continued to do the same throughout the trip, notwithstanding contracting an unshakeable head cold (later proven to be COVID) a few days afterward. On my previous trips to Scotland and Ireland, I had never broken 80, typically shooting in the mid 80's. I would break the 80 barrier on this trip on six of nine attempts. I think it was a combination of lowered expectations, a more relaxed atmosphere with my wife by my side (as an observer), playing from the next forward tees when called for by course length/ high slope rating, and experience adapting to the requirements of links golf. (Or, perhaps it was all about not worrying about handing over a Euro to Denis if I lost a match!)

The King's Course, with its gorse in bloom, reminded me of inland versions of Royal Dornoch and Bandon Dunes. It is a test, to be sure, but it is relatively open and usually possible to play out of trouble with a well-executed shot. After an amiable conversation with the starter, I teed off on the par-4 uphill first hole, in full view of the moorland glens. I was not prepared for the steeply sloped (back to front) green, which resulted in a dubious start to the round. The next hole, a straightforward two-shotter, heads downward to a receptive green. The par-3 5th can be a brute, as it was for me, given that its green rests on a tabletop with incredibly steep falloffs if you fail to land on or hold the green. The back nine is full of variety, its most famous being the par-4 13th, known as "Braid's Brawest" (best). This hole roller-coasters through gorse and testy bunkers to a tilted green. The par-5 18th affords the opportunity to reach the green in two shots if the tee ball makes it over the prominent fairway ridge. Since it is wide open, it is worth giving it a go with everything in the tank. For me, it resulted in, by far, the longest tee shot of my life - a thrilling 340 yards.

Kathy and I had a pleasant dinner in the clubhouse overlooking the 1st and 18th holes. The next day, following a made-to-order breakfast in Cairn Lodge's atrium restaurant, I returned to Gleneagles to play the **Queen's Course** - also laid out by James Braid. I was paired with a very pleasant French businessman on a short golf holiday. Fortunately, he spoke fluent English since my French is limited to broken present tense. We agreed that the course, though shorter than the King's, was sufficiently challenging while sharing similar topography and views and, therefore, quite enjoyable. The most memorable holes, besides the par-4 dogleg left number 10, with its green tucked amid the hills, were the final two par-3s on the back nine with singularly quirky greens. After a large beer in the clubhouse with my playing partner (whose name I have forgotten so I will just call him: "Mon Ami"), Kathy and I once again had an intimate dining experience at the Cairn Lodge.

Before heading to our next golf destination, Carnoustie, we took a short train ride from Gleneagles to the city of Stirling, a kind of mini-Edinburgh. Its historic castle is perched high above the river and city on ancient volcanic rock, with its sublimity in full view as the train pulls into the station. The Battle of Stirling Bridge, fought near the fortress, is featured in the film "Braveheart." Given its strategic location, the castle changed hands between the Scots and English many times during the Wars of Scottish Independence, circa 1296-1357. In times of peace, it served as a Royal residence. Mary Queen of Scots lived in the castle as a child and was later crowned there. After strolling the city's winding, hilly streets and taking the informative tour of the castle, we had an adequate lunch in the centuries-old Portcullis Hotel Pub just outside the stronghold's gates.

We then returned to the Cairn Lodge to collect our luggage and took a short taxi ride to the train station. An hour or so later we arrived on the east coast in **Carnoustie** and checked in at the Carnoustie Golf Hotel, with a room overlooking the course's famous 18th green. We had time to walk through the small town the next morning before my afternoon tee time. The first and foremost order of business was a visit to the nearby Simpsons Golf Shop. This small, well stocked store was founded in 1883 by golfer and famed club-maker Robert Simpson. (His brother Jack won the Open in 1884.) It sells modern golf equipment, apparel, a wide selection of antique hickory clubs, and vintage and reproduction balls. Hanging from the ceiling are over 2,500 bag tags from golf clubs all over the world.

I teed off on this Old Tom Morris/James Braid design with a degree of trepidation in light of Carnoustie's nickname of "Carnasty," derived from it being generally viewed as the hardest of the Open venues. The difficulties stem from a combination of its length, perilous pot bunkers, winding burns, speedy rumpled fairways, gorse, thick rough, and typically very stiff winds. The last few holes, in particular, are knee knockers. (Just ask John Vandevelde, who in 1999, orchestrated the most painful final hole collapse in Open history.) In the end, I liked the course and even managed to play decently - including a very conservative tap-in bogey strategy on the 18th to avoid being a Vandevelde doppelganger! My favorite hole is the par-3 13th. It has revetted bunkers in front of the green, and behind it a pair of large Scots pine trees and piles of gorse - the latter creating the illusion of the distant white hotel resting on top of them. Carnoustie does not have the stunning landforms and coastal views customary at the famous links courses. However, the layout is intriguing, and the greens are meticulously maintained. The experience can be fun if you allow it to be so. The new clubhouse facility next to the hotel provided an excellent dining experience.

The next day, we took a taxi a few miles down the road to play **Panmure**. (Kathy drove the buggy and tried to stay warm in her role as spectator.) This is another course with significant design contributions by James Braid. Here, Ben Hogan famously practiced prior to his one and only appearance at the Open, which he won at Carnoustie in 1953. There are a few uninspired, flat holes at the beginning and end but, in between, a number that incorporate the usual fine features of both links and heathland golf. Rivaling the course for impressiveness is the clubhouse, the exterior of which is modeled after the Royal Calcutta Golf Club in India, built during its Colonial period, and a wood-paneled interior with comfy stuffed chairs and wooden nook ("snug") with a large fireplace. The locker room is a complete throwback to late 19th-century wooden simplicity.

The following day, it was time to visit the home of golf yet again. The Carnoustie Golf Hotel arranged for an entertaining driver to deliver us to St. Andrews' famous old (but recently expanded and wonderfully renovated) Rusacks Hotel. Here, a century ago, Bobby Jones took up residence when playing in the championships. It was expensive, but we saved a considerable amount by choosing a room without a course view. (No problem, since we enjoyed a perfect panorama of the same when dining in the hotel's fabulous restaurant.)

As a single, I was not entitled to enter the daily ballot for a tee time on the Old Course. And, as was the case in my previous visit, I was unwilling to arrive at three in the morning the following day to stand in line for a possible walk-on opening. I stopped by late in the morning on the highly off chance that there might be a spot open for me. Not! My backup plan was to play the Eden Course, but it, too was booked due to a local tournament. Frankly, I didn't mind a bit as it was a very windy, cheek-freezing day. Instead, Kathy and I took in the town's castle/cathedral ruins, university and myriad shops. We wound up eating a surprisingly cheap and delicious fish and chips lunch in the golf museum behind the Royal and Ancient clubhouse. For dinner, I invited Kathy to join me for an encore visit to the Little Italy restaurant, where Denis and I had dined two years prior. She said the lasagna was the best she'd ever eaten!

The next day, the hotel's concierge set us up with a charming driver to take us south to Muirfield. It was about this time that a dry, tickly cough set in. Ugh oh! We checked in at Greywalls, and I determined I could catch a bus outside the hotel's entrance road that would take me to the links at nearby Musselburgh, leaving just enough time to play before it turned dark. **Musselburgh** contains only nine holes (inside a historic racetrack). It is one of the oldest courses in the world and is virtually untouched from its original design. At one time, it was part of the British Open rota, hosting the tournament six times between 1874-1889. Because of its ancient origins and relatively short length, many golfers visiting the course choose to play with hickory shafted clubs. I brought a handful of my steel shafted clubs, but the gracious pro shop attendant insisted that I borrow a set of hickories, retro balls, and a retro bag on a gratis basis. I felt giddy throughout the round, feeling conveyed back in time; the course all to myself as I was its final patron of the day. The most famous hole is the par-4 4th, named "Mrs. Forman's." Behind the green is Mrs. Forman's Pub (recently closed), which at one time served as an unofficial halfway house, with a walk-up window where one could secure a pint before proceeding to the next hole.

As I waited at the bus stop, I noticed that my nose was beginning to run. I hoped it was just a result of the evening chill. However, upon returning to the hotel Kathy also noted the onset of cold symptoms, which progressed throughout the night. So why not test for COVID? First, the symptoms were not as extensive or severe as those typically experienced with that virus, so there was guarded optimism behind our ignorance. Second, Great Britain and Ireland had discarded isolation requirements and most mandatory masking, assuming a stiff-upper-lip approach. So, when in Rome… (or Scotland). We decided to continue to mask up, carry on, and hope for the best. In any event, we assumed we would be negative by the time we were required to take a COVID test as a condition for boarding our flight home from Dublin.

A bit about the choice of Greywalls for our lodging. Perhaps most compelling is its location, immediately next to Muirfield's clubhouse, home of The Honourable Company of Edinburgh Golfers. Greywalls overlooks the course, as close as if it were part of the hotel's backyard. Needless to say, this concave-shaped manor home, turned inn, has served as the temporary living quarters for many famous golfers when the Open has been held here. Historic photos hang throughout, and the rooms can be traced to the golfers who stayed in them. We were assigned to the McIlroy quarters, where one could strike a chip shot over a short stone boundary wall to the tenth-hole tee box. The warm restaurant is five-star. Finally, a stay at Greywalls presents a unique opportunity to play Muirfield insofar as the course reserves a limited number of tee times for hotel guests during select months on select days. I was already on the waiting list through the club itself (singles can not reserve a tee time, but they can serve as fill-ins in the event of partial cancellations within a group). However, I figured that this Greywalls route would remove some of the suspense since I'd made my reservation a year in advance and, therefore, would be at the top of the list. In the months leading up to our visit, I kept in contact with the hotel, anxiously awaiting the announcement of Muirfield's release of the Greywalls tee times. Finally, the day arrived. The hotel informed me that tee time sign-ups were now available - but this season the privilege would not begin until two days after our departure from the hotel! Literally so close, yet so far. Unfortunately, I ultimately did not get to play the course, though we visited the pro shop and walked around the outside of the clubhouse. But, like my visit to Augusta to witness the Masters (covered in the next chapter), the Greywalls experience allowed me the opportunity to see and feel Muirfield's essence better than any television set or book could do. And a consolation prize came in the form of a round at a Hidden Gem up the road - The Glen Golf Club at North Berwick. But first, a bit of sightseeing in Edinburgh.

After a leisurely breakfast at Greywalls, we boarded a direct bus to Edinburgh. While this was my fourth visit to this legendary city, it was Kathy's first. Like everyone else on their maiden visit here, her mouth was agape as she gazed up from the park to the edifices, most notably the castle, high above on the massive, sloped crag ("craig" in Scotland). We toured the castle and then worked our way down the Royal Mile to Holyrood Palace at its base. Both are must-sees in terms of capturing the fascinating history of the Scottish and British royalty's presence here.

On the return bus trip, we hopped off in the golf town of Gullane (one stop away from Muirfield). We were fortunate to catch the proprietor of Jack White Gullane Golf Shop just as he was locking the door. He insisted that we come in as he was in no hurry to leave. There were enough hickory clubs to build a small warship! I hoped to find an affordable Forgan-made niblick, but he had just sold his last one the previous day. Nevermind, it was a pleasure just rooting around the little shop, perhaps better termed "museum," with its eclectic display of all things vintage golf. We then dined at The Old Clubhouse pub and restaurant just around the corner. This architecturally impressive building once served as the clubhouse of the members of the Gullane Golf Club, which consists of three courses on linksland where golf has been played for over 350 years.

The following morning, we boarded another direct bus in the opposite direction to nearby North Berwick. Since we wanted to explore the town before my tee time on North Berwick's East Links (**The Glen Golf Club**) I left my cart bag back at the hotel, carried a half dozen clubs, and wore my ribbed rubber soled golf shoes. I particularly enjoyed our visit to a small antique shop, where I had a nice chat with the owner. He happened to be related to Ben Sayers, who along with James Braid, designed the very course I was to play. Ben Sayers was also a North Berwick pro and fine club maker, some of which implements I own.

As at Musselburgh, I was a bit giddy playing the Glen GC course as its clifftop setting is amazing, and the layout is great fun to play. Despite my six clubs limitation, I managed to score quite well by using a little imagination. The first hole involves a steep ascent, and the final hole presents a steep drop. In between are a variety of holes that afford incredible views of the sea and massive Bass Rock set therein. The signature hole is the par-3 13th. It has to be as it is featured on the scorecard! The shot from an elevated tee box heads down to a green surrounded by jagged coastal rocks, with pounding waves next door. Afterward, my buggy driver, Kathy, was thrilled to calm her chattering teeth and thaw out next to the fireplace in the clubhouse restaurant.

After a final breakfast at Greywalls, the staff arranged for yet another fine storytelling driver to take us to the Glasgow airport for our flight to play the links of Machrihanish. The Kintyre Peninsula, upon which the courses of Machrihanish rest, near Kintyre's "Mull" (meaning rounded headland), is a remote but beautiful location in southwest Scotland. It was good enough for Paul McCartney; he chose to buy a farm retreat there half a century ago. He wrote a song about the area: "Mull of Kintyre," and another: "Long and Winding Road," describing the route to get there. We knocked off four hours of driving and got there via a more direct route - 30 minutes as the crow (10 seater) flies. This convenience did not come without a price. By now, our "colds" left us with classic sinus congestion. This, combined with the severe air pressure in the little puddle-hopper, had our eyes popping out farther than Rodney Dangerfield's. OUCH!!

Our plane set down at the tiny Campbeltown airport, after which we took a very short drive through the open fields to the Ugadale Hotel. This classic style 100-year-old building is very comfortably furnished and overlooks the first tee of the **Machrihanish Golf Club**. The lobby has a well-appointed golf theme about it. Next door, the small former clubhouse serves as a cozy pub restaurant.

Machrihanish GC, with its vast array of temperate-size dunes, rolling terrain, lush wide open hillside country in the distance, and sea shore, was designed by Old Tom Morris. He gave much of the credit to the natural handiwork of the Almighty. The first hole, a dog leg left requiring a tee shot over as much ocean and beach as one thinks they can take on, is generally regarded as the finest opening hole in the world. It is certainly pretty and offers strategic challenges. (The wave action is typically docile and the tide low, leaving an inordinate amount of beach leading to the low sea bank. The sand is in play, so all is not lost if one fails to reach the fairway with the tee shot.) However, I would not crown the opening hole as the world's King. Then what is? My candidates are Portstewart, Ardglass and Doonbeg. In any event, I took a safe middle- ground approach in terms of reaching the fairway and still easily reached the green in two. I was paired with an adorable octogenarian couple, a Japanese husband and wife who have come here to play over 30 times! Their mutual regard for one another and the course was readily apparent and moving. Both played a very respectable game for their age.

I can not identify any particular holes that I would define as exceptionally arresting. Rather, it was the overall nature of this remote place, with its naturally and generously undulating fairways and greens, all in excellent condition, that defined it.

After the round, I met up with Kathy (she'd opted for a nature walk full of sea otters, sheep, cows, and seagulls) at the modern clubhouse for a late lunch. From there, we took a short taxi ride to wander the streets of the peaceful and pretty harbor town of Campbeltown. In a little memorial garden rests a life-size statue of Linda McCartney.

Following a hearty breakfast in the Old Clubhouse pub, Kathy walked with me as I played Machrihanish Golf Club's new neighbor (opened in 2009), **Machrihanish Dunes Golf Club**. Yet again, that giddy feeling came a-calling. Why? Scotsman David McLay Kidd (of Bandon Dunes design fame) was required to build a course which, due to severe environmental restrictions, involved no earth movement, save for a little shaping of the tee boxes and natural green sites. No modern grass seeds or fertilizers were permitted. There is no irrigation system in place. The natural grasses were simply mowed down to create the fairways. Numerous sheep openly graze the course as supplemental members of the grounds crew. Blind shots (perhaps too many, but nevertheless understandable) over lanky grass, and sunken undulating greens are the order of the day. The early holes brought out the best of these. In short, I felt as if in another epoch, playing in the same environment as those shepherds centuries ago with their leather stitched balls and crude wooden clubs.

The clubhouse and pro shop are one, in a tiny little stone building where the genial attendant made us a couple of "toasties" (grilled ham & cheese). The airstrip is between the clubhouse and the terminal, so we took a short drive around it and soon boarded our plane for Glasgow, where we would transfer for a flight to Dublin. Fortunately, at this point, our health was back to normal, save for continued runny noses. Still, we wondered if we would encounter the head-exploding experience of the flight over. We chomped our gum like cud-chewing cows on fast-forward video mode and did quite well.

Late that evening, our plane touched down in Dublin, and we soon checked into the nearby Grand Hotel Malahide. Malahide is a small, upscale suburb of Dublin. The hotel is perfectly situated as it is just a short walk from the village shops, restaurants, castle, and train station. Moreover, my final golf destination of the trip, The Island Golf Club, could be seen on the other side of the estuary.

The following day had its share of ups and downs. We began with a thorough and satisfying breakfast in the hotel. We then went to a mall in the nearby town of Swords to take what we thought would be a pro forma COVID test at a drugstore recommended by Aer Lingus. We both tested positive. And we were scheduled to fly home the next day! There was nothing we could do but push back our flight departure a couple of days and plan to enjoy a little extra sightseeing. In the meantime, I had a late afternoon tee time to tend to.

The Island Golf Club, designed by Eddie Hackett, is an outstanding links course bordered by the sea on three sides. It is in excellent condition and has a variety of attractive holes amongst its giant dunes. Unfortunately, just as I teed off, the weather grew chilly, made even more so by a nonstop alternation of heavy drizzle and rain. This did not prevent me from appreciating its fine layout. Favorites include the solid dog leg right opening hole through the dunes, the short par-4 7th ridge hole, and the par-4 12th, its green tucked into a mini-amphitheater with Malahide in view across the water,

We retested for COVID the next day with self-testing kits. Kathy was negative. I bombed again. We did some research and discovered that some individuals will continue to test positive for up to 12 weeks even though they are asymptomatic and not contagious. Oh well, off to visit Malahide's castle, followed by some tasty fried chicken and chips at one of the sports bars. The next day, the same test results. We then took the short train ride to Dublin to visit the Guinness Brewery and the Jeannie Johnston Emigration ship. The following day, we again took an official test at the drugstore in Swords. Kathy passed. I flunked. We took a tour of the well-preserved ruins of Swords Castle, then returned to the hotel to push back our flight several more days (after listening to the painfully loud and repetitive "on hold" music for the customary hour and being told, in barely decipherable English, that we would incur yet another costly "change fee").

We checked out of the hotel and boarded a bus for Belfast, where we set up shop at the splendid Central Park Hotel a few blocks from the station. Everything from the staff to the beds to the food was first class, taking some of the sting out of our growing dilemma. The next day, the concierge set us up with an excellent all-day bus tour along the coast of Counties Down and Antrim, including the famous Giants Causeway. The following day, we visited the extensive and highly informative Titanic Experience Museum. With me continuing to test positive, we resolved to return to the Dublin airport the next day, get a hotel room, and put Kathy on the scheduled plane home the day after. We checked into the hotel and decided to walk the short distance to the airport's testing facility, expecting the usual result. The thought of saying goodbye to my loyal travel companion and best friend made me quite sad, as did the fear of not knowing how much longer and at what cost I would remain in Ireland. (While waiting for our test results, we bumped into an off-duty Aer Lingus representative who told us we could get a certificate from them to depart if seven days had passed since testing positive. She called the drug store, and they said they did not maintain records/certificates of positive tests; they only issued proof of negative testing.) So, just as I was preparing my plan of action to deal with my plight, the latest test results came in on our phones. We BOTH tested negative! Hasta la vista, baby!

TRIP 6 –
Doonbeg/Lahinch GC/Dromoland Castle/Enniscrone GC/Carne GL/Donegal GC/Rosapenna (St. Patrick's, Morris & Sandy Hills Links Courses)/Port Salon GC/Portmarnock Hotel GL/Corballis GL (July/August 2023)

An extended father-son golf trip was something I'd dreamed about for many years. All that was needed was a son who shared my fascination with the game. By 2023, my only son, Brian, and golf were attached at the hip. So, the time had come. His wife, Sara, daughter Claire, mother-in-law Mary, sister-in-law Liz, and her daughter Emily heard about the trip and entertained their own thoughts of *carpe diem,* albeit via a separate, non-golf itinerary. My wife's customary altruism made the trips possible - staying home and caring for Claire's "lively" one-and-a-half-year-old sister, Catherine the Great.

And so, we all flew to Shannon airport. Waiting for us was our perpetually gregarious driver, Tommy. We dropped the girls off in the town of Ennis, and Brian and I headed for the Trump **Doonbeg** Golf Links & Hotel. After checking into our stunning two-story country manor quarters in the main lodge, which overlooked the 18th green and the bay, with its long stretch of sandy beach, I was ready for a jet lag nap - but not before seeing an amped Brain off the first tee. He exuded a sports-related excitement that I had not seen since his grade school team took home the Parochial League basketball championship, and his high school football team snapped a 39-year curse against a powerful local rival en route to the West Coast Athletic League crown. Later, I watched from our large window as Brian bounded down the 18th fairway and putted out on the hole's impeccably maintained green, protected by several revetted bunkers. His broad, euphoric smile as he looked up at me said it all in terms of what he thought of his first British Isles links experience. He had taken a tour of golf heaven, and it was of no consequence that, on that day, St. Peter had dimmed the lights and turned the fan on high. As Brian put it: "I expected these conditions and loved it." The following day we played Doonbeg together. The weather was the same as the previous day, except for the added ingredient of torrential, sideways rainfall on one hole. Fortunately, it stopped as quickly as it came. The suddenly warm, high winds completely dried out our drenched clothes by the end of the next hole.

As great as the course is (see elucidation in the 2019 trip summary), the lodge compliments and enhances the golf beyond measure. As Brian framed it: "They nailed it with their combination of sophisticated golf-themed bedrooms, restaurants, bars, and lounge ambiance." The one suggestion I have relative to improving the course would be to cut the tall, thick seagrass back a bit near the fairways and around the greens, as has been done at courses such as Lahinch, Carne, Donegal, and Portsalon.

The following day Tommy's friend, Big Ray, picked us up for the short scenic drive to **Lahinch Golf Club**. (The girls had priority for Tommy's and his daughter's services for the week.) This course is also described in detail in the 2019 trip summary. Despite a dire weather forecast, we were blessed with great conditions that lasted right up to the time we got back in the car for the return trip to our lodging at Doonbeg. Upon entering the pro shop, Brian was like the proverbial kid in a candy store, enamored with the club's logo that features the course's mascot - a goat. Lore has it that the goats are more accurate and timely weather forecasters than the human experts. If they start heading toward shelter, it's time for the golfer to throw in the towel - or at least throw on the heavy rain gear.

Brian's driver was in high gear. The caddies and I were enthralled by his length and accuracy, given that he only has time to play about 12-15 rounds per year. We had a bit of competitive fun on the par-3 11th hole. I hit a high, soft shot that curled perfectly along the green's slope to within 15 feet of the pin. Brian countered with a similar-shaped shot that left him a mere four feet away. It was only fitting that we both made our birdie putts.

The following day we bid a reluctant adieu to the Doonbeg resort, and Big Ray took us to our new bivouac at the lovely Old Ground Hotel - conveniently situated in the spirited and tidy town of Ennis. While there, we visited its Cathedral, friary ruins, the County Clare Museum, and a couple of nice pubs (the Poet's Corner Bar in the Old Ground and the Diamond Bar, just down the road - where a group of locals played traditional Irish music).

Dromoland Castle Golf Club served as our next golf venue. Designed by Ron Kirby and JB Carr, this course would be hosting the KPMG Women's Irish Open tournament in a few weeks time. As such, it was in prime condition. Dromoland is a perfect location to experience Irish parkland golf. Aside from being in excellent shape, and offering varied terrain and hole variety, it rewards the golfer with the incomparable setting of the par-3 7th hole. From a highly elevated tee, one faces a pond at the green's left front as well as a small lake and the imposing castle in the background. This hole is followed by attractive par-4s at numbers 8 and 9. The par-5 18th hole is a sort of inland version of Pebble Beach's, in reverse. It is a dogleg right instead of left; the water to be negotiated (a small lake rather than the Pacific Ocean) is on the right rather than the left. And, like Pebble, a tall, stately tree in the fairway requires a strategically placed tee shot to maximize the approach options on the next shot. Both holes have a green overlooked by their memorable hotels - one a castle and the other a Spanish Colonial Revival lodge.

In the morning, Big Ray drove us a couple of hours north to the quaint and animated little town of Ballina in County Mayo. Before heading to play nearby **Enniscrone Golf Club,** we dropped off our luggage at the comfortable Ballina Manor Hotel, situated next to the river Moy and affording views of the spired St. Muredach's Catholic Cathedral and a nearly 200-year-old multi-arched stone bridge. Before departing the town limits, Big Ray drew our attention to a sign reading "Biden Corner." Here, President Biden's cousin, Jimmy, milked (or "Cup of Joe'd") the President's visit to his ancestral town in April of 2023. Just days before Sleepy Joe's arrival, Jimmy helped awaken the town by opening a drive-through coffee establishment across from the primary speech site and created 10,000 commemorative coffee mugs.

I knew that Brian would be immediately drawn to Enniscrone's links (see detailed course description in 2019 visit synopsis) as the first hole is one of golf's best openers - a par-4 dogleg right around an enormous dune toward an upward-sloping approach and green. Its secluded beauty amid many towering dunes and the sea further solidified Brian's love affair with links golf - which would reach its climax the following day at **Carne Golf Links**.

Lahinch is often described as the St. Andrews of Ireland. It seems only fitting, then, to label Carne as the Cruden Bay of Ireland. Carne and Cruden Bay are both rugged and quirky, with perhaps the largest and most numerous dunes in their respective nations. In both cases, the courses were laid out with minimal earth movement. Like Cruden Bay, Carne is a welcome sight for those who have no disdain for occasional "surprises" - such as blind shots, severely undulating terrain, and sharp dropoffs. There is no shortage of strategic options and shotmaking challenges. As far as combined beauty, intriguing play and sheer fun are concerned, these dunescape cousins have few rivals.

Carne boasts 27 holes - the original Eddie Hackett 18 (opened in 1992) and the Jim Engh/Ally McIntosh Kilmore 9 (2008). In recent years, it has been made possible to play the best of the best of these by creating a combo course called the "Wild Atlantic Dunes" 18. This creates some confusion for the first-timer when trying to follow the directions to the next tee - but the opportunity to engage the combined layout is entirely worth the mild logistical inconvenience.

Despite its irregular landscape both Brian and I felt that the typically generous landing areas offset its unpredictable effects. And, the tall, thick marram grasses in the dunes and around the greens were frequently cut back and/or integrated with other grass varieties of varied height and stockiness - which *sometimes* offered a jailbreak opportunity on errant shots. A buggy rental is strongly recommended, even for the young and fit linksters, particularly if playing a number of courses over a relatively short period of time. The inclines throughout, especially between many greens and tee boxes that afford such incredible views, are significant.

We were mesmerized by the remote and quiet nature of the course and the never-ending plethora of expansive seascape and countryside views from elevated vantage points. But it's not all about the scenery; there are virtually no weak holes. As such, it is a challenge to pinpoint the best ones. However, the par-4 dogleg right 11th hole has a little bit of all things Carne. A well-struck tee shot that traverses a downhill chute, bordered by a towering dune, is deeply rewarded, leaving a short approach over the highly lumpy fairway to a raised, undulating green backed by a natural amphitheater. There is also a great stretch of holes, beginning at the par-3 14th, with its lofty tee box offering a magnificent panorama, and a green abutted by a massive blowout bunker - a la the ones at Pacific Dunes, Royal St. George's and St. Patrick's, and continuing with the par-4 15th and par-3 16th that are equipped with well-raised tee boxes and greens, encircled by dunes. In short, the golfer here experiences a nonstop, picturesque joyride on a course filled with humps and bumps, ripples and ridgeways, and large hills and dales.

Given its combined isolation and relative newness, Carne's notoriety is only gradually gaining a foothold. (Hence, it is entitled to Hidden Gem status.) However, with acclaimed golf writers such as Tom Coyne and John Garrity touting it as their favorite links course, and the golf podcast/YouTube program "No Laying Up" bringing it to life and singing its praises, the number of rounds played there, and the course's conditions, are improving considerably. In any event, the Northwest of Ireland has many fine courses, including County Sligo, Enniscrone, Donegal, Rosapenna (Old Tom Morris/Sandy Hills/St. Patrick's), and Portsalon - and Carne should absolutely be included in an itinerary covering that area. Indeed, it should serve as the anchor of any such trip! (See Kevin Markham's great video tour of Carne on YouTube.)

Sadly, the father-son portion of the golf trip had to end. Thank God that, in this modern age, parental stoicism can give way to unabashed hugs and tears.

Big Ray spent the night at a B&B so as to be on hand to take me on my two-hour scenic journey from Ballina to Donegal. Donegal town was even better than expected, with my hotel (Abbey Hotel) overlooking the spiffy variety of restaurants and shops on Diamond Square in the center of town. Also included there is an obelisk that commemorates the Four Masters - four Gaelic monks who, in the 1630s, wrote "The Annals of the Four Masters", which records several millennia of fact and fiction and served as a frequent reference guide for future historians. Just steps from this center is Donegal Castle. The 30-minute guided tour of the partially intact fortress home was quite interesting and should not be missed if staying in, or passing through, this area.

Donegal Golf Club (aka "Murvagh") does not share the same level of dramatic terrain (though plenty of scenic rural/bay views are present) as the courses that Brian and I played, or the ones that I would be playing further north. It has a reputation for being one of Ireland's most challenging (particularly in the typically stiff winds) and long courses. However, it is a par 73, which helps account for its total of 6,500 yards - from the Senior tees! As things turned out, Donegal proved to be a diamond in the rough. However, the round began inauspiciously as the four weather seasons on the first few holes had me changing clothes faster than Clark Kent! After that, things brightened and warmed up.

The rough largely consists of relatively short, slender grass, so all was not lost, particularly new balls, if landing in it. There are five par-5s, and three of them (#'s 1, 6 and 14) were among my favorite holes on the well-groomed course - a solid blend of layout, challenge and extended vistas. And for dinner? La Bella Donna Italian Restaurant. Delizioso!

The next stop was a five-night encampment in the understated elegance and charm of the Rosapenna Hotel and Golf Resort in Downings. The hotel is juxtaposed with its three golf courses and Sheephaven Bay. Two golf layouts - Old Tom Morris & Sandy Hills - are a par-4 distance away (the hotel provides buggies to get there, if desired), and the third, St. Patrick's, requires a short taxi/rental car drive. On top of all this, the hotel television includes the Golf Channel!

Sandy Hills Links - designed by Pat Ruddy, opened in 2003 to incorporate the larger dune areas next to the Old Tom Morris course. However, I believe it would have worked out better if developed as a nine hole set-up (and blended, a la Carne, with the Morris course). Too many holes seemed forced into the natural landscape. There are an extensive number of blind shots (with virtually no directional aids) that leave "perfect" fairway tee shots, down narrow fairways, at the base of severe dropoffs, monster craters, and sizable rough - leading to head-scratching ball searches. It seems that Mr. Ruddy tried to offset this quirkiness overkill by inserting large, well-conditioned, and receptive flat greens - which did not blend well with the wild natural topography. Nevertheless, the course includes beautiful elevated views of land and sea. The par-5 first hole is unique as the dogleg left leads to a raised "infinity green." The par-4 15th presented an interesting visual, with a large dune fronting a mountain that looked like another, larger dune. The par-4 18th is a good finisher, allowing an accurate tee shot to scoot through a narrow gap.

Old Tom Morris Links - Perhaps Old Tom knew he should stick to the (relative) lowlands when designing this Hidden Gem in 1893. Subsequent revisions were made by an all-star cast consisting of James Braid, Harry Vardon, Harry Colt, and Pat Ruddy. (The latter was primarily responsible for an excellent new front nine (former back nine), designed to eliminate holes that crossed what had become a busy road, and better incorporate the dunescape. The new nine opened in 2009, thereby bringing Ruddy a form of redemption for the flaws which, in my view, exist at Sandy Hills.) I feel that this overall 18 hole layout is nothing short of a combination of fair challenge, significant beauty, and old-fashioned links fun. I had good vibes from the outset as the fairways and greens gracefully flowed with the natural landscape. Visible humps and dips were much more subtle and predictable in the outcome than the Sandy Hills course, and the dunes were used judiciously as both backdrops and strategic obstacles. This links has excellent, but not overly abundant or complex bunkering. My favorite holes are the par-3 2nd hole, with a marvelous undulating green, the par-4 6th, with its dunes encasing the low-lying green, and the short par-4 13th, with its long, narrow green.

The following day it was time to take on the newest kid on the block - **St. Patrick's Links**, which was designed by Tom Doak. It opened in 2021 and is already ranked #55 in the world by one of the major golf magazines. Soon after teeing off, I encountered, and continued to experience, shades of two Doak courses in the USA - Pacific Dunes and Ballyneal. The number of gigantic blowout bunkers is amazing. They are mostly visual candy unless one severely sprays the ball, as the fairway landing areas are quite generous and most of the greens huge. Strategic options abound. I can't place my finger on any single show-stopping hole, though they are all good. What I would classify as showstoppers are the greens. Their shaping is simply the finest I have ever seen. They have the appearance of virtually no earth movement in their creation as so often they are mirror-like extensions of the significant rises and dips of the adjoining landscape. Yet, the largeness of the greens makes it possible to place the pins in a variety of locations, that make putting them a fun challenge rather than a nightmare.

The par 71 course has a reputation for difficulty. However, a combination of playing from the 6,000 yard tees (heck, I'm 65!) and bringing my A+ game to the course resulted in my shooting a four over par 75. (Prior to our respective departures from Ballina, Brian shared with me a video he'd taken of my swing, and I noted that I'd reverted to some old bad habits. Here here for instant video phone feedback!)

The round was not without its amusements. On the 10th tee, a group of Irishmen invited me to play through. They said they'd been watching me and added that I played as well as I dressed. (A validation for tweed flat caps, pleated all-wool pants, and conservative shirts and shoes!) One of them said that he had a $20 bet with the others that I would hit another tee shot down the middle of the fairway. I managed to do so, and then chimed in that if I knew I would feel that much pressure to perform successfully I would have just hit my putter off the tee since the bet said nothing about the required distance! As for favorite holes, I will go with the par-4 7th, with its punchbowl green, the sharp dogleg right par-4 14th, where the option is to either hit a layup toward the sea-facing elbow or chew off a significant part of the fairway by aiming over the dunes on the right, the par-4 16th, with a tee offering splendid views of the dunes, mountains, and bay, the par-3 17th, with an incredibly deep furrowed green, and the short par-4 18th, playing into a strong headwind, with blowout bunkers on the left and a large crater fronting the right side of the green, along with a backstop on the back of the green that feeds the ball back to the pin if opting for a safer approach shot.

Mr. Doak certainly did Dr. MacKenzie and his minimalist design style proud here!

Portsalon Golf Club - Originally designed in 1891 by Charles Thompson, the course was lengthened and revised in 2000 by Pat Ruddy, along with input from accomplished professional Paul McGinley. The smart little clubhouse is a cozy place to have tea and enjoy the views before teeing off. The course has a distinct personality sitting next to the expansive, clean, bright sands of Ballymastocker Bay. It comes with more than modest dunes on the front nine and some steep parkland-like landscape, with large rock outcroppings set into the hills on the back nine. The Lough Swilly stream-like sea inlet flows across several holes, and the Knockalla Mountains are always in view. Despite being one of the oldest courses in Ireland, it is less well known than some of the other top courses, including those in the Northwest of the Republic and in nearby Northern Ireland. I suspect its day is not far off. Until then, it belongs in the Hidden Gem class.

There is certainly no bunker overkill here. The naturally lumpy landscape and raised greens with steep falloffs provide sufficient protection - and the pleasant dilemma of whether to pitch, chip, or putt to the pin when off the green. The greens, several of which are double in nature as at St. Andrews, are in excellent condition and roll true. I was partial to the long par-4 2nd hole, a dog leg right hit over a slice of beach on the tee shot and the Lough Swilly on the approach, with a rock ridge abutting the right side of the green, the par-4 7th, with beautiful views from the raised tee box, another dogleg right with a natural channel fairway to a raised green and the elevated par-4 dogleg left 14th (with trees lining one side) named The Altar - where Catholic Mass was secretly held amid a group of rocks wedged into a hillside during the Irish Penal Laws period, when public Mass was forbidden. (At least I think that's what was going on here - the descriptive plaque was in Gaelic!) Just past these rocks lies a beautiful green.

My only complaint about the course is that they could place more directional aids for the blind and semi-blind tee shots and approaches. In any case, Portsalon is a must if you are in the area.

The biggest challenge on this journey to Ireland was figuring out a practical means of transportation from the relatively remote Rosapenna Hotel in Downings to the Portmarnock Golf Hotel on the outskirts of Dublin. Months before the trip, I had looked into buses and combined train/bus/taxi transport, but the times and number of changes were prohibitive. Therefore, I resigned myself to hiring a driver, which I knew would not be cheap. Upon arrival, our driver pal Tommy made a few calls (as he did in setting us up with Big Ray), but informed me that the drivers up north wanted a thousand dollars for the three-hour trip, literally engaging in highway robbery. In the end, Brian did some digging and found that a summer bus schedule had opened up that involved the use of two private bus coaches with only one transfer stop (at yummy Mr. Chippie Fish and Chips Shop in Letterkenny) with a total time from Rosapenna to the airport being four and a half hours - for $80! So, the transportation worries were over, and I could focus on golf.

The quiet and tasteful Portmarnock Hotel and Golf Links (not to be confused with the nearby Portmarnock Golf Club) is conveniently located less than 15 minutes from the Dublin airport. Excellent meals were had in its bar - part of the Jameson whiskey family's former manor.

The Portmarnock (Hotel) Links opened in 1992 and was designed by Bernhard Langer. When I checked in at the pro shop I was told that I would be playing with two members. I had intended to play from the 6,300 yard green tees. (My home course plays at 6,050 yards from the white tees.) However, upon being introduced to the members, they said they planned to play from the 6,650 yard white tees since the weather conditions were pretty benign. Given that they were local Irish members, I felt it was only proper to join them on the whites. However, after the first couple holes, I quickly realized this round was going to be more than a question of length. Those familiar with America's Revolutionary War will recall the Battle of Bunker Hill. I soon labeled my round "The Battle of Bunker Hell." There were over 100 bunkers, a collection of the steepest faced (virtually all stacked sod), deepest, wildly and often beautifully shaped, sometimes unplayable on a direct line, bunkers I have ever seen. There were nine on one hole alone (though none on at least one hole). Often, they were in the middle of the fairways and, therefore, an automatic stroke loss if landing in one since, due to their nature, the ball could not be advanced very far even if making a successful escape. I was fortunate to land in only three of the bunkers and managed to extricate the ball on the first attempt. However, their looming locations and daunting character gave me a headache.

Setting aside my reservations about the length of the course and its bunkers, it did have its merits. The greens were very large, firm, and well-manicured as were the tee boxes and fairways. The par-4 first tee (the ruins of St. Marnock's church and its cemetery are just off the right-hand side of the fairway) and the par-4 18th (the hotel overlooking a beautiful, recessed undulating green in a small, grass-mounded arena) were my favorite holes.

It seemed only fitting that what would likely be my last golf sojourn to the Emerald Isle should conclude on a sunny warm day with light winds at a Hidden Gem - **Corballis Links Golf Club,** located near the Dublin airport and virtually next door to the Island Club (see 2022 trip description). The course bears a certain resemblance to its neighbor, along with shades of Carne and its quirky charm, as well as the cozy par-3s at the Bandon Dunes' Preserve course. But, there is one huge difference - the green fees! It costs only $30 to play Corballis, and getting a tee time there on short notice is easy. Indeed, it may be the best-kept golf secret in Ireland, save for the locals, who treasure its affordable fun. The course is not "championship" in nature (seven par-3s and only one par-5) but offers the full links experience. It roams through giant dunes, is filled with lumpy fairways, has large, undulating and well-maintained greens, and contains better than adequate bunkering. Views of the sea and beach strands can be observed from a number of tees and greens. The mixture of grasses in the rough generally allows balls on errant shots to be found and extracted.

I particularly liked the variety of holes on the front nine, which includes several newer ones designed by Ron Kirby to better incorporate the dunes and sea. The back nine also has some unique holes, but it is a bit helter-skelter, if not outright dangerous at times. Some fairways crisscross each other or are tightly joined despite blind tee shots. But, the overall joy ride here renders this as nothing more than a minor inconvenience. If a key factor in determining whether a course is great is that you would love to play it again and again, then Corballis belongs in the pack.

Irish Courses vs. Scottish Courses? And the Winner...
Scotland by a Haggis

In short, it comes down to personal preference. Ireland's courses are full of lush, undulating beauty, both on the course and in the vast, open surrounding areas. The dunes are bigger. The grasses are greener. Scotland's layouts abound in history and include classic wide-open links. There is better playability from the drier, wispy rough there as opposed to the thick, sugar cane-like marram grasses of Ireland, especially in the dune areas. The lost ball ratio is about 3-1 against Ireland. This is important if one subscribes to a fundamental MacKenzie tenet of course design; namely, an inordinate amount of time should not be spent searching for balls. I saw signs that Ireland is beginning to better recognize this principle - several courses have cut back their beautiful but menacing grasses further from the fairways, greens, and rough areas.

Generally, it is easier to get from primary groups of links courses in Scotland than in Ireland. This is more of an issue if your time is limited, since the scenery in Ireland otherwise tempers the longer drives and fewer bus/train options.

Watercolor of Ashford Castle by Katheen M. Hammel

Horseback Riding Near Adare Manor

Ballybunion Par-4 17th Hole

A Tee Box at Adare Manor GC (Abbey Course)

Rock of Cashel

Druids Glen Par-3 12th & 8th Holes

Dooks GL Par-3 4th Hole

County Sligo Par-3 9th Hole

Portstewart Par-3 3rd Hole

Village of Glenarm Antrim County   *Swords Castle*

LINKS TO THE LINKS · SCOTLAND/IRELAND

Doonbeg Hotel Main Lodge

Jack & Brian Lahinch 1st Tee

Doonbeg Par-5 Opening Hole

61

Dromoland Castle Par-3 7th Hole

Dromoland Castle Par-5 18th Hole

Across the Bay from Glenarm

Bushmills Inn

Enniscrone Par-5 16th Hole

Ardglass 1st Tee

Carne Par-4 11th Hole

Carne Par-3 14th Hole

Carne Par-4 15th Hole

Donegal Castle   *Rosapenna Old Tom Morris Statue*

View From Rosapenna Hotel & Golf Resort

LINKS TO THE LINKS - SCOTLAND/IRELAND

Old Tom Morris Links Par-3 14th Hole

St. Patrick's Links Par-4 16th Hole

St. Patrick's Links Par-3 3rd Hole

Portsalon Par-4 2nd Hole

Portsalon Par-3 10th Hole

Corballis Par-4 3rd Hole   *Corballis Par-4 5th Hole*

Corballis Par-3 6th Hole

Carnoustie Par-3 13th Hole

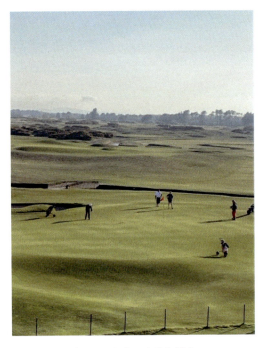

Carnoustie Par-4 18th Hole

LINKS TO THE LINKS - SCOTLAND/IRELAND

Panmure Clubhouse Exterior

Panmure Clubhouse Interior

71

St. Andrews Par-4 18th Hole (Tom Morris Shop Lft. & Rusacks Hotel Rt.)

Old Tom Morris Shop & Home

LINKS TO THE LINKS - SCOTLAND/IRELAND

Jack & Kathy at Rusacks, Overlooking St. Andrews Par-4 18th

Kingsbarns Par-4 18th Hole

Greywalls Hotel Muirfield

Greywalls' Neighbor - Muirfield Clubhouse

Glen North Berwick Par-3 13th Hole

LINKS TO THE LINKS - SCOTLAND/IRELAND

North Berwick Par-3 15th (Redan) Hole

North Berwick Par-4 13th Hole

North Berwick Par-4 18th Hole

THE BEST OF ALL THINGS GOLF

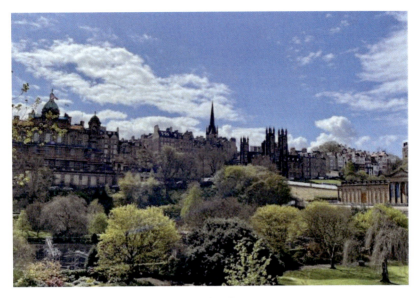

Edinburgh

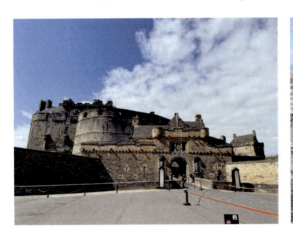

Edinburgh Castle

Urquhart Castle & Loch Ness

Glamis Castle

Machrihanish Dunes Misc. Holes

CHAPTER II

Golf in the Major Regions of the USA

Pebble Beach Par-3 7th Hole

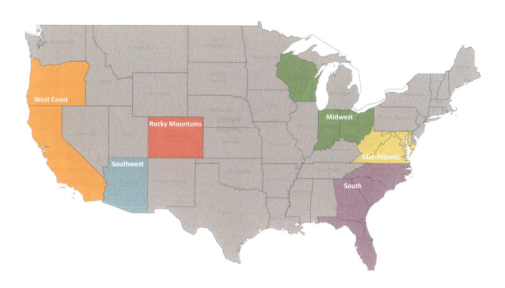

Given its vast size, few places on earth offer the variety of golf that one can experience in the United States. The USA has everything from true links golf (although relatively limited compared to Great Britain and Ireland) to mountain, desert, marshland, prairie, lakeside, and cliffside terrain. And, when the season is not conducive for golf in one region, a more receptive area is a short flight or manageable car ride away. What I find fascinating is an inescapable trend by major golf developers in America in recent decades. Namely, to bring the look and feel of the links of Great Britain and Ireland to all parts of this country. For Americans who do not have the time, money or desire to travel abroad to experience links golf, these developers have brought a reasonable facsimile of it to their doorsteps. And it has proven to be a wild success. Think Bandon Dunes, Prairie Dunes, Sand Hills, Sand Valley, Mammoth Dunes, Erin Hills, Whistling Straits, Arcadia Bluffs, Ballyneal, Lido, Kiawah Island, Streamsong and, coming soon, Rodeo Dunes. There are more, but I think you catch my sand drift.

In this Chapter, I will not engage in the laborious (or "bore-ious") exercise of describing all the courses I have played in the USA. Instead, I will highlight many of the best courses and/or experiences encountered in the country's major regions. (My apologies for the omission of the North East, where I traveled many times but never had the opportunity to play some of its fine courses.) The Appendix lists every course I have played, along with its star rating. This might be helpful, for comparison purposes, for readers considering a golf trip to a particular course and/or region. So, let's tee off on the West Coast!

THE WEST COAST

Bandon Dunes Oregon - Less than 25 years since the first of six courses opened for play (with two more in the development stages), this resort has taken the golf world by storm - literally and figuratively. It is one of the most unlikely success stories imaginable. Located in a remote southwest corner of Oregon, turbulent weather in the form of high winds, chilly temperatures and/or rain frequently looms over the golf landscape next to the rugged coastal cliffs. (However, calm, warm, sunny days are also known to weave in and out of the picture during most months.) Gorse plants spread here like weeds, providing colorful backdrops. Most holes were laid out over and around rolling natural landscapes and large dunes, with rangy grass ready to gather in wayward balls. The crashing ocean waves are frequently in view. Hmmm, it sounds a lot like the linksland courses across the Atlantic! That's what the resort's developer, former greeting card magnate Mike Keiser, thought when he conceived the idea of establishing golf here. However, at least the great links courses in Great Britain and Ireland (with a few exceptions, such as Machrihanish and Carne) are typically easily accessible within a short time frame by various forms of transportation. And, they have a comprehensive infrastructure with diverse activities and sights in nearby cities, towns and villages. Yet Keiser held steadfast to an "If you build it, they will come." mentality because golf enthusiasts would embrace "Golf as it was meant to be." And they have, at a pace that only increases with each succeeding year and additional course. It is the number one golf destination resort in the USA and has the most courses (all of them) in the Top 100 list of the major golf publications.

As for me, I have been to Bandon Dunes (where each course was designed by an architectural superstar) twice. I have played Pacific Dunes (Tom Doak) twice, and the Bandon Dunes (David McLay Kidd), Sheep Ranch (Bill Coore/Ben Crenshaw), and par-3 Bandon Preserve (Coore/Crenshaw) courses once. I have yet to play Bandon Trails (Coore/Crenshaw) and Old Macdonald (Doak) but narrowly secured a reservation to do so in the summer of 2024.

Of those I have played, I consider **Bandon Dunes** (the first to be built) slightly better than Pacific Dunes, even though the latter is typically ranked a few notches higher on Top 100 lists. The reason is that I feel Bandon Dunes most closely resembles a multifaceted Scottish links course, with a pinch of Scottish Moorland added in. More specifically, throughout my round I couldn't help but think of Royal Dornoch, Turnberry and Machrihanish (and later Gleneagles). Favorites are the "inland" par-4s at the opening hole, 5th, and 8th, and the coast-hugging par-3s at the 6th, 12th and 15th.

Pacific Dunes perhaps has the better layout and collection of dramatic holes (though not by much). I am most fond of the par-4 4th, close by the coastal cliffs, the par-3s at the 10th and 11th, which play out to the ocean over rugged terrain, the par-4 13th with a green sandwiched between the cliffs and a towering sand dune/bunker, and a fine par-5 finishing hole.

Sheep Ranch is raw, wide open, natural links golf and is a must for anyone who has not played, or does not plan to play, the links courses abroad. I place it a cut below the Bandon Dunes and Pacific Dunes courses because, if it was located in Scotland or Ireland, I believe it would be well regarded but not at the top of the lists. I am partial to the par-3 3rd hole with a shared green and ocean view, the par-4 6th, which cuts across the cliffs from the tee, par-4 9th, playing down to the coast, par-5 11th requiring a shot through a chute of sandhills fronting the green, and the par-4 15th and par-3 16th with greens perched against a small precipice overlooking the ocean.

The 13 holes that make up **Bandon Preserve** are short hole masterpieces. Each could fit in and be a par-3 signature hole at virtually any links course worldwide.

As for accommodations, the resort has a grouping of free-standing lodges consisting of upscale rurality. On my first visit, Kathy and I stayed in the main lodge. You won't find swimming pools and tennis courts here. The purpose and vibe is golf. (However, those who enjoy a fishing break between rounds will find opportunities nearby.) The resort continues to expand its guest room capacity, but "No Vacancy" is still a distinct possibility, even when planning a year in advance. No worries. Just a few miles down the road there are a few decent hotels at little Bandon Harbor. On my most recent visit, Brian and I stayed at the Bandon Inn. It was considerably cheaper and every bit as comfortable, albeit slightly less convenient.

California

The San Francisco Bay Area (Public Access Courses)

While New York (Long Island in particular) probably has the most remarkable assemblage of outstanding golf locations, most of them are not accessible to the public. The Bay Area certainly has its share of renowned private clubs, but it also offers a significant number and variety of public courses (where the tee times don't sell out in seconds and/or require you to stand in line in the pre-dawn hours in hopes of securing a walk on opportunity in the event someone cancels - a la Bethpage Black). Indeed, one could plan a week of golf playing just the San Francisco Recreation and Park Department Courses and still be rewarded with a rich (though somewhat chagrined "If only…") experience. Granted, these are far from being in mint condition due to the City's perennial refusal to invest in upgrades and best practices maintenance. However, the layouts by a couple of golf's greatest architects (five by Jack Fleming, who was also the former long-time groundskeeper for the San Francisco Recreation and Park courses in their heyday, and one by his mentor, Alister MacKenzie) and the views, coupled with the convenient locations and cheap cost, warrant looking past the current flaws relative to upkeep. (In rating these particular courses, I know that I have thought a little too much with my heart, rather than my head, given their enfeebled condition. But, the overall fun factor weighed heavily.) In any event, let's have a brief look at this group.

Lincoln Park Golf Course - This par 68 Jack Fleming design (original layout by Tom Bendelow) offers some of the best views in the country while you golf. Scenes of the cityscape, Golden Gate Bridge, Marin Headlands, Palace of the Legion of Honor Museum, and Golden Gate Park follow you around like a faithful dog. There are a number of elevation changes that enhance their presentations. While relatively short, it is nevertheless challenging and endearingly eccentric. Some of the best holes include the par-4 6th, where you tee off next to the grand old Legion of Honor structure that smacks of Paris, the short par-4 7th with its blind tee shot over a slanted rise to a green waiting in the hollow below, and the magnificent, long par-3 17th hole clinging to the cliff's edge, with a postcard view of the Golden Gate Bridge. A sign near the tee box on this latter hole states that it is forbidden to intentionally hit balls (i.e., aim at a 90-degree angle from the tee box) into the ocean. Not even once have I failed to heed this stricture. (Is my nose getting longer, or is it just me?) C'mon San Francisco, put a little money into restoring this splendid, well-situated course. It shouldn't take the lure of a major (in the manner of Harding Park) to polish up a gem.

Golden Gate Park Golf Course - Tucked away in the heart of this park is another Fleming layout, a charming little nine hole (Fleming's specialty) par 27 course with a nice variety of holes routed over and around the former sand dunes upon which Golden Gate Park was planted. Used more by casual tourists and local beginners, it is still a great place to play when it is not crowded. I used to frequent the course early in the morning after dropping my daughter off at nearby St. Ignatius High School for cross-country practice during the summers. What a wonderful way to ease into the workday it was!

Fleming Golf Course - Appropriately named in honor of its designer, this nine hole, par 30 course is surrounded by its big sister, Harding Park. Given its location, and the fact that Jack Fleming had a role in the ultimate layout of Harding Park (though it was primarily designed by Willie Watson and Sam Whiting of Olympic Club fame), the two courses share a similar look and feel. As such, Fleming is sometimes referred to as the "Poor Man's Harding Park." If you can't get a tee time at Harding or don't want to pay its relatively steep green fee, the Fleming course is an excellent consolation prize. The favored holes for me are the par-4 8th and par-3 9th, which blend right in with those at adjacent Harding Park. Both holes are nicely bunkered with contoured greens.

Harding Park (TPC at) - Most golfers are familiar with this course as it has hosted a WGC championship (won by Tiger Woods in 2005 in a playoff over John Daly) as well as the 2009 Presidents Cup (won by the USA) and 2020 PGA Championship (won by a young Collin Morikawa, which he secured by driving the green on the 300 yard 16th and making the seven-foot eagle putt). It plays long and is challenging, but it is not overly penal, and is easy to walk. The City does tend to let maintenance (but not the green fees) slide a bit between major tournaments. There are many nice holes, though I am partial to the final three (par-4, 3 and 4 respectively). They come with tall umbrella-like cypress trees and lakes in view.

Gleneagles Golf Course - This hilly, tilted par 36 nine hole course with Bay vistas is the least known and played of the Park and Recreation's courses, primarily because it borders some tough neighborhoods. It is also the most difficult. Lee Trevino is said to have played here and, after failing to break par, immediately played it again with the same result. It can be played from separate tee box locations if planning a second nine holes. The course has both a good opening hole and a closing one.

Sharp Park Golf Course - Your chance to play a rare Alister MacKenzie public course - which opened in 1932 - at the price of just a few beers. (Jack Fleming later relocated several holes after the originals were lost to the sea though, in view of their former partnership, the work of these two architects is sometimes indistinguishable.) When I lived on the Peninsula south of San Francisco, I played this course many times and retained fond memories, including pre-round breakfast in the old Spanish Hacienda-style clubhouse. While owned by the city of San Francisco, it is actually located 10 miles south in the seaside surfing town of Pacifica. The layout is situated next to the Pacific Ocean, though the shoreline is mostly obscured due to the necessity of installing a flood-reducing levy. But, the pounding surf can be heard, and the breeze delivers the aroma of the sea. (Formerly, one could take a short hike up the levy on the way to the next tee to remove the mystery, but recently some border fencing was added, making this option more challenging.) The surrounding headlands and mountains are always in view, as are the numerous wind-worn cypress trees. This par 72 course is very walkable, with a great variety of holes, and presents a unique opportunity to sample the artwork of Mackenzie's greens and bunkers. I like the par-4 3rd with its small undulating green, par-4 7th with a larger undulating green, par-3 12th (the original 2nd hole) where you hit straight toward the Pacific to a turtleback green, in typically stiff ocean winds, and the par-4 17th hole, adjacent to a large marshland/lagoon area modeled after the "Lido hole." (MacKenzie submitted a drawing of a hole for a contest sponsored by a golf magazine pertaining to the once famous, but subsequently closed, Lido Golf Club on Long Island. His winning entry essentially ignited his career in America.)

Other Public Access Courses in the Bay Area - Let's now examine several excellent courses where the conditions far exceed those found at San Francisco's muni courses.

The Presidio Golf Course - Located adjacent to the luxurious neighborhood of Pacific Heights, just inside a National park, this former military base course and super private club, became a public access facility a few decades ago. (It was five-time major champion and Hall of Famer Lawson Little's home course, where his father was a colonel in the army, and the reclusive Joe Dimaggio was perhaps its most famous member.) When the weather is nice (it is often prone to thick, wet fog and winds), there are few finer locations to play in the Bay Area. However, it is steep and tight in places and, therefore, a respectable challenge to walk and play at times. The holes are diverse and come with nice views. The course is well-kept, with splendid greens and picturesque bunkers, many fringed with the wispy grassed beardies that are so prevalent at Royal County Down. Favorites? The short par-3 4th plays from a highly elevated tee. It is a pretty hole, well guarded by bunkers. Therefore, it must be respected despite being the number 18 handicap hole. Hole number 9, a lengthy par-5, plays toward the original clubhouse and Pacific Heights. The par-4 11th takes you uphill/sidehill, then downhill to a green fronted by a massive bunker. The final hole is tight, with large trees lining the entire left side en route to another fine green/bunker complex. If you can hit the ball straight, there is an opportunity to finish the round with a satisfying birdie.

Half Moon Bay Links (Ocean Course) - This course opened in 1997 and is an Arthur Hills design on the Pacific coast, 30 miles south of San Francisco. In my view, it has it all. On steep bluffs overlooking the lofty waves that slam the expansive coastline, the Turnberry Hotel-like Ritz Carlton (including a Scottish bagpiper) is always in close view as you play the well-manicured links. In its earlier years, tall, thick, wet rough lined the fairways, making it not only difficult to advance the ball to any significant degree, but just finding it represented a moral victory. They then wised up, cutting the rough way back and down like most true links. As a consequence, they also speeded up the pace of play. I may be engaging in some hyperbole, but I think Half Moon Bay could fit right in in Scotland along the same lines as Kingsbarns. It is full of fun and varied challenges. The ocean can be seen on nearly every hole. (Try to schedule your tee time around the fog that rolls in, often like clockwork, during certain times of the year.) Notable holes include the par-4 2nd, par-3 3rd, and the fantastic three finishing holes (in order a par-4, 3 and 5) with the splendor of the coast in full view and play. Here, Paula Creamer won the 2008 Samsung World Championship, not far from where she grew up in Pleasanton across the Bay. The facility's other 18 hole layout, the Old Course (Palmer design), pales in comparison. It is, essentially, parkland save for the last two holes. Yet, ironically, its par-4 18th hole is simply stunning and surpasses any hole on the Ocean Course, as well as just about any in California. The hole runs parallel to the cliffs, with a downhill tee shot followed by an uphill approach to an amphitheater-backed green, clinging to the precipice of a bluff (with many "fans" observing from the S'mores fire pit on the Ritz patio).

Crystal Springs Golf Course - This is another fine public access course, 20 miles south of San Francisco just off scenic Highway 280 in Burlingame. It was designed by British architect William Herbert Fowler of Walton Heath et al. fame, though some of the original holes later had to be rerouted when the highway was constructed. It offers a picturesque countryside setting with elevation changes that maximize views of the glimmering blue water in the large Crystal Springs Reservoir. Numerous and varied wildlife sightings are frequent. The greens are well cared for and can be speedy, particularly those that slope more steeply toward the reservoir. Crystal Springs is challenging yet fair from the outset. The par-4 6th dogleg left provides both beautiful views of the reservoir (looking back from the tee box) and mountains from the elevated tee, and a risk/reward drive that can result in a relatively easy approach, or a missing in-action ball in the rough. The par-3 13th hole offers another tee shot from a lofty position to a small green embraced by bunkers and a large boulder on the side, and trees in back. The last three holes (par-5, 4 & 5 in sequence) are relatively flat compared to most of the previous holes, but their bunkers and greens have a certain links look and feel about them, which I enjoy.

Baylands Golf Links - Formerly known as "Palo Alto Muni," this course, alongside the South Bay, recently got more than a new name; it got an entire facelift. And a fine one at that. It wasn't a bad course (original design by W.F. Bell) before it shut down for renovation, but now it is an outstanding destination muni in the Bay Area. Architect Forrest Richardson added many touches that give the course a distinctive links atmosphere, such as more undulating fairways and greens, and gorgeous revetted greenside pot bunkers on the par-3 12th and par-5 13th holes. Greens are meticulously maintained and fast, sometimes too fast, when pins are placed on or about the base of significant contours. The par-3 8th is attractively bunkered with a nice two-tiered green. Hole number 9 is a long par-5, with a receptive green from most angles. The finishing hole is another par-5 with a challenging approach and green.

Poplar Creek Golf Course - One might say that I earned my golf playing stripes at this course, abutting the San Francisco Bay in San Mateo, not far from San Francisco International Airport. While I played a variety of courses when living in San Mateo for 18 years, this was the most frequented. And, like most individuals, I developed a particular biased affinity for my home course. Fond memories, therefore, result in a rating that is, no doubt, exaggerated. However, I do think certain things stand out, making it more than worth playing. Its original design architect appears uncertain, though there are hints that both MacKenzie and Tillinghast may have made suggested revisions. In any event, it developed into a heavily played municipal course, with some of the truest greens in the Bay Area and a nice variety of holes that can be sneaky tough, particularly in the often stiff winds. Numerous eucalyptus trees and water hazards come into play. Both are evident at the long, pretty (though a little artificial) par-3 3rd hole. Caution suggests leaving the driver in the bag on some of the short, but sharp and well-guarded doglegs, such as those on the 2nd and 8th holes. The 15th is a nicely bunkered par-3 cuddling the Bay, and the par-4 16th most often plays into a strong headwind, making par feel like a birdie. While the par-4 18th has an artificial water component, it blends in pretty well with a natural one, and both add to the drama of the approach shot. Landing in one would often determine the outcome of team match play competitions pitting Old Gino and myself against the two Franks; so good and bad memories are inescapable.

San Jose Muni Golf Course - This is one of architect Robert Muir Graves' many fine public access courses located throughout California. There is nothing spectacular about it. Rather, it is simply a steady, very walkable and fun layout. The fairways are generally wide open, and the greens tend to be on the larger side and are in good shape. My favorite hole is the long par-5 finisher, where three good shots present the chance for an indelible birdie experience. For those looking to play other affordable public courses in the San Jose area, I recommend Santa Teresa and Sunnyvale, and, to a lesser extent, Coyote Creek on a calm day. I regularly played these courses before my brother, Bruce, moved from San Jose to Florida. Despite his adoption of an unorthodox grip (baseball style) and taking vicious swipes at the ball (His stated goal being : "... to hit that ball just as far as I possibly can."), he always managed to give me a run for my money. Not that either one of us was counting the other's strokes. (Wink-wink.)

Cinnabar Hills Golf Club - The golfer is welcomed with a beautiful wide-open rural setting south of San Jose. Its 27 holes are set among small mountains, valleys and lakes unhindered by homes, business complexes, etc. It is far too hilly for my taste, and many greens are semi-hidden, so an approach shot that appears perfect winds up off the green due to hitting the "wrong" slope. Of course, if played more often, this latter problem would dissipate via local course knowledge. Many holes contain highly elevated tee boxes with expansive vistas. The conditioning here is outstanding. Even if you decide not to play the course, have a meal here. Why? Aside from the external views, the restaurant's large interior is literally surrounded by one of the world's most extraordinary private golf museums. There are many original items such as a Green Masters Jacket, Red Captain's coat, antique books, paintings/prints, clubs, and balls, as well as reproductions of the four majors trophies.

Northwood Golf Club - And then there is Northwood. Just nine holes (par 36), but what a unique history, setting and layout. If you are exploring the coast and wineries in the North Bay, take a day to dry out and try out this Hidden Gem. (And have breakfast or lunch in the informal and lively country lodge-like restaurant or on its deck that is nestled close to the first tee.) The famous Bohemian Club commissioned Alister MacKenzie to design this course, with tight undulating fairways and small greens tucked among the giant redwood trees bordering the Russian River in Monte Rio. It opened in 1928 and has changed ownership several times - with portions unfortunately developed for up-close housing on some holes. This, along with the overgrowth of the protected redwoods, has compromised some of the more open original layout/lines of play and pristine conditioning. In places, MacKenzie's touch was modified (e.g., some bunkers grassed over but still detectable), though his fingerprints remain throughout and are readily apparent. The current group of owners (since 1970) includes a family that has managed the course with pride for several generations. Hopefully, a full restoration will someday take place - not an easy task when the green fees are kept at such a highly reasonable level. In the meantime, the overall condition of Northwood is sound and it is still widely regarded as one of the finest nine hole courses in America. Standout features include the semi-blind approach to a sunken channeled green on the par-4 2nd hole, the steep back-to-front green on the par-4 4th, the beautiful classic greenside bunkering on the par-5 5th, a cozy two-tier green on the short par-4 6th, and the exhilarating par-3 8th from an elevated tee to yet another tiny, nicely contoured green guarded by a variety of attractive bunkering - a kind of "Mini-Me" of the 15th at Cypress Point, sans water. Additionally, at the 8th hole one can see an excellent example of one of MacKenzie's camouflage techniques. If you stand at the back of the green looking toward the tee box, the greenside sand bunkers you saw when teeing off "disappear" into solid grass. If the ultimate goal of a round of golf is fun, it begins here!

Yocha Dehe Golf Club - I am not much of a gambler, but I made the right bet in deciding whether to drive two hours to play this, then, relatively new course on the grounds of the Cache Creek Casino Resort outside of Sacramento. I invited Les, one of my best friends and one of the world's worst golfers, to join me. Since he lived (the kind, diminutive guy is now deceased) in San Francisco and loved to drive (no doubt influenced by his fear of flying), we agreed to go separately. I warned him that the course was in a remote Indian reservation area, so he might want to print out some directions. (GPS was not yet the norm for Les.) He declined. Having been in the real estate business for nearly 50 years, he prided himself on his sense of direction. Indeed, he dismissively explained that he had had a real estate deal in a nearby little town years ago and would just look for casino signs when he got near it. And, of course, he got lost. He called me on his cellphone and said he made a couple of turns on streets whose names he could not remember and had been driving for miles on a nameless single-lane dirt road amid billowing dust clouds. I told him to turn around and find the name of the nearest cross street. He said the few crossroads were also without names and paved in dirt, and he couldn't remember which one he'd initially turned off onto the current one. I suggested he pull over at a farmhouse or other facility for assistance. He said there were no such things in sight. I then told him to call the course for assistance. He tried, but they could not help without some coordinates. The battery on his cellphone was dying fast. I gave him a few more suggestions and said I would see if the course could push our tee time back a couple of hours. I encouraged him to remain calm as I would also ask them to be on the lookout for circling buzzards near the reservation.

Well, the old dog finally crawled into the clubhouse restaurant and after a stiff drink and a nice meal in his stomach, we teed off on a course that exceeded already high expectations. But, before sharing my impressions of the course, a few more words about my playing partner are probably in order since his name will surface again in connection with visits to other courses. In short, this loveable boob made the Absent-Minded Professor (Denis) look like a model of organizational skill and good fortune. A few examples will suffice to explain my meaning.

Les' penchant for mishaps began at a young age. At 14 his older "friends" introduced him to alcohol to such an extent that when he woke up (naked in a local garbage dump) he literally thought he'd died and gone to hell. He exercised an impressive case of thinking on his bare feet by wrapping himself in some cardboard and hailing down a taxi that somehow was willing to stop. After arriving home, he had to ask his dear mum to step outside and pay the good man!

He once bought a modest size boat and, after a proper christening, invited a few friends to join him on its maiden voyage to Candlestick Park, the former home of the San Francisco Giants. As he approached the nearby pier, he panicked and crashed, leaving both the boat and the dock in a serious state of disrepair. This earned him the dubious title of "Cap'n Crunch." He promptly sold the boat.

A few years later, he borrowed a friend's new motorhome for a family vacation. As they neared Death Valley (appropriately named), the engine caught fire, which quickly spread. There was no time to remove belongings. Everyone jumped out. He called his friend from a pay phone to share the bad news. The friend (soon to be a former one) said to have it towed and repaired. Les explained that there was nothing left to tow!

Undaunted, Les later decided to try his hand with a motorcycle. On his first trial run on the highway, a semi-truck flipped up a stone that hit him square in the forehead at 60 miles per hour, though it somehow avoided knocking him completely out. He sold it the next day.

God, I miss him. Now, back to golf.

Yocha Dehe, designed by former PGA Tour pro Brad Bell, was in mint condition from tee to green. Creeks meander throughout the property and moundings have a natural look. The bunkering is judicious in size, number and location and provides a colorful contrast to the greenery of the course and the surrounding brown hillsides. There was no delay in terms of excitement. The tee of the par-4 first hole (aptly named "Eagle Eye") is perched 160 feet above the fairway, offering a broad panorama of the course and the undisturbed countryside. Hole number 7 is a lovely par-3 with a challenging raised, quasi-Redan-like green. The par-3 13th is guarded by a long sand trap containing three grass islands. A long par-4 dogleg serves as the finishing hole, with a sizable lake on the right side. A large hill and clubhouse provide the backdrop to the contoured green.

Haggin Oaks - Besides Sharp Park and Northwood, this course, outside Sacramento, presents golfers with the opportunity to add another California public access MacKenzie layout to their quiver - at minimal cost. As for others, Delta View, in the East Bay city of Pittsburg, sadly closed a few years ago. A fifth, in the wine country town of Healdsburg (Healdsburg Golf Club at Tayman Park), has some grounds for claiming a design or revisions connection to MacKenzie. Pasatiempo, in Santa Cruz, is semi-private, but a tee time can be secured, albeit at a cost of $350- $375. Pasatiempo has retained the most original MacKenzie layout and features, particularly since a major overhaul by Tom Doak and Jim Urbina in 2007. A bunker/green preservation project is underway and scheduled for completion in December 2024. The club is proceeding one nine at a time, so two rounds on the same nine can be played for $275 until the work is completed.

A visit to Haggin Oaks is a must for more than one reason. First, it contains two courses, one of which is a very walkable, amateur-friendly Alister MacKenzie design. Second, Haggin Oaks claims to be home to the country's largest on-course Golf Super Shop. It sells all manner of modern golf apparel and equipment as well as hickory clubs and other antiques.

I played the MacKenzie course and paid particular attention to the bunkers to better appreciate the camouflage techniques he learned during his service in the Boer War and later utilized in his natural-looking golf course designs. Manipulating depth perception was one (e.g., placing a "greenside" bunker further away from the green than meets the eye). Another (see **Northwood** review) can be seen (or, rather, not seen) when looking back at a bunker - one makes out what appears to be a flat or elevated grass area - but not the sand fill within or behind it.

The course is fairly wide open and has few, if any, fairway bunkers that I can recall. Rather, its challenges come in the form of relatively small, speedy undulating greens defended by deep bunkers. Fairways and greens are in good condition, and majestic 100-year-old oak trees abound. Kudos to the course management for rebuilding the 9th and 18th greens to conform to MacKenzie's original design. The long par-3 14th and 16th holes have an array of oaks and a creek that add beauty to their challenges. The par-5 18th is also noteworthy insofar as it not only includes the restored three-section green but also has one of the phantom "greenside" bunkers (actually 50 yards from the green) that can confuse the individual in terms of appropriate club choice. (So, trust your GPS instrument.)

Bay Area Wine Country Golf - For those visiting the Bay Area with the primary purpose of wine tasting, there is ample opportunity to squeeze in a unique round of golf at some nearby courses. Both the Eagle Vines and Wente courses are virtually surrounded by Bay Area vineyards. And, Oakmont's Valley of the Moon and Sugarloaf courses (where I am a member) are just across Route 12 from the St. Francis Winery at the gateway to the Sonoma Valley and its dozens of renowned vintners. So, let's check in at these three courses.

Eagle Vines Golf Club - One thing is certain - this Johnny Miller-designed course and its surroundings are aesthetically pleasing. What is less certain is whether it is a great course. I have played it several times and remain ambivalent, though my taste for it is growing like an aging wine. I understand they have changed the order of the holes since my last visit. As such, I hope I will be forgiven if I mismatch a description with the current number. Now, back to my ambivalence. Some holes present too much awkward challenge and potential carnage. Others are somewhat testy, but fair. The following two holes will serve to illustrate this dichotomy. The par-4 13th hole (formerly the 5th) is a dogleg left around a lake to an elevated, severely sloped, two-tiered green. The upper tier is a mere postage stamp. When the pin is in this location, it is target golf at its worst. A birdie is out of the question. A bogey, or worse, is a distinct probability. It is easy to understand why the next hole is the course's signature one. The panorama from the highly elevated tee is stunning. After taking in the views of the vineyards, large rolling hills, stands of trees, and water features, one must focus on the task at hand - a one-shotter to a large island green complimented by several bunkers, trees and fairway level grass. This is not the tortuous 17th hole at TPC Sawgrass. Instead, it is sheer, relatively simple, fun. The next hole, a par-4, again presents the golfer with splendid elevated views. It doglegs around a vineyard hazard to a large, two-tier green guarded by large bunkers. The par-4 7th (formerly the 17th) plays to a hill crest from which one can attack a relatively flat and receptive green. The clubhouse has an excellent grill room from which to reflect on the day's round.

The Course At Wente Vineyards - Greg Norman put together a popular (though not cheap at $120-$170) East Bay layout amid the massive hills and valleys surrounding the Wente Vineyards Winery in Livermore, 50 minutes from San Francisco. This is not a walker's course. There are some long, often steep, rides from greens to the next tee box. Indeed, the 250-foot elevation change to the par-4 10th hole has so many switchbacks it has been likened to San Francisco's famously crooked Lombard Street. Big hitters will not be able to resist going for the green on this hole, despite a canyon waiting to gulp a sliced ball. The management defines the short par-4 2nd, with its attractive bunkering, as its signature hole, though I feel that trees unduly interfere with the intended line of play, even when laying up, which is the only real option for most. The par-3 7th has a steep drop to the green, offering excellent views. Wente's course is impressively manicured from tee to green. The grill room is noteworthy.

Oakmont Golf Club (Valley of the Moon & Sugarloaf Courses) - Ted Robinson Sr. designed this 36 hole layout. He was a pioneer in promoting the use of water as a significant defense and earned the nickname "King of Waterscapes." I am not a big fan of the overuse of water, but here, it (almost all natural creeks and ponds) blends seamlessly into the landscape. More importantly, it does not seriously come into play except for those hitting overly wayward shots or individuals casting aside apparent risks with hopes of rewards. The Valley of the Moon par 72 championship course has small, undulating frontside greens and larger ones on the backside. The bunkers are well designed, but many suffer from low-quality and/or quantity sand. (This is being addressed in stages due to the significant costs involved.) My sole but loud complaint is the overuse of huge oak trees in the middle of a couple of fairways or designed lines of play (the 12th hole being the most notorious). I don't know whether this was entirely intentional or a product of environmental standards. I prefer to give Mr. Robinson the benefit of the doubt since, generally, this is not part of the format on the par 63 Sugarloaf executive course. In any case, the great classic architects such as MacKenzie, Ross and Colt (and their progeny) disfavored planting trees as strategic weapons ("hazards") on or about the fairways, particularly in landing areas or in the intended lines of play. I believe it was Colt who said that one such fairway tree hole (but no more) on a course was acceptable (think Neville's cypress on Pebble Beach's 18th, or MacKenzie's copse of the same on the 17th at Cypress Point); particularly if there are ample alternative landing areas which allow for fair negotiation of the next shot. They also abhorred redundant straight holes lined with trees from tee to green. From their perspective, the primary purpose of trees was to serve as backdrops or other parts of natural but tactically non-intrusive landscape features. They further point out that a tree, or small grouping, might be planted by designers to assist with the intended shaping of the hole, as in the case of a dogleg. However, they note that these same designers often fail to look decades into the future, when the height and/or width of the tree(s) will either disrupt the lines of play and/or require expensive trimming.

Years ago, I thought I had a solution to the 12th fairway tree thing at Oakmont. I decided to call in a chit with my old foreign political friend. Actually, we were not that close. Truth be told, I'd never even met him. But, we both had large birthmarks, so I felt we were simpatico. And, in any case, I knew he was well versed in getting things removed - including himself from office. I phoned him up and minced no words. I said: "Mr. Gorbachev, tear down this tree!" He said: "Nyet." I responded: "Fine. Not yet. But when?" The son of a bitchski hung up on me! It probably had something to do with his diplomatic immunity having expired. Newsflash! Just days before sending this book off to print the management took down a large oak that blocked an alternative route past the humongous oak that remains in the center of the fairway. (It's unclear whether the old, leaning oak was removed for safety reasons or because someone slipped the management a draft of my book!). Now, I can't get the Elvis song "Peace in the Valley" out of my head! But, I digress.

Overall, both of Oakmont's courses have challenging but fair layouts, with nearby Hood Mountain and Annadel Park in frequent view. Robinson deserves extra credit for managing to weave two courses into an area teaming with natural water features and a sizable amount of housing - all the while leaving short walks from the greens to the next tees. Both courses have mild elevation changes and are easily walkable. The number and variety of wildlife on and about the courses are unparalleled. It is common to see as many as 20 deer casually grazing together in the fairway. Sometimes, they rest like dogs in the backyard shade of abutting homes. I have counted as many as 100 Canada Geese on the first fairway. It's confusing in terms of why they are not called "Canadian Geese." Something about the fact that the Canada species of goose is just one of a variety that make up the collective group of geese in Canada referred to as Canadian Geese. (These types of fascinating semantic issues presumably give the ornithologists something to squawk about at their annual conventions!) One thing is certain: while there haven't been any golden egg sightings on the course, one does see a lot of gooey green stuff. Recently, the management hired a man and his faithful sheepdog to address the situation. Other frequent visitors include foxes, hawks, wild turkeys, river otters, large turtles, squirrels, ducks, egrets, cranes, crows, quail, rabbits, raccoons, and occasional skunks.

On the Valley of the Moon course my favorite holes are the casual par-4 opening hole with a tee shot over a small creek and defended with a buried elephant green, the pretty but sneaky-tough number 18 handicap par-3 8th, the par-5 10th, with the second shot over a pond and creek to a green with majestic oaks that provide welcome shade as non-intrusive spectators, the par-3 16th with a similar tree setting and the par-4 final hole, which offers a links style run-up/air option to a green guarded by two large front bunkers. With one of Annadel Park's large forested hills as a backdrop, the par-4 6th probably would be my favorite - but for one of those blasted oaks in the fairway. The hole has a Redan-like raised green, further protected in the back by a steep hill to a creek that can catch overly aggressive approach shots. (So, there is plenty of defense without the oak tree.) For the time being, big hitters can easily fly it as it is only about one-third full-grown. The shorter hitters in this senior community are the ones who are unduly punished. (The existing tree actually replaced one that had come down in the same spot during a storm.) Oh well, let's move on to Oakmont's less controversial sister course.

The Executive (Sugarloaf) course is not your mother's Executive course. It has nine par-4s and nine par-3s, but the latter include several in the 170 yard range and a few more that exceed 200-plus yards. I like the drivable par-4 2nd hole, par-4 dogleg 6th with its birdie prospects, the par-3 16th with elevated green, creek along the left and oaks with hanging moss, and the par-4 17th with Hood Mountain watching over like a proud parent. While both courses are very nice, I believe Sugarloaf has the overall better layout and beauty. It is wonderful to have the option to play two courses within a three-minute drive from my home.

Oakmont's courses are open to the public for a more than reasonable green fee, though members have preferred morning tee times for their various golf groups. A full-service bar and grill overlooks the Valley of the Moon course. There is a standard artificial turf driving range. However, at the other end of the same, there is an excellent natural grass range and generous-sized pitching green with bunkers.

The San Francisco Bay Area (Private Courses)

There are many, but what follows is a breakdown of some private courses of particular renown that I have played - most notably the Olympic Club - which I have been fortunate to experience numerous times as a guest (and follow the pros as a spectator at two U.S. Opens). Omitted are a couple courses which some would die to play, or play again, but which simply did not meet my criteria for best course standing as set forth in Chapter III. These include, but are not limited to, Mayacama (quite rigorous walking-only course and too much target golf) and California Golf Club (very hilly, overly treed and bunkered, windy, foggy, and poor drainage - BUT this was before major renovations were completed in 2008 - which I understand has restored much of the original greatness).

Olympic Club (Lake Course) - During my more than 35-year relationship with this historic course, my sentiments have changed like its terrain - up, down and sideways. In part, this is because my game improved significantly over this period, removing some of the frustration related to playing such a challenging course. Similarly, there have been some significant improvements to the course itself, which has made it less demanding and restored original shot-making options intended by the designers Willie Watson and Sam Whiting. Primary among these were widening the fairways and shortening the thick wet rough (save for U.S. Opens), taking down/trimming back overgrown cypress and other trees, converting the greens from cantankerous poa annua to bentgrass, and shaving down the severity of the back to front slope on the 18th hole green following outcries at the 1998 U.S. Open. Architectural modifications by the great Gil Hanse are scheduled for completion in 2023 and will, with certainty, make it even more fun to play. I look very much forward to finding out. There are a variety of nice holes but, if forced to choose my favorites, I would say the solid par-5 opening hole, with good views of the surrounding complex from its commanding tee box, the long, picturesque par-3 3rd, the par-3 8th (which completely replaced the former one) set in a grass arena overlooked by the clubhouse restaurant, the treacherous par-5 dog leg left 16th (just ask Jim Furyk, whose apparent 2012 U.S. Open victory vanished here), and the iconic 18th hole filled with so much beauty (the clubhouse holds court from high above, a la Riviera's same) and history. (Billy Casper shocked Arnie and his Army in the final round of the 1966 U.S. Open by erasing a seven-shot deficit with nine holes to play and forcing an 18 hole playoff - which he won the following day by four strokes after Arnie had built a significant early lead.) But it is not just about the golf at the Olympic Club. It is the total experience: History (host to five U.S. Opens, including not only Palmer's 1966 loss to Casper, but Hogan's 1955 18 hole playoff loss to Cinderella Man, Jack Fleck); Understated elegance (A short drive through the gate past the immaculate practice area and first tee box to the Mediterranean style clubhouse); A classic wood paneled grill room.

How did I gain frequent access to this highly coveted, exclusive course? The answer requires a little context. While always prone to nostalgia-driven eccentricity (still wearing pleated cuffed pants and flat caps on the golf course), I have never been one for pretentiousness. Despite a high-level professional position, I dodged all black-tie affairs and fancy fundraisers. If I had to go to a large business/social affair, I always sought, if possible, to sit in an inconspicuous corner where I could quickly escape to return to my family. I got married at the tiny Santa Cruz Mission, with 40 attendees, and had a backyard reception with sandwiches. (I was attired in my blue business suit, and Kathy, wore an off-the-rack, on-sale, wedding dress.) The only jewelry I've ever worn is my $50 wedding band. So, what's my point? Well, while I have led a relatively simple life, I have never hesitated to brake for both animals AND great golf courses! As such, in the case of the Olympic Club, I made a deal early on with Paul, a partner at the law firm that handled most of our corporation's outside legal work. (I served as an In-House General Counsel.) Namely, don't invite me to any lavish outings or feel the need to court my favors in any way, shape or form. Let good work speak for itself and my loyalty will be secured. However, I added that I would accept an annual invitation to play at the Olympic Club, with the right to order one of the snack shack's world-famous burger dogs at the turn, and some French fries in the grill room afterward.

Olympic Club (Ocean Course) - For many years, I favored the Ocean (also designed by Watson and Whiting) over the Lake, primarily because it is every bit as scenic (though its name is a misnomer as the Pacific Ocean view holes succumbed to coastal erosion many years ago), but not nearly as difficult. However, with the aforementioned changes in my game and the improvements to the Lake course, as well as its rich history, the latter now wins the running for the Roses race. The Ocean has varied terrain and excellent bunkering, but less severe than the Lake, and it is relatively open. The last time I played it was about five years ago when a social member of the club (none other than the infamous Les of Yocha Dehe fame) secured a tee time as my birthday treat for my son Brian (heir to the family golf addict throne). And what a memorable day it was. Brian embraced the whole Olympic Club experience, and Les managed to score 123 (with some liberal number crunching by me as scorekeeper). The course has a fine array of holes. For me, the standouts are the opening dogleg left par-5, the par-3 5th with its steep elevation drop from the tee to the well-bunkered green, the dogleg left par-4 13th with a nicely undulating green, and the par-4 18th containing a back to front sloped green with run-up option between handsome bunkers, enhanced by a backdrop of a large cypress tree and the towers of the Golden Gate Bridge.

Olympic Club (Cliffs Course) - While it has become the norm in the past couple of decades to add nine hole par-3 courses to the championship layouts at private clubs, resorts, and even public facilities, the Cliffs Course has been a bonus feature at the Olympic Club since 1994. It was designed by the dynamic duo of Tom Weiskopf and Jay Morrish; the epitome of sheer beauty (the water nearly always in full view) and target golf. (Les would typically lose a baker's dozen balls here.) Virtually all of the holes are jaw-dropping gorgeous. The least fetching one, the first, is still a most memorable one for me. Nearly 200 yards long, it was the scene of the first of my career three holes-in-one.

San Francisco Golf Club (See comments in Chapter IV) - As a side note, the SFGC is not far down the road from the Olympic Club (and can be seen from the heights of at least one of Olympic's holes, just as Olympic can be seen from a couple holes at Harding Park). And then, just a little south of these courses rests Lake Merced Golf Club in Daly City. While not sharing the same level of notoriety as its sibling courses, Lake Merced is, nevertheless, a solid compendium of the others. Nearly a century ago, it held some tournaments on the men's professional tour and, since 2016, has regularly hosted an LPGA Tour tournament. The "Renovation Doctor" Gil Hanse recently got his "Hanse" on the course, so it is undoubtedly better than ever.

Peninsula Country Club - Of the more than 400 courses that Donald Ross designed in the USA, this one, located 45 minutes south of San Francisco in the city of San Mateo, is the only one he did west of Missouri (save for a pitstop in Colorado Springs, where he laid out some holes at the Broadmoor Resort). Ross had no interest in cross-country design work, but Peninsula (then named Beresford Park Country Club) made him an offer he couldn't refuse. (When I visited the Donald Ross room at the Tufts Archives in the village of Pinehurst, North Carolina, the curator pulled out the file containing the original correspondence, plans, newspaper articles, etc. This file was of special interest since I lived just a mile from the club for 18 years and played the course at least a half dozen times.) He completely gutted the original design by Tom Bendelow. A large Tudor-style clubhouse, a la East Lake, overlooks the compound. The terrain is hilly but manageable, with some good views of the Bay Area. Quintessential Ross bunkering is evident throughout the course. The greens are full of undulation and generally quite speedy. In my estimation, the best holes are the par-4 6th with beautiful fairway and greenside bunkers, the latter protecting a pleasant looking elevated green, the par-4 9th hole playing from an elevated tee with views of the Bay, the attractive downhill one-shotter at 15, which requires careful club selection due to shifting wind directions, and the par-5 18th, with an uphill approach to a classic Ross style green and the stately clubhouse in the background.

Burlingame Country Club - This ultra-private club, about 30 minutes south of San Francisco is situated in Hillsborough - the "Beverly Hills" of Northern California. Here, Bing Crosby relocated to raise his family, away from the Hollywood environment. So how did a bumpkin like myself manage an invite to this exclusive golf club? Well, indirectly, I owe it to Der Bingle himself. If legend is true, the Roman Catholic crooner was a regular church-goer who convinced the club board to offer the local parish pastor limited playing privileges so long as he held that office. In any event, a successor pastor was kind enough to host me.

The course ranks high on my favorites list because I can place a checkmark in virtually all of the best courses criteria boxes. Robert Trent Jones Sr. is listed as the architect. However, the club was founded in 1893 (three holes opened for play in 1895 - with 15 more added in 1912). So, unless Jones designed his first course at the age of 6, the name(s) of the original architect(s) is omitted. (It appears that the members hired William Robertson of Scotland to design the initial three holes and another Scotsman, Tom Nicoll, who plotted two other posh private courses in the area in or about 1912, to complete the task.) It's probably safe to assume that Jones was responsible for a major overhaul of the course, and his name carried more cachet in the world of golf - hence his sole accreditation as the architect.

The residential town of Hillsborough is one of the first places on the Peninsula where one normally breaks through the fog barrier of San Francisco. As such, it is typically much sunnier and warmer. However, it can get windy in the area. This influenced massive tree planting (e.g., eucalyptus/cypress) to serve as natural windbreaks. Fortunately, these do not unduly interfere with play, save for the case of more errant shots. As might be expected, the course is mint-conditioned. It is effortless to walk. At par 70, it carries a challenging but not crushing rating/slope of 71.1/125 from the white tees. There is a nice variety of holes, including an early front nine par-4 with a well-protected narrow green (I've forgotten the precise number) and a short par-3 (number 9, I believe), which is all carry over a gorge to a beautiful shaded green, supported in front by a stone retaining wall. The finishing hole provides a composite of the excellent "Goldilocks" bunkering throughout the course (i.e., not too many, not too few; not too big, not too small; not too deep, not too shallow; and lovely shapes and sand color that are just right).

Lake Tahoe Area

Schaffer's Mill - Located between Lake Tahoe and Truckee, this Johnny Miller design opened in 2008. I was fortunate to play there at the end of the club's inaugural year, when autumn's warmth and sun still reigned, just several weeks before the arrival of the area's snow sports season. At that time, the "clubhouse" was a trailer since the upscale housing development and club membership were still in their infancy. My genial lawyer pal, Dan, and I had the course nearly to ourselves. Its mountain setting is simply idyllic amid Sierra Pines, rumbling streams and rocky landscape. (There are nice elevation changes, but not exhausting ones, for the player.) According to their website, members of other clubs can obtain reciprocal rights to play the course by arrangement with their local pro. If you are one of those people, hit the "Full Speed Ahead" button. At one time, they also allowed limited public access on Mondays. I don't know if that is still the case, but it can't hurt to ask, or even beg if necessary!

From a playability point of view, I found Schaffer's Mill more enjoyable than Nicklaus' meticulously maintained, but longer and more difficult, Old Greenwood design in Truckee. The par-4 9th, par-3 16th and par-5 18th incorporate all the above-referenced topographical features.

LakeRidge - Generally, I am not fond of Robert Trent Jones Sr.'s courses due to their typically arduous nature. However, LakeRidge is "Jones Sr. Light." It certainly has its challenges, but the emphasis is on unique fun. This is embodied in the spectacular par-3 15th hole (220 yards from the standard tee). It resembles the island green at Eagle Vines, described earlier, but with at least double the elevation and a view of downtown Reno in the distance. The tee ball from the steep, rocky precipice stays suspended for hours. OK, minutes. Alright, many seconds. Due to the thinner mountain air, depth perception, wind, and the second-guessing of club selection, the ball's ultimate landing destiny remains a complete mystery until it touches down. The par-4 opening hole is a nice dogleg right over a creek. The par-5 8th is pretty and challenging, with a lake guarding the green. A par-5 dogleg left, with a narrow, back-to-front sloped green, serves as a solid finishing hole.

The Monterey Peninsula

Pebble Beach Golf Links - Let us cut to the chase. There is Augusta National, St. Andrews and Pebble Beach. And then there's every other place. Yes, there may be more difficult/strategic/comprehensive layouts (Pine Valley). There may be more dramatic/scenic ones (Cypress Point). But if you pressed golfers worldwide to pick the three courses they would most wish to play at least once in their lifetime, I believe the vast majority would pick these three. In each case, it is the total package: The setting. The history. Certain memorable holes. All etched in the mind like a favorite childhood happy place, shared experiences with a BFF, or the moment one says "I do" or hears the words "It's a girl!" or "It's a boy!"

Many courses have magnificent entrance roads leading to their bag drop area, but they need help to claim one 17 miles long! Most are familiar with 17 Mile Drive, which begins in Pacific Grove and ends in Carmel, just past Pebble Beach. Within this stretch lies a rugged coastline with crashing surf and multi-hued water glimmering on mostly sunny, warm days, sugar-white sand dunes, majestic cypress trees, and mansions in various styles, sizes and colors. Along the way, one passes a virtual Hall of Fame of golf courses, most offering glimpses of a few of their serene holes - Pacific Grove, Monterey Peninsula, Spanish Bay, Poppy Hills, Spyglass, and Cypress Point. And then you enter the small village of Pebble Beach. You park across the street from the Pebble Beach Lodge. You poke your head into its golf shops, with the usual array of logo items, as well as a golf antiques store with original clubs, prints, paintings, statuary, and ephemeral as well as certain playable reproductions, such as the set of clubs used by Bobby Jones to win the Grand Slam in 1930. Walking past the practice green and the first hole's starter clock, you can step into the Tap Room for a burger and fries, or perhaps splurge for a meal in the more formal restaurant overlooking the legendary 18th hole. And then, for the few, the proud, the addicted, there is a tee time.

My opportunity to play Pebble Beach occurred many years ago through a business connection. And, none other than Old Dog Les joined me. It didn't matter to him that he shot his usual 120+ score. He, like me, was just thrilled to walk the venerated ground and revel in its abundant history, much of it shared with us by our entertaining caddie. The caddie also happened to be pretty darn good at his job. He would confidently point to a small spot on the green and, if you trusted the sometimes incomprehensible line he gave and executed accordingly, you were richly rewarded. In my case, I was proud not to three-putt a single green.

Most readers have watched enough AT&T Pro-Ams (formerly the Crosby Clambake) and U.S. Opens held here, so I will refrain from engaging in an extensive course description. Let it suffice to say that the usual suspects all met expectations: the short par-3 7th on its little jutting peninsula - where Sam Snead once used a putter from the tee rather than face the ravaging winds with a conventional club - and parred it, the par-4 8th over a giant coastal chasm, where millions held their collective breaths watching the 2022 AT&T as Jordan Speith took a mighty swing from its very precipice, the par-3 17th into the headwinds, where Tom Watson snatched the U.S. Open trophy from Jack Nicklaus with that improbable chip-in, and the dream-state inducing par-5 18th.

Cypress Point Club - Few would argue with the fact that the par-3 16th hole represents the greatest combination of terror and beauty in the world. Designer Alister MacKenzie demonstrated both prudence and mercy by providing an all-land (and likely safe bogey) alternative to the 200 yard carry tee shot from a crag over the raging Pacific waters to a green perched on another cliff. When the winds are really up, even the best golfers, wishing to preserve a good score, might be wise to go the conservative route. It's easier said than done if the opportunity to play the hole occurs only once in a lifetime, as it did for me (through a connection of my Olympic Club guardian angel, Paul). The lure to go for it is at least as strong as the enticement of the dangerous sirens that Ulysses encountered in the Odyssey. (I achieved a moral victory, carrying the ocean-filled chasm and landing the ball in the sand bunker in front of the green.)

But, Cypress Point is not solely about rugged cliffs and water. Some holes are inland, with a bit of cypress-laced forestry, and others weave into white sand dunes with the ocean in a more distant view. All present fine examples of MacKenzie's genius for natural symmetry in greens, bunkers and general layout.

This is exemplified at holes such as the par-4 at the 8th, with expansive views of the course combined with a blind tee shot over a giant dune, the par-4 13th, with the green wedged into a dune ridge upon which rests a series of sprawling sand traps that appear to be part of the natural landscape, the par-3 15th, which is a shorter, more relaxing version of 16 with elegant bunkering, and the par-4 17th, playing diagonally over the cliffs, with a copse of cypress in the fairway requiring one to choose between a more dangerous shot to the right, or more conservative, albeit longer one, to the left. (Frankly, I would be much happier if they simply cut all or some of these overgrown specimens down or at least way back. I chose the conservative option and was still blocked out on the approach. Then again, given my experiences on the 12th hole at my home course at Oakmont, described earlier, I believe I suffer from PTTS - Post Traumatic Tree Syndrome!)

Pacific Grove Golf Links - Seeking a Monterey Bay golf experience, but short on cash and/or need a tee time on shorter notice than is necessary at the Big Boys? Give Pacific Grove a call. This place is the epitome of "Hidden Gem." If Charles Dickens was writing a book about Pacific Grove Muni, he might give it the title: "A Tale of Two Nines." The front nine plays inland over gently undulating grassland. Designed by two-time U.S. Amateur champion Chandler Egan, it certainly takes a back seat to the oceanfront back nine. And, for that reason, it is a bit overly maligned. It features many cypress trees, so ubiquitous at the high-end Monterey Peninsula courses, and some nicely shaped smallish greens. In fact, it provides a fun warmup for the exhilarating back nine (designed by Pebble Beach architect Jack Neville), where the holes are beautifully situated amid sandy dunes, with the slamming ocean waves in full view. It would be even more gorgeous had the environmentalists not forced the killing of the vibrant ice plant vegetation (because it was not "indigenous", even though it had been there for nearly a century). All of the back nine holes are fabulous, particularly 11-16. If you are en route to the course, but your GPS isn't working, look for the beautiful Point Pinos Lighthouse. It's part of the complex! There is also a great pro shop and restaurant on the grounds.

The Others - **Monterey Peninsula Golf Club** is well regarded, with two meticulously groomed courses, the ocean in view on many, and overlooked by an Old World, Mediterranean-style clubhouse. I played the then recently refurbished Shore Course (Mike Strantz design) and found it underwhelming, perhaps because I was subconsciously comparing it with Pebble Beach and Cypress Point. A testament to the same is I can't recall any particularly memorable hole save for the par-3 11th, with a tee box perched on boulders with a vast view of the sea. From what I have seen and read concerning MPCC's Dunes Course (designed by Raynor/MacKenzie/Hunter/Fazio), I think I would much prefer it over the Shore Course. **Spanish Bay** (Tom Watson/Robert Trent Jones Jr./Sandy Tatum design) is expensive but open to the public, and it shares some of the same look and feel as Monterey Peninsula and Spyglass. My two favorite holes are the par-5 1st, with an "infinity green" seemingly merging into the ocean, and the par-5 14th, with excellent mounding/bunkering leading to another green backed by the water. And, it comes with a sunset bagpipe player! The Robert Trent Jones Sr. designed **Spyglass** (which I merely walked as an AT&T spectator) has some beautiful opening ocean view holes, but it is too hard and expensive for my taste. So, I was content to skip Spyglass in favor of the Links at Spanish Bay as my retirement gift from my employer. **Poppy Hills** (Robert Trent Jones Jr.) is open to the public, well-maintained and fun. Nevertheless, with only a few distant glimpses of the ocean, and a good but not superb layout, it is a bit of a snoozer compared to the others. That said, if you ever have the opportunity to play it or any of the other above-referenced courses, you really can't go wrong.

Pasatiempo Golf Club - This is another Alister MacKenzie golf course shrine just north of Santa Cruz. It was at the top of his own list, and he lived out his final years in a home off the 6th fairway. (After he died, his ashes were spread over the course via airplane.) I played it a couple of times more than 40 years ago as a high handicapper and was a bit intimidated by its numerous barrancas and heavily contoured greens. I decided to play it again just prior to completing this book, even though it was necessary to engage the back nine twice because the front nine is undergoing a year-long green/bunker preservation project. (The same will be done to the back nine in 2024.) I was so glad I chose to play it for several reasons: I brought my A-game that day, so the former terrors of the course were welcome challenges. The green fees were reduced by $100, and a cart was thrown in for free - so my faithful companion, Kathy, joined me as a spectator, just as in Scotland the year before. The course was far less crowded than normal, so we finished the round in 2.5 hours!

They had two different pins on the generous-size greens to enhance/diversify the double back nine experience. The back nine is generally considered the better of the two. Indeed, Alister MacKenzie considered the par-4 16th hole to be not only the best he ever designed but the best that anyone ever designed! A blind tee shot over a wide crest is required. A long second shot (downhill lie unless you are a really big hitter) over a barranca is necessary to reach the steep, triple-tiered green, which is closely guarded by sprawling bunkers. He also considered the entire back nine to be the best combined nine holes in the world. (MacKenzie was not known for his modesty - though he did give most of the credit to female golfer Marion Hollins for the design of the 16th hole at Cypress Point, which he originally envisioned as a par-4.)

All of the holes on the back nine were great fun to play, though the award winners, for me, are the treacherous but beautiful par-3 15th, par-4 16th and par-3 18th. There are many things to like about Pasatiempo. I relished the undulating greens the most.

The MacKenzie Bar and Grill provides fabulous views and a wide selection of good food. Convenient, inexpensive and more than adequate lodging was secured next door at The Inn at Pasatiempo. The motel's Back Nine Grill and Bar is lively with an inspired menu.

Southern California

Oak Quarry Golf Club - When Les and I played this public access course in Riverside, California, we were just as amazed by an oddity there as by its stunning, omnipresent rocky namesake - namely, tame bunny rabbits - hundreds upon hundreds of them throughout the course. It brought to mind the Star Trek episode with the loveable, fuzzy tribbles that multiplied exponentially aboard the USS Enterprise. Equally surprising was that we did not see a single predator seeking them out like Grizzly bears after river salmon. At any rate, the rabbits exhibited better etiquette than some human residents who aimlessly walk my home course as if it were a state park. The course was designed by former PGA Tour pro Dr. Gil Morgan. It certainly suited Les' game as he (barely) broke 120.

The near mountain-sized rock dominating the former quarry had a color that was a mixture of tan and brilliant white. Juxtaposed against the greenery of the course, it is a one-of-a-kind specimen. The stars are the beautiful par-4 4th and 6th holes and the par-3 14th. This is not a "dumb blonde" course. It offers a challenging but fair layout with elevation changes and undulating fairways and is filled with a variety of well-kept holes. As for nearby lodging, it is well worth a few extra dollars to stay at the historic and architecturally stunning Mission Inn Hotel (A National Historic Landmark), which occupies an entire city block in downtown Riverside.

Torrey Pines (North & South Courses) - After watching the Farmers Insurance Open tournament held here every year, and recalling Tiger Woods' epic 18 hole U.S. Open playoff win (via sudden death on the 19th hole) here in 2008, I was certainly drawn to play it. With some "Use it or lose it" flight credits, I decided to make a destination trip there in 2022, staying at the reasonably priced Hilton, just a short walk or courtesy cart ride to the pro shop. The Bell father-son team designed both courses, and Tom Weiskopf made some relatively recent revisions. It was fun to play, as much for its history as its several scenic holes near the cliffs. (Warning: There are a number of others that are relatively flat, bland and repetitive.) I was not amused with the pricey, antiquated, and impractical two-wheeled pull carts, but I got over it. Of the two, I thought the North Course had the more scenic and enjoyable layout, though I did not find it to be appreciably easier than the South Course, considered to be the more demanding of the two. On both courses, it is the par-3s that remain etched in my memory. On the North Course, the two best, in my view, are the 12th, over a canyon away from the ocean and the steep-dropping 15th, with wonderful views of La Jolla and the Pacific Ocean. On the South Course, the par-3 3rd hole is also exhilarating, playing toward the ocean. And, then, there is the par-5 18th, unique because it is the only hole with water (a pond fronting the green) and because it is where Tiger made "The Putt" that forced the playoff.

Arrowhead Country Club - William P. Bell (designer of Torrey Pines) was the architect of this unassuming and thoroughly enjoyable, formerly private club course. (It was sold in 2017, after which I played it and was sad to discover that it had fallen into a serious state of disrepair as a semi-private facility. I am informed that under recent new ownership, things are fast improving.) Arrowhead is named after the 1,400-foot high, 450-foot-wide, always visible, natural quartz rock image located in the foothills of the San Bernardino Mountains. For decades, this course served as my happy place whenever I had the occasion to visit Wil, a close fellow-lawyer friend. He was a member of the club and lived just across the street. The former home of PGA Tour professional Dave Stockton is just a short wedge shot away from the tee box of the third hole. The course is flat, but the small greens are well contoured. The shade from the large oaks, pines and sycamores is a welcome retreat from the desert sun. Assuming the owners complete the restoration here, it clearly belongs near the top of the "Hidden Gem" class.

Redlands Country Club - After Wil got married, he moved to a home across the street from Redlands CC. The irony is that he seldom played golf, except when I visited. But, it worked for me, particularly since Redlands is an Alister MacKenzie design. This course has a hilly layout and is best played using a cart. It is solid but not awesome, in part because it appears that MacKenzie was not the original architect, and had limited acreage to work with in his redesign. As such, because some holes run close together, large trees apparently were planted in places for safety reasons, sometimes interfering with the course's equilibrium and intended lines of play. Nevertheless, Redlands conforms to two core MacKenzie principles: 1. A great course must be a constant source of pleasure to the greatest number of players. 2. It must give the average player a fair chance, while requiring the utmost from the expert. (Robert Trent Jones Sr. and Pete Dye must have cut class the day MacKenzie taught these!) It seems he was saying that, as a starting point, par means par if the hole is played reasonably close to the way it was intended, not par means bogey or worse with the slightest deviation. The most I can say about these principles is that I have played over a dozen courses primarily designed by MacKenzie and I have only exceeded 90 once, shot below 80 on several, and most often scored in the low to mid 80's - all the while admiring, rather than cursing, the signature features of his work. Can't ask for more than that.

The opening hole is an uphill par-4 dogleg left to a classic MacKenzie-style green. Number 9 is another par-4, moving downward to an attractive back-to-front sloped green setting. The somewhat steep, uphill par-3 10th dominates the landscape as you enter the property. It has imposing bunkers as a defense. The par-4 finishing hole heads down from the tee, then back up to a good-looking green at the base of the clubhouse restaurant. Not surprisingly, the course is kept in excellent condition. The clubhouse is situated on high ground, affording pleasant views. It is well appointed, but neither the furnishings nor the membership seemed stuffy.

La Quinta Resort (Mountain Course) - Close, but no cigar. It is hard to argue with the setting of this Pete Dye-designed course in the Palm Springs area. Up close and personal mountains surround it. Unfortunately, it is also fraught with the usual Pete Dye excesses, often contrasting with the natural setting - Railroad ties and bulkheads and severities - Oh my! There is an abundance of obviously manufactured mounding, target approach shots to many elevated small greens - and vast waste bunkers. (In the latter case, Pete is excused since, after all, the course sits in a bloody desert!) The greens were in excellent shape save for being surprisingly slow, yet with more break than meets the eye. Some greens come dangerously close to the next tee boxes, though you don't realize it until you drive up to park the golf cart. (Perhaps the installation of air raid siren buttons at the tee boxes would be fitting at this golf battleground.) Nevertheless, I did like four holes. The par-3 5th and 16th offer scenic target shots. The par-5 15th is beautiful, challenging, but fair, as is the par-4 17th.

The Central Valley

Dragonfly Golf Club - Located 15 miles north of Fresno, this fantastic public access course was designed by Gary Roger Baird. It boasts that it is the longest course in California at 8,073 yards. Do they know something we don't know about future equipment enhancements? Les and I played from the more reasonable 6,300 yard white tees. (Despite his advanced age and horrific golf skills, Les always stubbornly refused to play from senior tees. But he rented carts and did not hold up play.)

The front nine has a distinct links feel with its undulating fairways and greens. The par-4 first hole is wide open with no bunkers. Number 3, a pretty one-shotter, presents a perfect example of the course's high-quality bunkering and greens. The par-4 9th has a split fairway with a 100-foot tall hill along the entire right side, evoking images of the dunes in Scotland and Ireland. The back nine is similar, except there are several holes with lakes and more trees. The course is well-manicured from tee to green. The bunkers are creative in shape and size, and some have unique features (e.g., wooden staircase down to one of the deep bunkers, grass mounding in, and/or beardy grass fringes around, others). The par-3 16th is picturesque, with a tee shot over a curving lake. In all the years I played with Les, I never saw him happier. He had one of his best putting days ever (41 - including two one-putts and no four-putts) and a limited number of his customary worm burners. He was so excited to get to the next tees that, a few times, he was halfway there before I'd putted out. Since this is the last course described in this book that Les and I played together, it seems appropriate to share one final story about the Loveable Boob.

On our way to San Diego to witness the installation of a good friend as a bishop, Les and I decided to spend the night and play the course at the Pala Mesa Resort. It is noted for its very speedy greens. One of these, in particular, had a steep back-to-front slope, and there was virtually no stopping a ball putted from above the hole. A putt tapped ever so gently from 8 feet, if missed, would roll 30 feet past. I repeatedly tried it with the same result. I whined to Les that this was the silliest combined green/pin placement I had ever seen. He proceeded to the green's highest edge, nearly 20 feet from the cup, and said: "Let me show you how it's done." Against trillion-to-one odds, he knocked in the putt on the first try! A few weeks before he died, he reminded me that he once hit the greatest shot in golf history.

Les was living proof that anything in golf and life is possible and the most important thing is to keep smiling. As with Annie in the musical with the same name, for Les: "The sun will come out tomorrow." Just give him his 24 cans of Diet Coke per day (really 12 because he typically tossed the can when half empty because it was no longer, in his narrow estimation, cold enough), his giant-size Reese's Peanut Butter Cups for breakfast (I tried to change this bad habit by confiscating them whenever possible, but always found more in rotating "secret" locations), and his daily pack of cigarettes. (He had quit the habit for 20 years, but a "friend" talked him into joining her for "just one," and that was that.)

The irony is that he managed to remain on this earth for 81 years. But he was more than hapless. Indeed, he was a genius when it came to real estate matters, and if the questions on "Jeopardy" were limited to sports and movie trivia, he would be the perennial champion on the show. On top of that, he was an accomplished handball champion. No matter what fate befell him, he was always humming, singing and telling stories about growing up in the Golden Age of San Francisco. He would do anything for anyone at any time of the day or night, expecting nothing in return. If love is defined as willing the good of another, then Les loved the world, and the world loved Les. OK, that's it. I'm out of stories. Oh, but wait a minute. Did I tell you the one about how not once, but on two occasions, he parked his car, dined in his favorite restaurant, came out a couple of hours later, and discovered that he'd left the keys in the car - with the motor running? Or how about the time a valet pulled up with an elderly woman's car, after which she tipped him and drove home, not realizing until the next day that the vehicle was actually Les'! Then there was the time…

HAWAII

Mauna Lani (South Course) - If your idea of a great course is one that is challenging but not brutal, can be walked if desired, has a unique landscape with profound colors and beauty, is consistently played in warm but not stifling weather, and has a bit of history, then Mauna Lani is the place for you. Located on the Big Island, my son and I were overwhelmed by the course's singular contrasts, such as the perfectly maintained green playing areas spotted with bright sand bunkers that meander through ancient black lava beds, with the shimmering deep blue ocean delivering a steady stream of waves that collide with the craggy shoreline. The virtuoso of the course is the par-3 15th, one of the most photographed over-the-water holes in the world. You may have seen it on television if you are old enough to remember the annual Senior Skins Game, hosted here from 1990-2000. My other favorite hole is the par-4 14th, which plays into a green fronted by a large lava rock and backed by a cooled magma amphitheater.

It has been nearly 40 years since I played Kauai's Princeville Resort (Makai Course designed by Robert Trent Jones Jr.) on my honeymoon. All I remember is that it was lush and difficult, with severe elevation drops and headwinds. I managed to make par on three holes, but a 10 on one of the par-5s, and an 8 on a par-4 left me with a mind-numbing total of 101! I understand that the newer layout at the Resort (the Prince Course, also designed by Jones Jr.) is even more lush and difficult. No thanks!

THE ROCKY MOUNTAINS

Ballyneal - A couple of months after Kathy and I returned from our COVIDfest trip to Scotland/Ireland (see Chapter I), it was time to play the exclusive Tom Doak-designed Ballyneal, a "links" course magically built on remote prairie land outside (way outside) of Denver. I had read somewhere that a non-member was entitled to play there once in their lifetime, on select days of the week, if any tee times were available. I kept in contact with the staff and submitted my application the minute that that season's signup opportunity opened. Huzza, it worked! However, the ride there was less than ideal.

After landing in Denver, we secured our rental car and endured a non-stop three-hour Armageddon-like lightning storm followed by a six-mile unmarked and unlit dirt road drive to the club's entrance in pitch blackness. Upon arriving, we received a midnight welcome from a quartet of howling coyotes and a slithering something in the grass as we unloaded our luggage. I played the round in 105-degree heat (but it felt like "only" 95 with the winds). The course has an authentic high dunes isolated links look and feel about it. I told the caddie that my brain had me expecting to see the ocean whenever I reached the next elevated tee. The course was in perfect shape, and the layout was phenomenal and natural looking. I have only two complaints: First, I am not a fan of their no set-colored tees policy. You go to whichever unmarked tee box area the caddie happens to take you on a given hole. So, the actual total yardage you play is highly fungible, rather than pre-determined as at other courses. Second, if you land in the outer rough, such as the areas on or about the dunes, the ground is a mixture of hard, eroded, pock-marked dirt and scrub. At times, the ball is virtually unplayable in these locations (unlike the tall, often wispy fescue in the rough at most links courses in Scotland and Ireland). There are so many nice holes that it is difficult to pin down the most elite. If pressed, I will go with the par-3 3rd hole to a punch bowl green fronted by massive natural bunkers, par-5 4th, which rewards good shot-making with a birdie opportunity, the naturally haphazard fairway and green on the par-4 12th, and the long par-3 15th with a large slope in front of the green and generous-size hills surrounding it. The lodging and restaurant reflect provincial golf elegance.

Whether you trek to Ballyneal or not, if you ever decide to stay in Denver, the Omni Interlocken Hotel in nearby Broomfield is an excellent place to set up headquarters. It also has a 27 hole golf course. The nine (Eldorado) which you see from the back of the hotel, is by far the best. The hotel is conveniently located between the cities of Denver and Boulder. We toured somewhat avant-guard Boulder and its beautiful university campus at the base of the mountains. The next day, we made a loop from Boulder taking in the thorough, but not exhausting, Peak-to-Peak Trail road that provides a perfect sampling of the vast Rocky Mountain scene. It took us to Boulder Falls, the stunning panoramic setting at The Chapel on the Rock visited by Pope John Paul II, and a gondola ride at Estes Park Aerial Tramway, which offers expansive vistas that capture the snow-capped mountains and green valleys. While in Denver, we also took in a terrific outdoor evening concert in the natural setting at the Red Rock Amphitheater - featuring the Beach Boys and Chicago. We wrapped up our visit with a quick tour of downtown Denver and watched the Rockies play for a few innings at Coors Field.

As a quick side note, on a separate occasion, we visited Colorado Springs on a business trip many years ago and I played the West Course, designed by Robert Trent Jones Sr., at the stately Broadmoor Resort. I was not impressed, though some friends who played the East Course (Ross & Jones Sr. design) were very pleased with their experience.

Soon, golfers will not have to travel three hours from Denver to experience the atmosphere and exclusivity of Ballyneal. Dream Golf Resorts (Bandon Dunes, Sand Valley, Cabot, et al.) is building two courses in the plains about 45 minutes from the Denver International Airport, with as many as four more to follow. The Resort's name is **Rodeo Dunes**, a tribute to the activities of the property's former owners (the largest producers of rodeos in the country).

THE SOUTHWEST

Sedona Resort - Keep your eye on the ball *and* the scenery here, as there are few places quite like Sedona. Yes, there are many mountains and varied rock formations around the world. But, the red rock colors of Sedona, and the way the sunlight plays upon them, is something to behold. Bell Rock looms over this par 71 course designed by Gary Panks. No more so than on the mesmerizing par-3 10th hole. If you haven't played it, you've probably seen a picture at some point. As is the case with courses at most top destination resorts, the holes at the Hilton Sedona Resort are very well-manicured and sufficiently watered This heightens the stark contrast between the lush green of the course and the red rock backdrops. This is not a "target golf" style course. The fairways are generously wide, and punishment for a mishit to the green is a bunker, not a lost or otherwise unplayable ball. At the same time, it provides more than sufficient variety and challenge (6,127 yards from the white tees with a rating/slope of 68.5/126).

Troon North (Pinnacle Course) - An outing at this pristine Tom Weiskopf/Jay Moorish design includes its share of dart board golf. While I wouldn't want to play the course on a regular basis, it certainly is an attractive specimen for the desert golf experience given its setting amid large boulders, giant cacti and mountains. I was not bothered by the homes visible throughout. Instead, between shots, I enjoyed looking at the architecturally impressive structures which tastefully blend into their surroundings. Fortunately, the visually appealing par-3 holes are short to medium length from the standard tees. Hence, a relaxed swing to relatively good-sized greens provides a reasonable opportunity for par or better. The four-hole stretch of 8-12 (par 3/4/4/5) offers the best combination of challenge, variety, beauty and fun.

We-Ko-Pa Golf Club (Saguaro Course) - I stayed at We-Ko-Pa's Casino Resort, which was semi-dormant, presumably due to the lingering effects of the COVID epidemic. The main restaurants were closed, and the a la carte offerings in the open one would not pass muster at a college cafeteria. Nevertheless, the hotel was comfortable, clean and favorably located in relation to the course. This Ben Crenshaw/Bill Coore design is generally recognised as the best public access course in the state. While the scenery is not as dramatic as at Troon, far less target golf is involved. With wide open, undulating terrain, it projects a hint of links in the desert. And, as is typical of this minimalist architect team, they moved little earth when constructing the course. There are no homes or other signs of civilization here. Just an immaculate golf course in a world of its own.

However, in desert territory, these impressive links traits are both a blessing and a curse. You can find beautiful layouts in great condition in any state. But, what most golfers coming to play in the desert expect is close-up boulders, cacti and mountains as at Troon North. As far as favorite holes, I liked the par-5 dogleg left 8th, the little par-3 at the 9th and the split fairway option at the par-5 14th.

TPC Stadium Course Scottsdale - As was the case with the trip to play Torrey Pines, I had some flight credits that needed to be used up by the end of the year, so that is how the golf journey to the Scottsdale area came into being. And, like the annual Farmers Insurance Open at Torrey Pines, I'd seen enough Waste Management tournaments on television that it seemed logical to choose the TPC Stadium course as one of the Scottsdale venues. And, again, like Torrey Pines, I found the TPC, designed by Weiskoff and Morrish, to be enjoyable because of its notoriety and a few excellent holes; but, overall, I did not consider it a great layout. I brought a pretty good game that day, but it seemed like the sand bunkers always crept just a little too close to the intended fairway landings/lines of play. And, several par-4s were long and played longer. The greens were in excellent condition and appropriately contoured. While the rowdy 16th hole is the most famous one during tournament week, it was surreally sedate and isolated the day I played as the management had recently taken down the stadium facility. (Due to building code restrictions, the structures can stay up only for approximately seven months per year.) Consequently, the contrast between the television version of the hole and my playing version was akin to how the house looks the day after all the Christmas decorations are taken down. While I'm generally conservative in my approach to the game, I decided to skip aiming for the center of the fairly generous green. Instead, I went directly for the pin, even though it was located tightly in a back corner. The phantom crowd booed as the ball did not hold the green. But, then again, that tough crowd would have booed a ball hit to the middle of the green as well! For me, the real star, with or without stadium seating, is the immediately preceding hole - a beautiful and challenging par-5. It has an island green with a mountain backdrop that is not terribly difficult to negotiate if one lays up with the second shot, but presents great risk/reward for those going for the green in two.

THE MIDWEST

Indiana

Warren & Burke Courses at Notre Dame - Playing here in the spring of 2016 was part of a couple of bittersweet weeks. The trip began at the University of Notre Dame, where our son, Brian, and long-time girlfriend, Sara, both Domers, were married in the University's Basilica of the Sacred Heart. The day before the wedding Brian and I, along with a herd of his high school and college buddies, gathered at the Warren Course to celebrate the occasion. I had played this relatively new Ben Crenshaw/Bill Coore design once before, but this round was more memorable for obvious reasons. The University's original 18 hole Burke Course was located adjacent to the Rockne Center in the heart of the campus. I have fond memories of it - particularly as they relate to the spring of my final year of law school there. Classmate Paul (with whom I played at St. Andrews the previous year while studying abroad) and I decided to remain on campus during the Easter break to prepare for the Multistate Ethics Exam. To make things more palatable, we engaged in a daily regimen of study followed by golf, study, a box of South Bend's famous Bruno's Pizza, and a final study session. We had the course, and pretty much the whole campus, to ourselves. Nine holes of the flat, steady old Burke course remain, but the Warren Course is now the main attraction.

Crenshaw and Coore managed to lay out a course on the outer edges of the campus that is not only student/alums/visitor friendly (and affordable), but also adaptable for use as a professional tournament venue - no less than the 2019 U.S. Senior Open. The course weaves in and out of woodlands and has nice little bonuses, such as old-school pot bunkers, other traps with beardy fringes, and run-up options to greens. My favorite holes include the par-3 9th, with excellent bunkering and green undulation, the par-4 16th signature hole, playing over a creek past heavy left side bunkering, then uphill to a two-tier green fronted by a pot bunker, and the par-4 dogleg left 18th, with a fine green at the base of a hill on which rest the modest sized, nicely appointed brick clubhouse and pro shop.

After giving our farewell hugs to the newlyweds the morning after the wedding, Kathy and I drove to Ohio for what would prove to be the last visit with my dear, sweet, saintly mother, who would pass away a month or so later. As is often the case with married couples joined at the hip for well over half a century, her health declined rapidly after the death of the family's revered patriarch, my dad, six months prior. Fortunately, shortly before our arrival, her mental faculties had improved considerably with a medication change recommended by Kathy, a retired nurse. And, so, we could share photos of the wedding and engage in many treasured conversations about the distant past and present. Then, it was time to work our way back to Chicago for our flight home. But, first, there were a couple of courses to visit in Wisconsin.

Wisconsin

Erin Hills - Forgive me if I gush a little too much, but I believe Erin Hills, designed by the trio of Dr. Michael Hurdzan, Dana Fry and Ron Whitten, is the most underrated course on the planet. The same holds for its clubhouse and lodging. Together, they exude an Irish-inspired landscape and warm, tasteful country comfort, with Holy Hill (a Catholic basilica sitting on the tallest point in southeast Wisconsin) dominating the scene from a distance like the Wizard of Oz' castle. Erin Hills is among the growing number of inland links facsimiles in the USA. While it may not have as many dramatic dunes (whether natural or manufactured) as some others, it rolls naturally over glacial moraine, with amber waves of grain-like grass alongside the lush green fairways and putting surfaces. The bunkering is perhaps the most innovative, varied and beautiful I have ever seen. They are masterfully shaped (some with grass mounds sitting on or jutting in them) and often rest naturally in the hillsides. Yet, unlike the creator of its neighbor at Whistling Straits, the designers exercised restraint in terms of the size and number. The first hole has none around the green. Instead, it, like the signature 14th hole at Royal Dornoch, relies on the shape of the green and the slopes approaching it to serve as its defense. That said, the par-3 9th is a beast, surrounded by treacherous bunkering. My favorite two holes are the par-5 14th, with its green set into a large hillside, and the driveable (at the player's peril) par-4 15th, with a bunker-guarded raised green situated inside a grass arena.

I played Erin Hills a year before it hosted the 2017 U.S. Open - where Brooks Koepka won his first major title. He did so with a total score of 16 under par, aided considerably by the fact that Mother Nature set the usually high wind button on low mode that week.

If you visit the spiritually moving basilica on Holy Hill, I offer you the following words of caution: Do NOT climb the 178 narrow, curved steps to the top of its spire just prior to your round - at least if you are nearly 60 years old and struggle with serious fibromyalgia! I did so and then literally limped my way around the course like a bow-legged cowboy. Perhaps, however, my pilgrimage was rewarded with an Irish blessing. As was the case with my 54 hours without sleep round at Gleneagles and the post-horseback-riding one at Ballybunion, I managed to play well, for me, despite the infirmity - shooting a 78. Go figure!

Whistling Straits - It's now time to visit the polar region. I am not referring to the course's location in Wisconsin, home of the frozen tundra of Lambeau field. Rather, I'm alluding to the fact that Whistling Straits is yet another polarizing "Dye-abolical" design by Pete Dye. Here, he was given a former flat, World War II military training airfield on a bluff overlooking Lake Michigan and moved three million cubic yards of dirt, and imported 7,000 truckloads of sand, to create a dunes-filled "links" course with over 1,000 bunkers. The attempt was certainly bold, but a couple of Alister MacKenzie's 13 principles of golf course design were breached, with Dye's typical combination of design overkill.and brutality. MacKenzie believed a course should have beautiful surroundings and artificial features should appear so natural that a stranger cannot distinguish them from nature itself. He also believed a course should be an enjoyable experience, even for the duffer. I have played approximately 50 natural links courses in Scotland and Ireland and have never seen one resembling Whistling Straits. I don't recall anywhere else walking to a port-a-potty or restroom surrounded by pot bunkers! The sheer number of bunkers throughout the course and its surroundings can give you a headache, even if the number you play out of is kept to a minimum which, fortunately, was the case for me. That said, despite the artificiality and difficulty of the course, there are some unquestionably pretty settings, particularly the cliffside par-3s. Whistling Straits is more than sufficiently challenging for top-tier golfers with its combination of length, bunkers, narrowness, undulating greens, and high winds, as evidenced by the fact that it has hosted three PGA

Championships, one U.S. Senior Open and one Ryder Cup. But, the average foozler is likely to leave this course frazzled.

Ohio

Growing up in Ohio in the city of Massillon (about 50 miles south of Cleveland), golf as a sport was more an aberration than an avocation. The big three for most kids were football, baseball and basketball. However, my oldest brother, Bill, was introduced to golf at an early age by a couple of uncles with low handicaps. He would spend hours pitching balls to a big box in the lot next door or go to a nearby alfalfa field and hit a driver and other long clubs in one direction and then back the other way. I would sometimes tag along, watching in awe at the prodigious length that the balls carried - particularly in relation to those I hit with the little club he made for me - a sawed-off hickory nine iron wrapped with green duct tape that served as the grip. I would assist in gathering the balls and placing them in a duffel bag before rushing home for dinner at the sound of my dad's two-fingered whistle (with a range of half a mile). Bill always called me his "little protégé" but never explained its meaning. When asked, he would just pat me on the head and repeat the term. Thirty-five years later, I think I had an idea as to what he meant. Bill went on to play as a four-year starter on the high school golf team and at Xavier University for a few years before getting married and joining the work world, and later various country clubs. During my summer breaks from undergraduate and law school studies, I would join him for a round, now and then, at Congress Lake - a Donald Ross design (said to be one of Ben Hogan's favorites) in the nearby little town of Hartville. To put it mildly, I was neither very adept at the game nor a quick learner. But, I always enjoyed those rounds (especially the picturesque par-4 dogleg left 7th hole, with water on the left and front of its lovely green, and the par-3 finishing hole, requiring one to land the ball on the green or face having it devoured by one of the many deep bunkers circling the green like sharks). I was hell-bent on joining him in breaking his personal record of playing 54 holes (on foot) in one day. My otherwise athletic muscles simply were not trained for golf, so we never made it past 36, even though riding in a cart. But, these early life experiences slowly fueled what would later develop into an extreme passion for the game and some memorable golf trips involving Bill and his little protégé.

Brookside Country Club - This Donald Ross sister course of Congress Lake is not far from our former Massillon home. During the summer after my sophomore year of high school, I showed up to caddie there on a hot, humid day. It was my first and last time doing so. Later that day, I ran into an acquaintance. He told me he was leaving his job as a tennis court maintenance assistant at the club and would happily recommend me as his replacement. I got the job. It's probably a good thing since a snooty member gave me the bare minimum for my caddie services. Perhaps it was because I did not respond like a bobblehead when he told me early on what a privilege it was to serve as a golf course "gofer." Then again, maybe it was because during the round I sought out a shade tree and sat the bag down at the apex of a steep hill and, a few seconds later, it began tumbling down toward a pond. I intercepted it just before it and I made the "Nestea Plunge." I smiled 30 years later when I passed that pond while actually playing the course.

Brookside is frequently mentioned in Top 100 course listings for its creative Ross layout and impeccable conditioning. It is both lauded and criticized for having lightning-fast, sometimes severely undulating, greens.

Legends of Massillon - After graduation from law school, I moved to California. Whenever I returned to Ohio to visit the family, I would play several rounds of golf with my dad, who earnestly took up the game following his retirement as a pharmacist. He had worked six days a week, 51 weeks per year as the owner of a pharmacy, and then, after handing out his final bottle of pills, the Legends course became a more enjoyable worksite twice a week. It began as an 18 hole facility and later expanded to 27. It is a well-maintained public access club and worth a play (as is the Wilkshire Golf Club course in the Amish country south of Massillon and Clearview Golf Club in East Canton) if ever in town to visit the Pro Football Hall of Fame in the nearby city of Canton.

Glenmoor - It was here that I befriended, for the first time, a Jack Nicklaus course design. Located close to Brookside, it is super private. However, I learned that one could gain access by staying (at a surprisingly reasonable cost) as a guest at the Glenmoor Inn - a former Roman Catholic Seminary - to which are attached the clubhouse and pro shop. It was love at first sight. In an almost eerie manner my visualization for playing the course suddenly opened wide. It was as if Mr. Nicklaus himself (born and raised in Columbus and also the son of a pharmacist) was playing alongside, sharing his design strategy and course management suggestions on this superbly gromed layout. It is not target golf here or otherwise terribly difficult or penal. However, it presents fair challenges throughout. The Golden Bear knew his playing audience - decently skilled club members, not members of the pro circuit. The result is pure enjoyment in a tranquil and aesthetically pleasing setting of water, woods, gentle slopes and hollows, and manageable contoured greens. My favorite holes are the par-3 7th over a pond to a two-level green with the red-bricked campanile of the old seminary overlooking the scene, the short but tight par-4 8th, which includes a small green with a steep bank in front that leads to a pond, a downhill par-4 dogleg at number 16, also fronted by a pond with a lovely green backed by mature trees, and the par-5 finishing hole, which plays blindly from the tee over a hill, then works its way downward to a punch bowl green.

Clearview Golf Club - I could write a whole book about this course and the unmatched uniqueness surrounding the people involved in its creation and legacy. However, I will limit myself to providing you with a thorough summary.

Located in the tiny village of East Canton, Ohio, Clearview is no ordinary public golf course. William Powell overcame racial barriers to become (and continues to be) the only African-American to design, build, own, and operate a golf course. (This distinction ultimately led to Clearview's inclusion in the National Register of Historic Places.) A World War II veteran, William was denied a GI Bill loan for this purpose but managed to begin construction of the course in 1946 (via private loans from a couple of local black physicians) despite working the night shift as a security guard at the Timken Roller Bearing Company. As a result of his accomplishments, the PGA of America awarded him its highest honor, The PGA Distinguished Service Award, as well as PGA of America Life Member status (retroactive to 1962, when African-Americans were first entitled to join the PGA).

The daughter of Bill and Marcella Powell, Renee Powell, graduated from Central Catholic High School in Canton, Ohio (my alma mater) and, after serving as Captain of the Ohio University and Ohio State University ladies golf teams, she joined the LPGA in 1967. Renee continued on the tour through 1980 despite receiving the "Jackie Robinson" treatment as its second African-American player. I had the opportunity to play the Clearview golf course for the first time about ten years ago and, that same day, the honor of meeting Renee. We developed a treasured friendship through subsequent regular correspondence on golf and life. Renee is a humble, dignified, genuinely caring individual with no bitter bone in her body. Named the 2003 PGA First Lady of Golf, she became, in 2008, the first female golfer and the ninth golf professional in history to receive an honorary Doctor of Laws degree from the University of St. Andrews in Scotland. In February of 2015, Renee, along with Annika Sorenstam, Louise Suggs and Laura Davies, were the first lady professionals named honorary members of the Royal and Ancient Golf Club of St. Andrews.

Bill Powell passed away at the age of 93 in 2009, and Renee continues as the teaching pro at Clearview, at which her brother, Larry, does an outstanding job as golf course superintendent. The heartwarming story of the Powell family (who in 1992 received the Jack Nicklaus Family of the Year award from the National Golf Foundation) has been featured on the Golf Channel and Golf Digest Magazine.

The Clearview Foundation was established in 2001 as a non-profit organization dedicated to golf education, course preservation, and turfgrass research. The Foundation runs a youth program for young people in foster care, an LPGA/USGA girls golf program that teaches youth the etiquette of golf and life, and the country's sole year-round female military veterans rehabilitative golf program. Future plans include an Education/Learning Center for youngsters and adults, regardless of race or gender, a new clubhouse that will connect to a museum chronicling the history of one of America's most unique golf centers, and the development of an upgraded course maintenance program, including an automatic irrigation system."

Through Renee's untiring efforts, and the promotional and/or financial support of organizations such as the LPGA and PGA, and individuals such as Hall of Fame football player Franco Harris (RIP), the voice of the Masters ("Hello, friends") Jim Nantz, Michelle Wie West, and Ben Crenshaw, many of the above-referenced plans have come to fruition, or soon will. I hope you will add your name to the list of Clearview Legacy supporters. More information can be found at clearviewgolfclub.com - or simply send a check to Clearview Legacy Foundation P.O. Box 30196 East Canton, Ohio 44730.

And now, a little bit about the course itself. For someone with such limited resources and no formal architectural training or experience, William Powell did a fantastic job designing and constructing a layout with a wide variety of holes that require you to think and execute. If both are done well, you can score well. Clearview's setting is bucolic amid rolling terrain, creeks and forests. The greens are large and in excellent condition. Improvements to the bunkering are ongoing. I like all the holes, but claim partiality to the attractive and diverse par-4s at 5, 6 and 9 and the fabulously fun uphill par-4 18th to a clever punchbowl green.

I can't depart from this visit to Clearview Golf Club without mentioning Renee Powell's kindness toward my niece, Rose, when my brother Bill and I took her to play there (and visit her cousin who worked in the pro shop). Renee welcomed us with a huge smile and a firm embrace as if we were a long-lost family. She then told the cousins to go out and play a few holes while she minded the store. Later, she joined us on the back nine and did a Golf Channel-like "Playing Lessons With the Pros" show with Rose. I love Renee, and I know you will, too, if you ever have the opportunity to meet her at this wonderful place.

THE MID-ATLANTIC

The Cascades Golf Club - This William Flynn design is located in Slamin Sammy Snead territory, adjacent to the Omni Homestead Resort in Hot Springs, Virginia. Due to its crude terrain, particularly on what would become the front nine, Flynn had to use everything at his disposal, including dynamite, to carve out the holes in 1923. However, adhering to MacKenzie's design philosophy, he managed to do so in such a natural way that the land alterations were not easily detectable. Unfortunately, the course has been significantly altered over the years and, with excessive overgrowth, it has become somewhat tired and tight-looking. It's not that it isn't worth a play (good holes include the long par-3 downhill 4th, and the par-3 18th with a steep back to front green towards a pond). It just doesn't seem to belong in the top-tier of America's courses. The

Sam Snead Tavern, located in town, with its golf decor and memorabilia, is worth a stop after your round.

The Greenbrier (Meadows Course) - Not far from the Cascades Course sits the Greenbrier Resort in White Sulphur Springs, West Virginia. It has the look and feel of a mountain version of the White House. (It is appropriate, then, that tucked deep into the mountainside is the once top-secret Cold War fallout shelter for use by Congress.) Brother Bill and I played the Meadows Course, redesigned by Bob Cupp, and it was OK. But, in hindsight, we wish we'd spent the extra dough to tee it up at The Old White, as it offered the rare opportunity to play a public access course designed by the great Charles Blair Macdonald.

Congressional Country Club (Gold Course) - Speaking of Congress (which never had to retreat to the safety bunker at Greenbrier), I had the opportunity to play this Maryland golf refuge for members of Congress while on one of my semi-annual business trips to Washington, D.C. The U.S.Open has been played many times on the Blue Course. The Gold was initially designed by Devereux Emmet and revised by George Fazio and nephew, Tom. It was in great condition but, other than the pretty finishing hole over a lake, I remember most the cool looking U.S. Capitol Building dome tee markers and the enormous clubhouse.

East Potomac Park Golf Course - Hidden Gem alert. Walter Travis, who won four majors in the early 1900s, was also a golf journalist and golf course architect. His design of this dirt-cheap muni, located on Hains Point Island on the Potomac, is a blessing for its mostly blue- collar local patrons - as it was for me as a visitor. Whenever I was on business in Washington, D.C., I knew that as soon as "class" was out, I only needed to take a 10-minute taxi ride for instant golf fun. You know just how close you are to the city's hub when your primary target line on a number of holes is the Washington Monument (most notably the signature par-3 8th), and the Jefferson Memorial watches over the facility from less than a mile away. The clubhouse itself could fit right in as a small government memorial to some lesser personage. The condition of the course is only average. However, according to a recent article in Golf Digest, National Links Trust is planning a sizable investment in a full restoration to be overseen by famed architect Tom Doak. In any event, as they say in the real estate business, it's all about "Location.

Location. Location." - and timing. If you are prudent (and a little lucky) with your planning, you can, in the springtime, arrange to be in the very heart of the city's blossoming cherry trees as you tee off. What a capital idea!

The USGA Museum - About an hour outside of New York City (and just 10 miles from the historic and very interesting Revolutionary War winter encampment site of General Washington's army at Morristown) sits a large, elegant building serving as the United States Golf Association Museum in Fall Hills, New Jersey. It has all manner of original items pertaining to the game and its stars. Entire rooms are dedicated to Bobby Jones, Ben Hogan, Arnold Palmer, Mickey Wright, and Jack Nicklaus. There is a large archival center and a thorough gift shop. You have the option to play its 16,000 square foot, nine hole putting green inspired by the wildly undulating Himalayas putting course at St. Andrews. The facility provides a reproduction vintage golf ball (which you get to keep) and a choice of hickory shaft putter. This museum will surely provide both the golf expert and neophyte with an edifying experience. If you cannot squeeze a visit into your travel schedule, then the museum's website provides a "Plan B" - a close-up virtual tour of the entire complex.

THE SOUTH

North Carolina - The "Tar Heel State" offers some of the most diverse golf experiences in the nation. Mine focused on the Sandhills and Mountain regions.

Pinehurst - This area belongs in the same conversation with Bandon Dunes and the Monterey Peninsula in terms of offering a combination of numerous and excellent public access golf facilities in close proximity.

Pinehurst No. 3 - I passed on the opportunity to play Donald Ross' most famous (and also most difficult and expensive) No. 2 Course. Instead, I chose the "Poor Man's No. 2" (said to most closely resemble No. 2's features, without the same level of length and pain). The layout, with less extensive bunkering, was terrific. The member with whom I was paired assured me that the greens were similar to those on No. 2. I had no reason to doubt him as they proved to be quite treacherous at times. The par-3 4th, over water, is both beautiful and testing. At number 5, a short dogleg right par-4, two well-placed shots provide an excellent opportunity for a birdie. The same holds true at the par-5, dogleg left 13th if one can avoid the lengthy sand trap on the left. The final two holes, both par-4s, present the golfer with a memorable combination of charisma and challenge.

Mid Pines Golf Club - Kyle Franz renovated and restored this course in 2013 to conform to the original Ross design and condition. He did an excellent job. It was my clear favorite on my golf destination trip to North Carolina. I imagine it is somewhere between the length and difficulties of Pinehurst Nos. 2 and 3. I was paired with an entertaining young trio from Ohio, who make a buddies trip here every year. I believe they were not particularly thrilled at first to be joined by an old fart. They were all long-hitting, former high school team players with low, single-digit handicaps. I was both pleased and honored when, after being the only one to par the first three holes, they called me a "sandbagger." The opening hole is a solid par-4 with all the anticipated Ross features, as is the pretty 9th. The 11th is an attractive par-3 that requires accuracy to a small well-protected green and the same can be said with regard to the longer par-3 13th. Number 15, a dogleg left par-5, slopes nicely and rewards good play. The par-4 18th is difficult, but incredibly scenic. The historic Mid Pines Inn is perched above the green, with a wandering swale in its center.

The Cradle - Donald Ross said: "Golf should be a pleasure, not a penance." It seems he did not always adhere to this principle, at least as it relates to the design of some of his infamous greens, and as applied to the average golfer on his tournament course layouts. However, when Gil Hanse designed a nine hole, par 27 short course that opened in 2017 below Pinehurst's clubhouse, he did so with pleasure in mind. The holes are very short and not overly complex. They share the same general characteristics as the other Pinehurst courses. Fine so far. However, in my view, the management went overboard in creating a Spring Break party vibe here and on the adjacent practice green (with shoes optional, and alcohol and cigars promoted thereon). The obvious intent is to provide a quick, light-hearted warm-up before a more serious round on one of the challenging championship courses or to satiate the golf appetite after one of those rounds. Rock music blares from amps hidden behind trees and rocks. I get it; they are reaching out to Gens X and Z, and the Millennials. However, this Baby Boomer prefers the sedate atmosphere and standard length of the par-3 short courses at places like The Preserve at Bandon Dunes.

The Village of Pinehurst - Just down the road from Pinehurst's clubhouse, this idyllic little New England-style business district is suspended in time. It looks today much as it did over a century ago, when it was carefully planned by the Tufts family to serve as an escape for visitors suffering from harsh winters elsewhere. There are several historic hotels with excellent restaurant ambiance and food such as the Carolina Hotel, Holly Inn and Pine Crest Inn. (I dined at each of these but opted to stay at one of the nearby convenient and comfortable economy hotels just outside the village.) The Given Memorial Library and Tufts Archives building includes research materials and artifacts covering all things Pinhurst and Donald Ross (whose former home can be seen next to Pinehurst No. 2's third fairway). And, then, there is the golf antique shop to end all golf antique shops - Old Sport & Gallery. (As I write this book, I note that the long-time owner is apparently retiring and selling the store. Hopefully, another golf enthusiast will grab the baton.) No visit to Pinehurst is complete without spending some time in the village.

Duke University Golf Club - Duke University is just an hour and 20-minutes drive from Pinehurst and 20 minutes from Raleigh International Airport. I first saw the Duke University Inn and the golf course it overlooks while on college campus tours with the kids when they were in high school. I thought then, that one day I would love to stay and play here. The opportunity presented itself in connection with the golf trip to Pinehurst. And, I made the arrangements despite discovering that the course was designed by the "Paragon of Penality," Robert Trent Jones Sr. Oh, wait, that sobriquet belongs to Pete Dye. It would be more appropriate to call Jones the "Sovereign of Severity." In any event, the course turned out to be about a 5.8 temblor on the Jones scale. Like a cheap steak, a little too tough but fairly tasty. I played with a man and his wife, both University Hospital doctors, who were pleasant company and decent players. Overall, it is a good layout, in excellent shape, with generally charitable tee shot landing areas. However, nearly all the holes require long approach shots to either raised, back to front sloping greens and/or ones guarded by steep slopes with deep bunkers or water. So, landing the ball in the center of the green is the safe route. But, easier said than done. My favorite holes include the par-5 uphill/downhill 7th hole, with a creek fronting the green, the long and difficult but beautifully situated uphill par-5 9th, and the par-3 12th signature hole, requiring an accurate tee shot over a large pond. The Bull Durham Bar is the perfect spot to have a hamburger, watch sports, and dissect your scorecard after the round. The Inn is pure, understated elegance and is just a short walk from one of the country's most artful campuses.

Grove Park Inn - Sad at having to say goodbye to the great Donald Ross courses in the Sandhills, but also looking forward to a cooler climate? Then, go no further than three and a half hours to the mountain area surrounding Asheville. The Omni Grove Park Inn Resort offers optimum lodging (10 Presidents have stayed in this hotel, built with eye-catching rustic boulder facings and red roofing) and is home to a splendid Donald Ross course. It follows rolling terrain, and its elevated tees provide panoramic views of the undulating greens, the lodge and the Blue Ridge Mountains. The somewhat tight, well-manicured layout is nicely, but not overly, bunkered. Excellent examples of these features can be found at the par-3 second and par-4 15th holes.

Asheville Golf Course - Donald Ross designed this municipal course, which has its ups and downs in terms of topography and maintenance. However, the city recently agreed to underwrite a significant capital improvement project. So, a good inexpensive course will only get better and deserve coveted Hidden Gem status. It also has the distinction of being the first municipal course in North Carolina to be racially integrated. Of average length and difficulty, it offers the perfect opportunity to combine a great time with a great score. There is a pleasant variety of holes. All of the par-5s provide good birdie opportunities, and the long par-3 18th is a great finishing hole.

Wolf Laurel Country Club - W.B. Lewis drew up the plan for this private course, which is little more than a half-hour drive from Asheville. My brother Bill had a summer cabin home here for a while, so I had the opportunity to play it four times. It is a bit tight and overly sloped in numerous places, but it can also boast of having one of the most spectacularly situated par-3s in the country. The tee on the 185 yard 6th hole rests at an elevation of nearly 5,000 feet, with a 200-foot drop to the green, and a backdrop of a broad mountainscape. Numbers 10-15 offer the best stretch, with an excellent mixture of par 3, 4 and 5 holes. My best memory here was playing nine holes with hickory clubs while wearing our flat caps. Bill initially said: "No!", but relented when I reminded him that I traveled 3,000 miles to come see and play with him. (There's nothing like a bit of guilt to get the retro golf juices flowing.) My worst memory was playing in a team charity tournament and hitting the ball to within two feet on the above-referenced par-3 signature hole and, for some unknown reason, they didn't provide their customary closest-to-the-pin prize that day. Grrrrrrrr!

South Carolina

Cobblestone Park Golf Club - This is the University of South Carolina Gamecocks' home course. The University's website claims that the course, located 20 miles north of Columbia, provides its men's and women's golf teams with the country's finest playing and practice facilities. This claim is not without foundation. I had read that the 27 hole layout, designed by Pete Dye's son, P.B., was a former private club turned semi-private (i.e., public access for wandering golf minstrels like me) and still well regarded. As such, it seemed like the logical final stop on a golf journey for Bill and I. It took us from Ohio to the Virginias to the Carolinas before arriving for some more golf at Bill's long-time home in Jacksonville, Florida. As we approached the clubhouse, we were awed by the views of the 1st and 9th holes of the respective nines and the immaculate and immense (30 acres) practice facilities. A massive driving range containing eleven greens with pin placements, a practice pitching green and sand bunker area, and a 14,000-square-foot practice putting green with varied terrain is included. The course was equally impressive, featuring a rolling landscape, elevation changes, contoured greens, and an array of water and trees accentuating the serenity of the place. We played the Black and Gold nines. The Black does not long detain before presenting its signature hole. The par-3 2nd plays downhill to a green with water on three sides, and the fourth side is protected by bunkers and trees. The challenging par-5 9th has a little of everything, including a double fairway. The short par-4 5th on the Gold offers intriguing strategic options and related potential perils. The par-3 9th is full of tests and character.

Georgia

Augusta National Golf Club - I have always hated the expressions "VIP" and "VIP Treatment." Everyone puts their shoes on one at a time. We all die, and when we do, we leave behind our possessions, whether many or few. We then account for ourselves, not by what others did for us, but what we did for others. Indeed, one who could justifiably claim to be the ultimate VIP came into the world over 2,000 years ago courtesy of a stable.

Aside from the privilege of playing as a guest at some excellent private golf clubs, I have taken advantage of extraordinary special treatment only three times in my life. The first was assuming the honor of marrying my beyond-all-description wife. The second was accepting the opportunity to sit in a front pew at St. Mary's Cathedral in San Francisco and be introduced by the Archbishop to my hero, Pope (now Saint) John Paul II, during his 1987 visit to the USA. The third was reluctantly acceding to the request of Denis (The Absent-Minded Professor) to share one of the two hospitality tickets he'd received from a corporate mogul to attend the Masters.

I was never fond of attending big venue sports or musical events. This was even more the case following the advent of high-definition, big-screen home TV's that allow commercial skipping. There is simply too much logistics, time, expense, and comparative discomfort involved in attending these live gatherings. And, so, I turned Denis down when he initially invited me to attend the Masters with him. A few weeks later, he lobbied again, reminding me that the only cost would be our airline tickets. Ultimately, I determined that I could combine the trip to watch the tournament with a visit to see my brother, Bill, in Jacksonville. Denis agreed to these terms, and off we went. Little did I know what "all-included" really meant. It turned out that we would be wearing "Berckmans Place" badges, which entitled us to a mind-boggling amount of Masters golf candy!

The Berckmans Place hospitality center was built in 2012 and named after Belgian doctor Mathieu Berckmans. Prior to the Civil War, he purchased a former indigo plantation, which included a modest two-story mansion. There, he established a nursery (which, among other things, had all sorts of azalea shrubs and peach trees) on a sprawling hilly area on the outskirts of Augusta, about

140 miles from Atlanta. Some decades later, the nursery closed and the property passed into other hands. By the early 1930's, the Antebellum-style home became Augusta National's clubhouse and the former nursery land was converted into the club's famed course (designed by Bobby Jones and Alister MacKenzie).

The cost to build Berckmans Place, a 90,000 square foot, air-conditioned, multi-storied, multi-pillared white structure built in the style of the other buildings on the property, and located across from the 5th fairway, was reportedly $30,000,000. It is lavishly furnished like a Ritz Carlton and contains five themed restaurants, a Whisky bar and a cigar room. Display cases with a wide variety of Masters memorabilia and a merchandise shop with items not available elsewhere on the grounds are thrown in for good measure. Conspicuous signs make it clear that admission is by invitation only. That restriction also applies to the Media - unless a sponsor has forked over the $6,000 necessary to secure one of the limited Berckmans Place badges for the week. In our case, I think the two-day badge cost was "only" $3,000. Save for merchandise purchases, everything is included. No bills. No tipping. No limits on the type, number or frequency of food and beverage choices. The facility is full of tour pros - past and present - as well as other sports stars and celebrities. My favorite restaurant was the least formal - MacKenzie's Pub - with external stone walls and internal dark woodwork. Fortunately, the pub offered hamburgers and fries as an option. Shortly after we were seated, the former Chairman of the club, Billy Payne, along with his wife, sat down at the table next to us inconspicuously - except for his wearing the club's customary green jacket. Members wear their jackets at Berkmans Place more as a sign of welcome and assistance rather than prestige. The affable former Secretary of State, "Condi" Rice, has been known to stand at the complex's entrance door, donning her green jacket as she greets badge holders.

Another option available to Berckmans Place guests is the opportunity to putt on replicas of the 7th, 14th and 16th greens accompanied by a caddie dressed in the familiar Masters white jumpsuit and green cap. From what I have read and heard, Berckmans Place is nothing short of being the most lavish hospitality experience in all sports. Would I do it again? No. Am I glad I did it once? I must answer, albeit a little sheepishly, yes.

As for accommodations, our host secured two large homes for eight people overlooking a nearby private golf club. (I'm unsure if that was part of the badge cost, but I doubt he cared.) And then, if all this wasn't enough, the host and his companion had to bow out of their tee time at Palmetto Golf Club (located just over the Georgia border in nearby Aiken, South Carolina). They invited Denis and I to assume the duty. It opened in 1892, and the course was redesigned by Alister MacKenzie while he was in the area mapping out Augusta National. The clubhouse alone was worth the non-price of admission. This small, old-school gem was designed by noted New York architect Stanford White, who also served as the architect of the clubhouse at Shinnecock Hills. From 1945 to 1953, a pre-Masters Pro-Am tournament was held here (with many of the usual Crosby Clambake suspects in attendance). Its winners include Ben Hogan, Byron Nelson and Lawson Little. The course was quite nice, but seemed in "poor" condition after having walked the grounds of Augusta National the prior two days!

Oh, yeah, I almost forgot. The badge also includes patron viewing rights. We visited every hole, spending the most time at the par-3 6th, 12th and 16th holes, the par-4 10th and 11th, and the par-5 13th and 15th. All are mesmerizing. We watched the tournament's final round, won by Patrick Reed, on good ole fashion TV at my brother's home. But, all of the above-noted experiences flowed in and out of my brain as we did so.

Florida

San Jose Country Club - After our trip to Augusta, Denis and I drove to Jacksonville. We stayed with Bill and my charming sister-in-law, Chris, for a few days before our return to California by way of Atlanta. I had played Bill's home course several times in prior years but was glad that Denis would have the opportunity to visit Florida and play one of its better courses. Donald Ross did a tremendous amount of design work in the south, and San Jose is another club that can proudly claim his authorship - and their faithful restoration of his original work. It has a good layout and is kept in pristine condition, though (like many in Florida) it has too many holes with water in play for my taste. It has all the usual features of a Ross design and, fortunately, rests somewhere in the middle of Ross' work in terms of difficulty and length. The 3rd, 4th and 5th holes (par 5,4 & 3, respectively) provide good early-round scoring opportunities if shots are executed well (the short par-3 being resistant due to its small sloping green jutting out over the water). On the back nine, the par-5 17th and par-4 18th are attractive holes with generous but exacting greens.

If unable to secure access to San Jose CC, one can visit nearby **Hyde Park Golf Club**, an inexpensive public course designed by Donald Ross (though some evidence has surfaced suggesting that another famed architect, Stanley Thompson, deserves some or all of the credit). It certainly is outside the prime condition of San Jose (or the local, private Timuquana, designed by Ross) though I understand that the owners are committed to restoring the layout to its former glory. In the meantime, it offers the opportunity to play a course that was a fixture on the PGA Tour in the 1940s and 1950s. (Ben Hogan infamously scored an 11 at the par-3 6th hole in the 1947 Jacksonville Open!) It is full of tall, stately Southern Pines and Spanish Oaks with hanging moss. The course was sufficiently challenging, with a diverse range of holes.

The Breakers - The Breakers Hotel is a towering and stunning Italianesque legend overlooking the Atlantic Ocean in Palm Beach. Its Ocean Course is decorative, filled with flowers and tropical plants that blend nicely with the sugar-white sand bunkers, lakes and lush fairways and greens. I played here many years ago with Brian while on a family vacation. It was a very good and fun resort-style course to play then. From what I have read, it is now even "gooder" following the extensive redesign work done by Rees Jones, completed in 2019. One-third of the bunkers were eliminated and others more strategically placed. Additional contour was placed on the fairways and enlarged greens. Overgrowth was removed to open up the course and enhance sights on the intended lines of play. Top holes include the par-4 6th, with a green that wraps around a lake and, if you really love water, the dogleg par-4 9th that requires a tee shot over agua followed by an approach shot over more of the same. If in this part of Florida, stay and play here. You'll have a lot more fun than you will at TPC Sawgrass!

TPC Sawgrass - Everyone has seen this Pete Dye course on television, so it is unnecessary to describe it at length. Suffice it to say that almost all either love or hate it, particularly the entirely manufactured 17th Island green hole. (Diggings used to enhance course elevations elsewhere left a gaping hole. Dye's wife, Alice, suggested filling it with water and leaving a tiny target green.) In general, I appreciate that Dye was able to fulfill the PGA's desire to build a very challenging tournament course with elevated grass mounds on flat land to maximize the visual experience for fans. Many pros have embraced the course because of the evolution of improvements to the original design (the excessive difficulty of which caused bitter outrage), its mint condition, and its challenge to identify the best. However, I deplore the 17th hole, which skews my feelings about the rest of the course. The only thing missing is a clown and a windmill. As much as some like to see the pros suffer like the rest of us on tough holes, no tournament (especially a "5th major") should be decided so late in the round on a hole with so little margin for error. This is accentuated when, as is often the case, there are sudden and significant changes in wind direction and speed when the player attempts to select the proper club (or, worse, seeing this happen after the ball has already taken flight). In short, the overall course is nothing but an expensive torture chamber for the average golfer, or even a very good one. It is best left to watch the greatest in the world play it. If you are hell-bent on tackling an island green, there are plenty of imitations, albeit less difficult ones, around the country.

THE BEST OF ALL THINGS GOLF

Pacific Dunes Course at Bandon Dunes Par-3 10th Hole

Northwood Par-4 7th Hole

GOLF IN THE MAJOR REGIONS OF THE USA

Lincoln Park Par-3 17th Hole

Cypress Point Par-3 16th Hole

Olympic Club Par-4 18th Hole

Sharp Park Par-4 17th Hole

GOLF IN THE MAJOR REGIONS OF THE USA

Pasatiempo Par-4 16th, Par-3 15th & Par-3 18th Holes

Crystal Springs Par-4 6th Hole

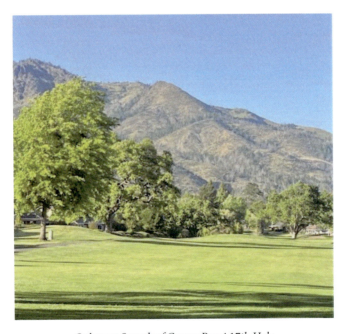

Oakmont Sugarloaf Course Par-4 17th Hole

Harding Park Par-4 16th Hole

Harding Park Par-4 18th

Half Moon Bay Links Course Par-3 17th Hole

Half Moon Bay Old Course Par-4 18th Hole

Torrey Pines North Course Par-3 15th Hole

GOLF IN THE MAJOR REGIONS OF THE USA

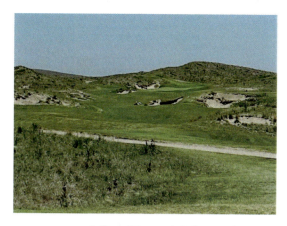

Ballyneal Par-5 8th Hole

Troon North Pinnacle Course Par-3 8th Hole

TPC Scottsdale Stadium Course Par-3 16th Hole

Erin Hills Par-5 14th Hole

Erin Hills Pub

Jack & Clearview Pro Renee Powell

Clearview Par-4 5th Hole

THE BEST OF ALL THINGS GOLF

USGA Museum

Mid Pines Par-4 1st Hole

Old Sport & Gallery Pinehurst Village

GOLF IN THE MAJOR REGIONS OF THE USA

Jack & The Absent-Minded Professor (Denis) at Augusta National

Old Dog Les

CHAPTER III

The Best Courses
*(Ranking of the Top 100 Courses Played**
Plus Architect & 5 Star Scale Rating)

St. Andrews Par-4 18th Hole

Ardglass Par-4 1st Hole

Royal County Down Par-4 9th Hole

Rating courses is no easy task. One could certainly question the order of this ranking or the omission of certain courses among the roughly 250 I have played, many of which are routinely placed on the "greatest" lists by various golf magazines, books, etc. (For a complete listing of all courses played - by region, their architects, and their number of stars on a five-star rating scale - see the Appendix). However, for me, it comes down to the best possible combination of uniqueness, history, natural setting and design, scenery, flora and fauna, layout and diversity of holes, challenges without over-the-top difficulty, ability to be walked, condition, number of memorable holes, clubhouse setting and ambiance, unforgettable experiences and, perhaps most important, fun. In short, is it a place ("famous" or otherwise) where I would look forward to playing again and again, or a course where, afterward, I felt mentally and/or physically exhausted (and my hard-earned handicap seemed like a fraud)? Since I have not played Augusta National, but only walked it as a patron, it is not included in this ranking. Nevertheless, I consider it to be the hands-down best in the world. It is golf's Garden of Eden, and no attempt should be made to replicate its diverse collection of holes AND their incomparable beauty/condition. (I looked everywhere on the grounds and could not find a single weed!) At Augusta, despite its supernatural aura, everything comes together in an ironically "natural" way but would seem contrived and counterfeit anywhere else. As such, I retain an overall aversion to the Disneyland nature of tortuously manufactured courses (for example, those with obviously fake waterfalls and lakes, large spewing pond/lake fountains, expansive and overly abundant "artistic" sand bunkers, bulkheads, railroad ties, etc.) and/or those often target-like modern courses that are hopelessly difficult for all but the scratch golfers. (Can you say Pete Dye?) My strong preference/admiration is for "minimalist" golf course design. That is, take the ground that God gives you and create a layout that incorporates as many of the ranking factors listed above as possible and, if played from the proper tees, can be enjoyed with the possibility of a decent score on a good day, by pros as well as foozlers.

1. St. Andrews Links (Old Course)/God & Old Tom Morris/5.0+
2. Pebble Beach GL/Neville/5.0+
3. Royal County Down GC/Old Tom Morris & Vardon & Colt/5.0
4. Carne (Wild Atlantic Dunes Course)/Hackett & Engh & McIntosh/5.0
5. Doonbeg GL/Norman/5.0
6. North Berwick GC (West Course)/Strath/5.0
7. Turnberry/Fernie/5.0
8. Cruden Bay GC/Old Tom Morris & Fowler & Simpson/5.0
9. Cypress Point Club/MacKenzie/5.0
10. Lahinch GC/Old Tom Morris & MacKenzie/5.0

11. Bandon Dunes/Kidd/5.0
12. Prestwick GC/Old Tom Morris/5.0
13. Pacific Dunes/Doak/5.0
14. Gleneagles GC (King's Course)/Braid/5.0
15. Royal Dornoch GC/Old Tom Morris/5.0
16. Mauna Lani/Flint & Cain/5.0
17. Bandon Dunes (The Preserve Course)/Coore & Crenshaw/5.0
18. Half Moon Bay GL (Ocean Course)/Hills/4.5
19. Olympic Club (Lake Course)/Whiting & W.Watson/4.5
20. Ardglass GC/Misc./4.5
21. Burlingame CC/R.T Jones Sr./4.5
22. Druids Glen/Ruddy/4.5
23. Portsalon GC/C.Thompson/4.5
24. St. Patrick's Links/Doak 4.5
25. The Island GC/Hackett/4.5
26. Northwood GC/MacKenzie/4.5
27. Erin Hills/Hurdzan & Fry & Whitten/4.5
28. Machrihanish Dunes GC/Kidd/4.5
29. Kingsbarns GL/Steele/4.5
30. Mid Pines/Ross/4.5
31. Carnoustie GL/Old Tom Morris & Braid/4.5
32. Enniscrone GC/Hackett/4.5
33. Old Head GL/Misc./4.0
34. Rosapenna (Old Tom Morris Course)/Old Tom & Ruddy/4.0
35. Pacific Grove/Neville/4.0
36. Sharp Park GC/MacKenzie & Fleming/4.0
37. Harding Park (TPC) GC/Whiting & W. Watson & Fleming/4.0
38. Olympic Club (Ocean Course)/Whiting & W. Watson/4.0
39. Corballis Links GC/Kirby/4.0
40. Pasatiempo GC/MacKenzie/4.0
41. Gleneagles (Queen's Course)/Braid/4.0
42. Portstewart GC/Giffin/4.0
43. Castle Stuart GL/Hanse/4.0

44. Arrowhead CC/W.P. Bell/4.0
45. Ballybunion GC/Misc. Members & Simpson/4.0
46. Machrihanish GC/Old Tom Morris/4.0
47. Brookside CC/Ross/4.0
48. The Presidio GC/Johnstone + modifications by Tillinghast/4.0
49. Ballyneal/Doak/4.0
50. Peninsula CC/Ross/4.0
51. Glenmoor CC/Nicklaus/4.0
52. Royal Troon/Braid/4.0
53. Dooks GL/Hackett/4.0
54. Poplar Creek GC/Unknown/4.0
55. Adare Manor Golf Club (Abbey Course)/Hackett/4.0
56. Panmure GC/Braid/4.0.
57. Sedona Resort/Panks/4.0
58. Pinehurst (#3 Course)/Ross/4.0
59. Royal Portrush GC/Colt/4.0
60. Whistling Straits/Pete Dye/4.0
61. Schaffer's Mill/Miller/4.0
62. Stanford/Thomas & W.P. Bell/4.0
63. Musselburgh Links/Unknown/4.0
64. Lake Merced GC/W. Locke & MacKenzie/4.0
65. Spanish Bay (Links At)/T. Watson & Tatum/4.0
66. St. Andrews Links (New Course)/Old Tom Morris/4.0
67. Lincoln Park GC/Bendelow & Fleming/4.0
68. Yocha Dehe GC/Brad Bell/4.0
69. Cancun Hilton (Now Iberostar)/Dye Jr./4.0
70. San Francisco GC/Tillinghast/4.0
71. LakeRidge/Jones Sr./4.0
72. The Breakers (Ocean Course)/Findlay & Ross & Rees Jones/4.0
73. Bandon Dunes (Sheep Ranch Course)/Coore & Crenshaw/4.0
74. Troon North (Pinnacle Course)/Weiskopf & Morrish/4.0
75. Adare Golf Club (At Adare Manor)/Jones Sr.& T. Fazio/4.0
76. Dromoland Castle/Kirby & JB Carr/4.0

77. Redlands CC/MacKenzie/4.0
78. Baylands GL (Palo Alto Muni)/W.F. Bell & W.F. Bell/4.0
79. Dragonfly GC/Baird/4.0
80. San Jose CC (Jacksonville)/Ross/4.0
81. Torrey Pines (North & South Courses)/W.P. Bell & W.F. Bell/4.0
82. Crystal Springs GC/Fowler/4.0
83. Cobblestone Park/Dye Jr./4.0
84. Glen Club (North Berwick East Course)/Sayers & Braid/4.0
85. Oakmont GC (Sugarloaf Course)/Robinson/4.0
86. County Sligo GC/Colt/4.0
87. Elie (The Golf House Club)/Old Tom Morris/4.0
88. We Ko Pa GC/Coore & Crenshaw/4.0
89. Donegal (Murvagh)/Hackett/4.0
90. Monterey Peninsula CC (Shore Course)/Strantz/4.0
91. Notre Dame (Warren Course)/Coore & Crenshaw/3.5
92. Notre Dame (Burke Course)/Kelly/3.5
93. Oak Quarry GC/Morgan/3.5.
94. Oakmont GC (Valley of the Moon Course)/Robinson/3.5
95. Clearview GC/Powell/3.5
96. Cinnabar Hills GC/Harbottle/3.5
97. San Jose Muni GC/Graves/3.5
98. East Potomac Park GC/Travis/3.5
99. Eagle Vines GC/Miller/3.5
100. Duke University/Jones Sr./3.5

* In the final chapter, I outline several planned future trips that will complete my lifetime golf journey. No doubt most, if not all, of the fine additional courses that I will play will be added to the Top 100 list. This will result in a shift in the rankings and the necessary removal of some beloved courses.

CHAPTER IV

The Best Golf Architects (Top 10)

Just as there was a trend in America over the past century away from downtown shops with integrated, intimate baseball parks to large, bland suburban malls and nondescript mega baseball/football stadium combos - then back again, so too has a full-circle trend in golf course design/revision largely taken shape. Perhaps, in both instances, this can be attributed to nostalgia and/or an innate appreciation for what looks and feels most natural, relaxing and fun. In the case of golf course architecture, the current movement can, in its most simplistic terms, be summed up as a return to minimalist design. That is, utilizing and/or blending in with the natural landscape without significant alterations while offering strategic alternatives, rather than heavily manufactured and often artificial looking and/or overly penal (particularly as regards the average golfer) layouts. The stalwarts of this revival are Tom Doak, the team of Bill Coore and Ben Crenshaw, and Gil Hanse. The minimalist designers (both past and present) dominate the ranking of the 100 best/favorite courses that I have played. At the very top is Old Tom Morris, who designed Royal County Down/Lahinch/ St. Andrews' New Course and revisions to its Old Course/Cruden Bay/Royal Dornoch/Prestwick and Carnoustie. Many of his courses were subject to later modifications, not because of poor design, but to avoid becoming obsolete due to shortness of length following the switch from the gutta percha ball to one with a rubber core, and from hickory shaft clubs to steel shafts. In the process, some holes were rerouted to reduce the number of original blind shots - to the satisfaction of those golfers desiring an open tee to green view. Most of the revisions to Old Tom's work were carried out by other minimalist designers who happen to be at the top of my list, including Alister MacKenzie, who designed Cypress Point, Northwood, Sharp Park, Pasatiempo and Augusta National (the last at which, as previously noted, I was a mere awed spectator).

The thought did occur to me as to whether Old Tom and MacKenzie stand out as designers because they were such geniuses *or* because they happened to be handed the most naturally beautiful settings upon which to design their courses. Would much less renowned architects have designed similar icons if presented the same prime locations? I believe there is some merit to this query. Still, I also think that the particular vision/styles/philosophies of Morris (e.g., revetted bunkers/double greens) and MacKenzie (e.g., a Boar War-trained master of camouflage techniques) resulted in unique signatures on the somewhat singular topographies they developed. Moreover, both designed a number of other courses that bear their appealing stamps, yet on relatively average settings. That is, they created challenging and fun layouts, with telltale signs of their authorship, on good but not great locations without unlimited budgets and moving or importing thousands of tons of dirt, adding man-made water hazards, waterfalls, etc. (Unlike, for example, Pete Dye at Whistling Straits and Kiawah Island, or Tom Fazio at Shadow Creek and Trump National Westchester.)

Given my admiration of the works of Alister MacKenzie, it is no surprise that I am attracted to the courses designed by his protégé, Jack Fleming. He served as the architect of several fine private courses as well as some unique municipal/ public courses in the San Francisco Bay Area of California. Unfortunately, many of the latter are now in a state of sad and embarrassing disrepair. Yet, if one

THE BEST GOLF ARCHITECTS

looks past their current conditions, he or she can still enjoy Fleming's legacy of magnificent layouts for a song.

While I have played only three Harry Colt-designed courses (Royal Portrush, County Sligo and Royal County Down – the latter at which he made modifications to Old Tom's original), I believe this reductivist's name will move up the list after I have had the opportunity to play some more of his courses on planned future golf trips (e.g., Swinley Forest, Alwoodley (teamed with MacKenzie), Formby, Muirfield, Royal Liverpool, and Sunningdale).

Another "hands-off nature" proponent at the top of the list, Eddie Hackett, is the king of Irish golf course design for good reason. He crafted the following layouts on my favorite courses-played list: The Island Club, Enniscrone, Dooks, Donegal, and his opus, Carne.

Perhaps the most underappreciated of the group is James Braid, in part because he is remembered more for being a member of the "Great Triumvirate" alongside Vardon and Taylor and because his prolific course designs (over 250 in the British Isles) do not include any in the USA (save one done from home using topographical maps). Yet, his resume rivals them all. (Examples include Gleneagles, St. Enodoc, Pennard, and Brora, along with remodel work at Troon, Carnoustie, Royal Aberdeen, Royal Cinque Ports, Prestwick, Elie, Nairn, Fraserburgh, Murcar, Ganton, and Berwick-upon-Tweed (Goswick.)) Not to say that I don't grumble on occasion when landing in one of his treacherous bunkers!

Who knows just how much higher Jack Neville, five-time winner of the California State Amateur Championship, might have climbed in the golf architect world had he more than dabbled in the profession. One might say that he did passable work at Pebble Beach and Pacific Grove! (He also assisted George Thomas with the design at Bel Air CC and Bob Baldock at the Shore Course at Monterey Peninsula CC.) A testament to his work at Pebble is that relatively few changes have been made since it opened in 1919.

As for Donald Ross, America's most prolific golf course designer (more than 400) and among its most revered, one might be surprised that this master of integrating a course with its natural surroundings is not ranked higher than number seven. I have had the opportunity to play quite a few of his courses (favorites being Mid Pines, Brookside, Peninsula, San Jose, and Pinehurst No.

3). I appreciate his minimalist approach to design and his links-inspired layouts and bunkering. But, I am less than enamored with the notorious nature of some of his "signature" green complexes, the most frequent features being their so-called "inverted saucer" or "turtle back" shape and severe undulations, resulting in runoffs and excessive speeds. After all, as pointed out earlier, it was Ross who favored pleasure over pain as a design philosophy. However, Ross may be entitled to some slack in this regard, at least with respect to his most famous and demanding course, Pinehurst No. 2 (and frequent host of the U.S. Open). During my stay at Dornoch, Scotland, I had the privilege of being invited to attend a talk on Donald Ross (at a facility located a short par-3 distance from Ross' modest, early-life home). It was given by Bradley Klein, the former longtime architecture editor of Golfweek magazine and perhaps the foremost expert on Ross and his work. If I recall correctly, he pointed out that at Pinehurst No. 2, the difficulty of the greens has been magnified beyond Ross' original intent insofar as the initial "greens" of 1907 consisted of more receptive sand surfaces that were oiled in to allow smooth putting. Then, after replacing the sand with grass in 1935, the steepness of the greens increased as a result of nearly a century of top dressings. My question (which, unfortunately, I neglected to ask him) is why, when making significant restorations to the course in 2012 and changing the grass type on the greens in 2014, did they not also shave down the greens and/or why not raise the mower blades or reduce the weight of the rollers to better reflect Ross' original idea of highly challenging, but more reasonably manageable green contours and speeds? Perhaps there is a fear that the course would lose some of its mystique and become easier for the pros to conquer (which U.S. Open officials hate to see on one of their host sites). But, what about the rest of us? As for me, when I was at Pinehurst, I chose not to pay $500 to be tortured on this particular Ross design.

And now, without further delay, here is my biased ranking of the best architects* of the courses I have played.

1. Old Tom Morris
2. Alister MacKenzie (One-time partner of Colt)
3. Eddie Hackett
4. James Braid

5.   Jack Neville
6.   Harry Colt
7.   Donald Ross (Mentored by Old Tom Morris)
8.   Jack Fleming (Mentored by MacKenzie)
9.   Tom Doak
10. Ben Crenshaw/Bill Coore
     Honorable Mention - Gil Hanse

Three fine minimalist architects, David Strath, A.W. Tillinghast and William Flynn, are not included in the top ten list because they each designed only one course I have played. In the case of Strath, it's the masterpiece at North Berwick - home of the most copied hole in golf - The Redan. Apparently North Berwick was Strath's only foray into course design. He was a professional and sometimes playing partner of Young Tom Morris. And, like Young Tom, he died at an early age. With regard to Tillinghast, it's the San Francisco Golf Club. This very famous, challenging course is not higher on my favorites list due, in part, to its numerous and massive bunkers, many of which encroach too close to primary fairway landing areas. Still, the secluded, pristine course and the old, unmodified clubhouse/locker room exude a pure old-school golf atmosphere. While Tillinghast's other most famous designs such as Winged Foot, Baltusrol and Bethpage Black were primarily created to challenge the greatest golfers, he also designed or made revisions to many other courses that present a fair test for all golfers. But, perhaps his lasting legacy to golf course design, besides the several major championship venues still in regular use for that purpose, is his whistle-stop course consultation tour across America - undertaken during the Depression on behalf of the PGA of America. Many of his suggested revisions were acted upon and can be appreciated today, such as various bunkers at Lake Merced and remodeled and/or newly designed greens at the Berkeley, Peninsula and Presidio golf clubs in the San Francisco Bay Area. Significantly, he found two of my favorites (Harding Park and Lincoln Park) to be sound and made no suggested revisions. As for Flynn, I played his Cascades course in Virginia. A very nice course, though with the passage of time it has lost some of its original luster. Several of his other courses are widely recognized as among the best in the world - Shinnecock Hills, The Country Club in Brookline (Primrose Nine), Merion, and Cherry Hills.

The names of the following architects typically show up on greatest lists - but they are not included on mine - because their work generally fails to meet the minimalist criteria and/or other key Best Courses rating factors referenced in this chapter and the previous one: Robert Trent Jones Sr., Pete Dye, Jack Nicklaus, and Tom Fazio. Jones did state that a course should "follow the land" (minimalism), but he also said: "Every hole should be a difficult par but an easy bogey." (Reference the review in Chapter I of his Cashen design at Ballybunion to see why this combination of philosophies can be disastrous - at least from a fun course standpoint for the average player.) He did manage to tone down his exacting standards on a couple of courses on my favorites list (Burlingame CC and LakeRidge). Nicklaus contributed one at Glenmoor by doing the same.

*A few of the undisputed great architects, who are omitted from my list because I have not had the opportunity to play on a course they designed, include C.B. Macdonald (National Golf Links of America), Seth Raynor (Fishers Island) and George C. Thomas, Jr. (Riviera CC). I did play the solid course at Stanford University, which Thomas designed on paper but due to his illness was completed by William P. Bell.

CHAPTER V

The Best Golfers
(And the Greatest of Them All)

Golf's Mount Rushmore - Drawing by Gerald K. Hammel

Mount Rushmore literally and figuratively represents the larger-than-life nature of four of the United States' all-around greatest Presidents. These men not only had varied lengths of service in their presidential role, they also were necessarily confined to the particular times and circumstances under which they operated. Thus, judging their relative merits and achievements is challenging, to say the least, particularly when trying to determine which of the four Presidents deserves the title of "Greatest." However, when pressed, most students of the subject will name one, even if influenced as much by visceral instinct and sentiment as by specific achievements. (I believe the answer to the greatest on Mount Rushmore question is Lincoln, by a granite nose, over Washington.) The same framework and challenges apply if one engages in the exercise of identifying who belongs on golf's version of Mount Rushmore. However, in my view, establishing golf's top five (OK golf's Mount has five figures instead of four!) is far easier than selecting the greatest individual in that illustrious grouping. In any event, set forth below is my case for both. But, first, a listing of the top 25 golfers of the post-1920 era,* and the top 10 golfers of the pre-1920 era.**

Top 25 – Post-1920 Era

Rank	Golfer	Major Wins	PGA Tour Wins	Of Note
1	Jack Nicklaus	18	73	2nd place in 19 majors
2	Tiger Woods	15	82	Made 142 straight cuts
3	Bobby Jones	13	-	Grand Slam in same year
4	Ben Hogan	9	64	Won 6 of 9 majors 1950-'53
5	Walter Hagen	11	45	4 consec PGA Championships
6	Sam Snead	7	82	Won same event eight times
7	Arnold Palmer	7	62	17 straight years with a win
8	Gary Player	9	24	165 Worldwide wins
9	Tom Watson	8	39	5 British Opens
10	Byron Nelson	5	52	18 wins (11 straight) in 1 year
11	Lee Trevino	6	29	Nicklaus' nemesis in majors
12	Gene Sarazen	5	38	Albatros on Augusta #15
13	Phil Mickelson	6	45	Oldest to win a major (50)
14	Billy Casper	3	51	20 Ryder Cup wins
15	Seve Ballesteros	5	9	50 Euro / 20 Ryder Cup wins
16	Nick Faldo	6	9	30 Euro / 23 Ryder Cup wins
17	Raymond Floyd	4	22	PGA Tour win in 4 decades
18	Cary Middlecoff	3	39	Tied for 10th all-time wins
19	Rory McIlroy	4	24	Won 3 of 4 majors by age 25
20	Jimmy Demaret	3	31	Won Masters three times
21	Johnny Miller	2	25	1st 63 at a U.S. Open (1973)
22	Ernie Els	4	19	7 World Matchplay wins
23	Greg Norman	2	20	331 career weeks at No.1

24	Hale Irwin	3	20	Won U.S. Open three times
25(T)	VJ Singh	3	34	Record 22 wins after age 40
25(T)	Bobby Locke	4	15	4 British Opens
25(T)	Brooks Koepka	5	9	2 consec. U.S.Opens & PGAs

Hon. Mention: Jim Barnes/Tommy Armour/Lawson Little/Peter Thompson

* Some may wonder why still active modern greats such as Dustin Johnson, Jordan Spieth, Justin Thomas, and Jon Rahm are not listed in the Top 25. Before their careers are over, they might significantly add to their current impressive resumes and, thereafter, make the cut. In the meantime, which members of the existing group can you remove in view of their actual number of career PGA Tour/major victories and other worldwide professional wins? Koepka has only 9 PGA Tour wins, but five of them have been majors (only 20 golfers have achieved this feat), and he has finished in the top 4 eight times in the majors - all over a six- year span and by the age of 34.

Top 10 – Pre-1920 Era

1. Harry Vardon
2. J.H. Taylor
3. James Braid
4. Young Tom Morris
5. John Ball
6. Old Tom Morris
7. Willie Park Sr.
8. Harold Hilton
9. Francis Ouimet
10. Sandy Herd

** The names of Old Tom and Young Tom Morris, and to a lesser extent Willie Park Sr., are more widely known than some of the others on the above list because they were pioneers of professional golf. These men played many exhibition challenge matches against other single or two-man team competitors, with a large number of spectator bets on the line. They also dominated the first dozen or so British Opens. However, it would be difficult to rank them any higher since the fields in those early Opens typically included a mere 8-12 entrants. Contrast that with Taylor's and Braid's full-field five British Opens each, and John Ball's record eight British Amateurs and one British Open. Nevertheless, Young Tom Morris deserves special recognition since he won four straight Opens (beginning in 1868 at age 17) utilizing his invention and/or perfection of some significant modern-day shot-making techniques. He undoubtedly would have won many more majors but for his early death at age 24, a few months after the tragic passing of his wife and son during childbirth.

GOLF'S MOUNT RUSHMORE

Jack Nicklaus - "The Golden Bear" (The Greatest)
Tiger Woods - "Tiger"
Bobby Jones - "The Scottish Terrier" ***
Ben Hogan - "The Hawk"
Harry Vardon - "The Greyhound"

*** A little poetic license is used here. Jones was not regularly referred to as any particular animal as far as I am aware. However, given his special relationship to Scotland and the Scots, and the fact that each of the others on golf's Mt. Rushmore has a nickname associated with an animal, a Scottish Terrier seems apropos - particularly since the name of the country's most famous Terrier is, coincidentally, Bobby!

JACK NICKLAUS

Without question, Jack Nicklaus is the greatest golf champion of all time, with his record-setting total of 18 major wins (and numerous near wins in the majors). However, it is also important to remember that this record and his many other PGA Tour wins were spread out over a long career, covering several eras that included most of golf's all-time best players. As such, when identifying not only the sport's greatest champion, but also its greatest ever golfer, any "wouldas", "couldas" or "shouldas" pertaining to the other members of golf's Mount Rushmore must be set aside in favor of the one and only "dida" that applies to Big Jack.

So, let's look at some of Jack Nicklaus' incredible achievements, including a few comparisons with those of other mountaintop members. Naturally, one is drawn to Jack's record in the major championships (today consisting of the annual Masters, U.S. Open, British Open and PGA Championship tournaments). He won 18 majors (vs. Tiger Woods' 15), spanning a period of roughly 25 years (with the first 17 wins occurring over a 20 year stretch). Between 1970 and 1980 he made 44 consecutive cuts in the majors, winning ten times and finishing in the top five 30 times. Jack won his first at the age of 22 - in a U.S. Open playoff against Arnold Palmer on Palmer's backyard course at Pennsylvania's Oakmont Country Club - and won his last major at the age of 46 at Augusta National's Masters tournament in 1986. This compilation includes a record-tying four U.S. Opens, three British Opens, a record-tying five PGA Championships and a record six Masters wins. He is one of only five players to achieve the Career Grand Slam (winning each of the current four majors), and he did it a record-tying three times. Nearly as impressive as Nicklaus' win record in the majors is his record of most top ten finishes in the majors (73 vs. Tiger Woods' 41) and his record 19 second-place finishes (vs. Tiger's 7), including four times in the U.S. Open - golf's most exacting championship in terms of difficult course set-up. Five of those second-place finishes came by one stroke or in a playoff. And he had a record 9 third-place finishes (vs. Tiger's 4). Jack finished in the top six in the U.S. Open for a record 14 consecutive years. No golfer since has finished that high more than three straight years. Nicklaus' playoff record in the majors was 3-1. He had eight final-day come-from-behind wins in majors (vs. Tiger's one). As for the other members of golf's Mount Rushmore club, Bobby Jones won 13 majors (over the course of eight years!), Ben Hogan won his 9 majors in an eight year stretch (and another one a few years earlier if the Hale America tournament, played for one year in place of the U.S. Open with the same format, is included) and Harry Vardon won 7 majors, including a record six British Opens, despite wartime disruptions and several extended, near-fatal encounters with Tuberculosis.

  Jack's focus was undoubtedly on the majors (often playing a limited PGA Tour schedule to allow more time to mentally and physically prepare for them) yet, with unparalleled course-management skills, he still managed to win 73 times on the PGA Tour. That total is behind only Sam Snead and Tiger Woods with 82 career wins each, though it is worth noting that the Golden Bear finished second 58 times vs. Tiger's 31. Nicklaus' overall PGA Tour playoff record was 13-10. Both his total major and total PGA Tour wins, particularly when compared with Woods, also must be placed in the context of the top-level competition he faced. During his prime major-winning years, Jack's chief ten rivals were Hall of Famers Arnold Palmer, Gary Player, Billy Casper, Lee Trevino, Tom Watson, Johnny Miller, Raymond Floyd, Gene Littler, Hale Irwin, and Julius Boros (Five of the top 15 all-time greats listed above). These ten players won on the PGA Tour a combined 319 times, including 46 majors. Ben Hogan and Sam Snead were still competitive during Jack's majors run, but they were winding down their careers, and Nick Faldo, Fred Couples, Mark O'Meara, and Nick Price were top-level, but they were relative newcomers - so these old-timers/babies, and their tremendous career achievements, are not included in this rivals/wins list. At the same time, if the career achievements of just a dozen more of Jack's contemporaries (Tom Weiskopf, Dave Stockton, Doug Sanders, Lanny Watkins, Hal Sutton, Corey Pavin, Ben Crenshaw, Seve Ballesteros, Greg Norman, Curtis Strange, Tom Kite, and Hubert Green) were added to the totals of the above ten players, the numbers would swell to 518 PGA Tour wins and 66 majors! By comparison, Tiger Woods' top ten rivals during his prime major-winning years were Ernie Els, Phil Mickelson, VJ Singh, Jim Furyk, Padraig Harrington, Davis Love III, Sergio Garcia, Adam Scott, Hal Sutton, and David Duval (only one of whom is among the top 15 all-time greats listed above). These players combined for 194 PGA Tour wins, including 22 majors. It should be noted that modern stars such as Justin Rose, Jason Day, Bubba Watson, Dustin Johnson, Rory McIlroy, Jordan Spieth, Justin Thomas, Jon Rham, Collin Morikawa, and Brooks Koepka accumulated virtually all of their major and PGA Tour wins after Tiger had won all but one of his majors. This suggests that a combination of Woods' injuries AND the quality and quantity of his top-level competition caught up with him in the second half of his career.

Nicklaus' Ryder Cup Record was 16-8-3 (vs. Woods' record of 13-21-3). Another remarkable fact is that in 1998, at the age of 58, Jack shot what was then the lowest final round (68) for a senior in Masters history and tied for 6th place. (At the 2023 Masters, 52-year-old Phil Mickelson shot a final round 65 to finish in a tie for 2nd.) As for the Champions Tour, Jack only played six seasons, with a limited schedule focused on the majors. He won 10 times and - surprise,

surprise - eight of those wins were majors! (That is third all-time behind Gary Player's nine majors over 13 years and Bernhard Langer's 12 majors over 16 years on the Champions Tour.)

Finally, one can only wonder what Jack Nicklaus' total records might have been if he had access to today's equipment. (Add the fact that it is generally acknowledged that the MacGregor clubs he used were inferior to other top brands at the time.) Lee Trevino speculated that if Jack, in his prime, had played the clubs and balls used in 2010, his drives would have been 400 yards! Or, what if Jack had the advantage of the modern-era players' benefits of traveling coaches, physical trainers and sports psychologists? But, then again, the same can be said for golf's other Mount Rushmore members who played in previous eras.

Now, having made the case for Jack Nicklaus as the greatest golfer of all time, Tiger Woods must be given his due as the most dominant golfer over a significant period (roughly 12 years), though, as we shall see, fans of Bobby Jones, or even Ben Hogan, might have something to say about that!

TIGER WOODS

Tiger seemed born to golf. From his television appearance at age two on "The Mike Douglas Show," where he demonstrated an effortless proclivity with a golf club, through his mind-boggling performances in the Junior Amateur (3 consecutive wins) and U.S. Amateur (3 successive wins vs. Nicklaus' 2 non-consecutive wins), his Hall of Fame-level success as a pro was never in doubt. However, the speed with which he physically, mentally and statistically dominated his sport is unprecedented. He won twice in his rookie season on the PGA Tour and four times the following season, including his first major (The Masters) by 12 strokes! While not the most accurate driver on tour, he simply overpowered courses, mentally intimidating and demoralizing the competition by hitting the ball prodigious lengths with every club, having the strength and shot-shaping skills to extricate balls from the most difficult of lies, and to make seemingly every "must make" putt. His work ethic was unprecedented in terms of combined practice and physical training. (Sophisticated workout trailers at PGA Tour sites quickly became the norm in response to Tiger's example and success.)

Tiger is, without question, the greatest front-runner the game has ever witnessed. When the outright leader after 54 holes, he won 44 out of 46 times (96%), including each of his first 14 majors. The PGA Tour tournament average is 45%. When leading or co-leading after 54 holes, he won 55 out of 59 times. This indicates, however, that Tiger has not been a great chaser, most notably in the majors. By way of contrast, Jack Nicklaus won eight majors when not holding the 54 hole lead, patiently waiting for the others to make mistakes and lose their nerve.

Woods was blessed (or cursed from a comparisons standpoint) with perfect timing in terms of his run at the majors. As noted above, Tiger's top-level competition was nowhere near that which Jack Nicklaus (and, for the most part, the other members of golf's Mount Rushmore) faced when accumulating majors and other PGA Tour wins (though the overall field that Woods played against was certainly deeper). However, one can not manufacture the level of competition; they can only respond to it in the best possible manner. And Tiger certainly did that!

Here, then, is a list of some of his chief accomplishments:

Won 15 majors (second to Nicklaus' 18). His first 14 majors were won over a period of 12 years (vs. 14 years for Nicklaus), with his last coming 11 years later.

Won 82 times on the PGA Tour (tied for first with Sam Snead).

Won four consecutive major championships (not all in the same calendar year so not, technically, a "Grand Slam", but instead referred to as the "Tiger Slam").

11-1 record in PGA Tour playoffs.

Held the World Number 1 spot in the Official World Golf Rankings for five continuous years - twice!

Won the 1997 Masters by 12 strokes.

Won the 2000 U.S. Open by 15 strokes.

Won by 7+ strokes a dozen times.

Won by 5+ strokes 17 times.

Won by 3+ strokes 32 times.

Made the cut in 142 consecutive PGA Tour tournaments.

BOBBY JONES

Nothing can quite compare to the playing career of Robert ("Bobby") Tyre Jones Jr. Unlike the other individuals on golf's Mount Rushmore, Bobby remained an amateur. And, unlike the rest, he essentially was a part-time "hobby" golfer, confining his competitive play almost solely to the summer's four major tournaments for which he was eligible. The rest of the year he was earning degrees from Georgia Tech (Bachelor's in Engineering), Harvard (Bachelor's in English Literature) and Law (Emory – passing the bar after only three semesters), and then practicing law. Imagine any of the other greats attempting to do this and achieving the same results. During his era, there were still as many outstanding amateur golfers as professional golfers. As such, the "majors" (for "Grand Slam" purposes) consisted of the British Open, the British Amateur, the U.S. Open, and the U.S. Amateur (As a non-professional, he was not eligible to play in the PGA Championship, established as a fifth major in 1916.) After his retirement in 1930, Jones, along with Alister MacKenzie, designed Augusta National. The tournament held there beginning in 1934 (the Masters) became the fourth major after it, and the PGA championship replaced the two Amateur Opens in the Grand Slam grouping. In short, Bobby Jones was Tiger before there was a Tiger. He was a child prodigy for whom unprecedented greatness was assumed. (Jones won the inaugural Georgia Amateur Championship at age 14!) The difference between Bobby and Tiger was that, despite repeated knocks on the door at the majors, it took Jones several more years than Tiger to open it to a win. (His career effectively began in 1920, at the age of 18, since only two majors were held during the World War I era.) Jones clearly felt the weight of the expectations of the media and general public, not to mention his own obsession with perfection. But, once he opened that first door in 1923, there was no closing it until he chose to walk away from the game in 1930 at the age of 28. Many of the greats (e.g., Mickelson, Singh, Hogan) had not even won their first major at that age, let alone 13 of them! Jones dominated golf in a manner that the world of sports had never seen. He did so against competition, which, at its highest level (e.g., Walter Hagen*, Gene Sarazen, Tommy Armour, Macdonald Smith, Wille MacFarlane, Bobby Cruickshank, George Von Elm, Jim Barnes, Francis Ouimet, Jess Sweetser, Leo Diegel, Johnny Farrell, Cyril Tolley, Chick Evans), was below what Jack Nicklaus faced but at least as good, if not better than that which Tiger Woods encountered when collecting his first 14 major trophies. (Furthermore, both the U.S. Amateur and the British Amateur were match play formats, with elimination rounds played over a mere 18 holes and the championship round over 36 holes, leaving no room for "off days.") So, why isn't his name, rather than Tiger Woods', regularly thrown into the ring against Jack Nicklaus as the greatest golfer ever? Indeed, a strong argument can be made that it should be. Here's why:

Won the U.S. Amateur five times (1924, 1925, 1927, 1928 and 1930) and came in second twice.

Won the U.S. Open four times (1923, 1926, 1929 and 1930) and came in second four times.

Won the British Open three times (1926, 1927 and 1930).

Won the British Amateur (1930). Entered the tournament only three times.

Only player to win all four majors in the same calendar year (1930)

Played in a total of 31 majors, winning 13 (44% !!) and placed among the top ten 27 times (87% !!).

In the end, Jones' primary achievements, like Woods' and Hogan's, occurred within a short time frame relative to Jack Nicklaus'. And, so, the dominant nature of, and the win totals achieved by, each of these three players for a significant, but nevertheless limited, period must be stacked against Nicklaus' long and steady years of greatness playing against the very best over several epochs. This especially applies in terms of total wins/placements in the majors, which present an unimaginable test of combined skill and nerves far beyond regular professional tournament golf. (Hence, the primary reason that Sam Snead, despite his 82 PGA Tour wins, is not on golf's Mount Rushmore; he won "only" seven majors, and none of them was a U.S. Open title.) In the case of the three others, the elements of "woulda," "coulda," and "shoulda" inevitably enter the equation. What if Woods' had not encountered several major injuries and self-induced disruptions in his personal life? What if Hogan had learned earlier in his career the "secret" to pure shot-making and accuracy, which enabled him to continue to dominate despite serious injuries sustained in a major traffic accident? And, what if he had managed to avoid, or at least learned to manage, the putting yips that plagued his later career?

What if Jones had continued playing for another 10 years (or more if he hadn't later contracted a severely crippling and ultimately terminal case of syringomyelia)? This is perhaps the most difficult "What if?" question to answer. Jones certainly left the game when he was at its absolute summit. He had nothing left to prove, and he felt it was time to keep his promise to his beloved wife, Mary, to devote more time to his family, law practice, golf equipment promotion, and instructional film opportunities. But, by his own admission, he was also simply burned out. Tournament golf at the most elevated level had taken a tremendous toll on his mental and physical health. (He lost an average of 14 pounds during each tournament due to anxiety and stress and often could hold down only tea and toast for lunch.) The pressure to meet the public's expectation that he would win every time he played was overwhelming. That being the case, how much longer could he have continued at this altitude? In addition, as Bobby was winding down his career, a new era was beginning. The hickory shafted club was being replaced by those made of steel. In the 1930s these clubs were utilized with rapidly increasing success by a new age of youthful and expanding number of skilled professional golfers. Of course, with regular play Jones may have been able to adapt to the new equipment and set aside his growing issues with nerves, particularly if he chose to turn professional and play a full tournament schedule. But, there are some hints that perhaps the glory days would not have continued, at least at the same pace. When his new home course opened at Augusta, Georgia in 1934, and became an annual major tournament (initially called the "Augusta National Invitation Tournament" rather than the "Masters"), Jones acceded to requests that he participate. After a respectable 13th-place finish the first year, he was never remotely in contention again, often experiencing the yips on the lightning-fast greens set up for the tournament. Again, while he had long given up tournament golf he did, nevertheless, play the game on a regular year-round basis at Augusta and other local clubs. As such, given his still relatively young age and home course advantage, one might have expected better results. Ironically, after Bobby's final, and finest, season in 1930, perhaps his star was about to fade had he continued. Who knows? In any event, his actual career achievements, rather than possible additional ones, must (as in the case of Woods, Hogan and Vardon) be weighed when comparing him with Nicklaus and his accomplishments. And, in this regard, his supporters' claims that he was the best may be as good, if not better, than those of Tiger Woods.

*A few words about Walter Hagen. "Sir Walter" was a Babe Ruth-like charismatic character who lived a flamboyant lifestyle and elevated the status and financial rewards of professional golfers. He frequently passed up formal tournament play in favor of lucrative exhibition matches, becoming the sports world's first millionaire. During his nearly three decades on the professional tour Hagen won 45 tournaments (tied for 8th all-time) and 11 majors (4th all-time). He is unquestionably the greatest match play competitor ever, having won the PGA Tournament five times, including a record four straight. (The match play format was used for this tournament until 1958). He also had five Western Open wins, at a time when it was considered one of the top three events on the professional golf schedule behind only the U.S. and British Opens, yet for some reason, is not recognized as a "major" in golf's official record books. (Unofficially, then, Hagen won one more major than Tiger Woods!) So, why isn't he on golf's Mount Rushmore? Primarily because he was not quite even the best golfer of his era, since he overlapped with Bobby Jones. Hagen won two U.S. Opens but never won the event when Bobby Jones (winner of four U.S. Opens) was in the field. Since this version of Mount Rushmore includes the best golfers of their respective eras and the arguments for each as the greatest player ever, Sir Walter falls just short of placement on that coveted facial carving. But, perhaps room should be made at the park entrance for a statue of both Sam Snead and Walter Hagen!

BEN HOGAN

As remarkable as Ben Hogan's career was, what makes him the sentimental favorite of many is the fact that he was the Godfather of incessant practice and determination, which ultimately led to awe-inspiring shot-making, a flawless-looking swing, and continued tournament success - even after a near-fatal high speed, head-on, car collision with a bus in 1949. After that, due to residual damage to his legs, he confined his play almost exclusively to the majors, yet won six of his nine (tied for 5th all-time) under such circumstances. His small stature and focused, steely nature, particularly on the course, earned him the moniker of "The Wee Ice Mon" from admiring Scottish fans in 1953 during his only appearance (a win) at the British Open. He was also called "The Hawk" for his intimidating stare and assiduous study of the courses he played.

Ben's career on the PGA Tour began in 1931, but he won only once prior to 1940. He played on the tour for over four decades, gathering a total of 64 wins - 4th all-time - but his nine major victories did not begin until 1946 (by which time he substituted his tendency toward wild hooks with a reliable fade) and his last occurred in 1953. The competition he faced at the top level (e.g., Byron Nelson,* Sam Snead, Jimmy Demaret, Henry Cotton, Tommy Bolt, Ken Venturi, Cary Middlecoff, Lloyd Mangrum, Lew Worsham, Julius Boros, Jack Burke Jr.) during his majors run exceeded that which Woods faced in his. The most significant blemish on Hogan's career is that he was 8-12 in PGA Tour playoffs (0-4 against his two primary rivals, Byron Nelson and Sam Snead), including a 1-3 record in majors playoffs. The highlights of his career include the following: Won nine of the 16 majors that he entered between 1946-1953 and eight majors out of the 11 that he entered between 1948-1953.

Won all three of the majors that he entered in 1953.

One of only five players to win the Career Grand Slam, including a record-tying four U.S. Opens (along with two playoff losses in the tournament).

Six Second place finishes in the majors (including one playoff loss and one loss by one stroke in the U.S. Open, and two playoff losses and one loss by one stroke at the Masters).

---

* Hogan won only one of his majors before Byron Nelson's premature retirement, at the peak of his career (at age 34), following the 1946 season. Nelson won 52 times on the PGA Tour (11 straight and 18 total, in 1945), including five majors. As such, one must assume, had Nelson remained on the PGA Tour, he would have won at least a couple of the majors Hogan won after Nelson's retirement.

HARRY VARDON

Harry Vardon is the clear dark horse among the four behind Jack Nicklaus, whose faces are sculpted on golf's Mount Rushmore. Indeed, many with short sports memories might wonder why he is even on that mount, given that he won only seven majors. His name most often comes up in the context of the overlapping grip (the "Vardon Grip") that he adopted and is used by the vast majority of golfers. Others may have heard his name in connection with the Vardon Trophy, awarded annually to the PGA Tour golfer with the lowest per-round stroke average. Still others may associate his name with the book, or the Disney movie based thereon, which casts him as one of the giants slain by gifted young amateur Francis Ouimet in the biggest upset in golf history - a playoff at the 1913 U.S. Open. Yet, if I were to judge with my heart rather than my head, I could convince myself that "The Stylist" was a fraction better than even the Golden Bear. To understand why, it is necessary to engage in the "What if?" game and probe deeper into some amazing statistics that do not show up on Tour record books. But, before suggesting that the men in white jackets, not green jackets, should be contacted concerning my sentiment, it is worth examining what three of golf's great writers, familiar with his play, had to say.

A.J. Tillinghast (1876-1942) was not only one the best golf course designers ever, he also was an accomplished player and wrote extensively about the sport for several major journals. He played against or watched nearly all of golf's finest players from the 1890s through the 1930s. He felt that Harry Vardon was the greatest, followed closely by Bobby Jones. (Of course, we don't know if that opinion would have changed had he lived to witness Hogan, Nicklaus and Woods.) Golf's greatest writer (in my view, though the general consensus is that Bernard Darwin was the best), Herbert Warren Wind (1916-2005), opined that there had never been a better golfer than either Vardon, Jones, Hogan, or Nicklaus. However, in 1983, after Nicklaus had won two more majors, Wind acknowledged that while Vardon, Jones and Hogan were as preeminent in their eras as Nicklaus, he could readily understand why many people close to the game considered Nicklaus to be nothing less than the greatest golfer ever. In 2002, shortly before his death, Wind was asked about Tiger Woods. He responded that Woods was remarkable but said nothing about his comparative greatness. Darwin (1876-1961), an outstanding amateur golfer and prolific golf writer, stated that there was no greater genius at hitting a golf ball than Vardon but hedged a bit as to who, Vardon or Jones, was better. The point is that Vardon was undoubtedly in the equation when informed contemporaries discussed the relative greatness of the figures on golf's Mount Rushmore.

Harry Vardon's career coincided with two other stalwarts from Great Britain, J.H. Taylor and James Braid. Together, they were known as "The Great Triumvirate," much like Hogan, Snead and Nelson in their era and Nicklaus, Palmer and Player in their prime. From 1884 to 1924 the Triumvirate won the British Open 16 times and finished second 16 times. Vardon won a record six British Opens (coming in second place three times, third place twice, and in the top ten 20 times over a 30-year span). He finished first in 49 professional tournaments, as well as 21 team events and numerous high-stakes challenge matches, confined mainly to Great Britain, though he did enter three U.S. Opens. What set him apart from the rest was his swing's tempo and synchronized nature, resulting in a rare combination of power and uncanny accuracy. He was so consistently straight that he once went seven consecutive tournament rounds without ever hitting into the rough or a hazard! In 1898-1899, he played in 17 tournaments and won 14 of them, coming in second place in the other three. He was often called "The Greyhound" based on his penchant for catching and overtaking his opponents. He won the first U.S. Open that he entered in 1900. In 1913 he was defeated in a three-way playoff with fellow Jerseyman and good friend Ted Ray, and the winner, Francis Ouimet. Ouimet had won the Massachusetts State Amateur just prior to the 1913 U.S. Open. He also was a former caddie at the U.S. Open's host site, The Country Club in Brookline, outside Boston. Vardon had a measure of revenge the year following his loss to Ouimet. After Ouimet won the 1914 U.S. Amateur, he entered that year's British Open and Vardon bettered him by 26 strokes en route to his victory.

Vardon was a virtual lock to win his last appearance (at age 50) in the U.S. Open, held at Inverness in 1920. He led by five strokes with five holes to play but then encountered gale-force winds and a torrential downpour that would have suspended a tournament under such conditions in the modern era. It took him four strokes on one of the par-5s to reach the green! The storm, which physically drained Vardon, ended just as he entered the clubhouse. This paved the way for the powerful Ted Ray, who had teed off a number of holes behind Harry, to win by a stroke. Bobby Jones' close friend and biographer, O.B. Keeler, afterward noted: "Fate and nothing else beat Harry Vardon that day."

Vardon was not eligible to play in the British and U.S. Amateurs. The Masters did not yet exist. The PGA Championship, which Vardon never entered, was not established until 1916 and was suspended in 1917-1918 after America entered World War I, and the British Open was suspended five times during that war. As such, Harry had few opportunities to accumulate major trophies outside the British Open tournaments, and the three U.S. Opens he entered. He also missed many other professional tournaments due to severe Tuberculosis, which he contracted in 1903. This necessitated an initial eight-month stay in a sanatorium followed by severe respiratory challenges throughout the remainder of his career - several times confining him to bed for months. It also left him with what was diagnosed as permanent nerve damage to his right hand. (He had broken a bone in his right wrist some years prior.) This seriously impacted his putting. However, I wonder if an element of the yips might have exacerbated the effect of this condition since the resultant shaky hand condition surfaced most frequently when putting inside four feet!

As impressive as Vardon's formal tournament play was, his performance during several exhibition tours in America is nearly beyond comprehension. In the months leading up to the 1900 U.S. Open, he played a series of 88 exhibition matches, primarily in the eastern half of the United States and Canada. He logged over 60,000 miles, mostly by train, playing a vast number of courses. In nearly every match, he played against the better ball of two, and sometimes three, of the best local pros (meaning Vardon's score on a given hole was pitted against the lowest score on each hole made by the two or three people he was playing against). He beat the defending U.S. Open champion, Willie Smith, in all three of their individual head-to-head matches. In fact, he lost only one head-to-head match (to Ben Nicholls on the grassless "greens," of a Florida course, made up of compacted sand). His overall record, despite the stacked-deck nature of the formats, was 75-13! Moreover, on this trip, he often set the course record at many of the clubs he was playing for the first time.

Before the 1913 and 1920 U.S. Opens, Vardon and Ray played together in a series of exhibitions against another two-man team at each locale, including

America's top players. They played 40 matches in 50 days prior to the 1913 Open. They won them all (including a "redemption" game against Ben Nicholls and his brother the day after Vardon and Ray got off their ship from England and took an overnight train from New York City to the course in Philadelphia). During one portion of their 1920 tour, they played nearly every day for six consecutive weeks (sleeping on trains between stops) across the United States and Canada. They won 60 of 84 matches along with a few halves. (Recall that Vardon was 50 years old at this time!) One of the losses was to a team that included the young Bobby Jones (with whom Vardon was paired in the first round of that year's Open and was beaten by Vardon by six strokes). Imagine anyone, past, present or future, matching Harry Vardon's individual and team exhibition tour feats under the same conditions.

There simply are not enough official statistics to objectively crown Vardon as the greatest player ever, but subjectively? In any event, he certainly belongs in the group on Mount Rushmore.

CHAPTER VI

The Best Golf Books (Top 50)

I estimate that at least 10,000 books have been written about golf. I have read upwards of a thousand of them, retaining only those hundred or so worthy of "Hall of Fame" recognition. I reduced the number even further for this book, listing the top 50 by category. You can easily locate all of these books and, with a few exceptions, purchase them cheaply (e.g., $5-$20 used) via eBay, Amazon, etc. Just type in the name of the book and/or author, and away you go!

Some will think I took leave of my senses when compiling the list since several "icons" are missing. For example, where is Michael Murphy's "Golf in the Kingdom," one of the best-selling sports books of all time with a cult-like following? I'm sorry. I tried. I read the book and waded through the complicated brogue. Saw the movie as well. But, in the end, I was left with the same impression I had after reading some of the famous golf psychology books. Namely, they can all be reduced to a few simple, worn-out cliches along the following lines: "A respectful, joyous, and determined spiritual approach to the challenges of golf is a microcosm of that which leads to a meaningful and rewarding life."; "Be the ball laddie."; "Stay in the present."; "Play the course, not your opponent."; "You can't control what others do - You can only control what you do."; "Stay positive." Not that any of these aren't laudable. It's simply a question of overkill - when entire books say the same things dozens of different ways.

Then what about Tom Coyne's series of golf odyssey books, beginning with "A Course Called Ireland"? The first, in particular, was quite novel in nature. He *walked* the entire island, with a golf bag and travel clothes strapped to his body, and played *all* its links courses! It is definitely worth a read if you enjoy links golf and travel adventures like I do. I just can't put his books, as a group, at the very top of the list (though the first one deserves an honorable mention, at a minimum) as they contain a certain sense of redundancy of theme (like "Rocky" movies). An idea sets in for an extended golf trip to search for the secrets of golf and better understand a nation's soul. But first, one must wrestle with guilt over the travel costs and being away from family responsibilities for an extended period. With a degree of trepidation, he approaches the wife with the idea. She ultimately gives her full support (easier, no doubt, with each book's subsequent financial success). Then come the physical and mental travails of so much self-inflicted travel and golf, second guessing his plan, but persevering. And (particularly in books two and three), just a bit too much personal detail about shots, competitive prowess, scores, etc. Good, humorous books. Just overdone.

Fine, but why is Harvey Penick's "Little Red Book" series omitted from the list. These best-selling books, which share simple lessons on golf and life (without the lengthy redundancy and sappiness of "Golf in the Kingdom" etc.), are welcome friends in my library. It is evident that Harvey was a kind, gentle, and wise coach and instructor, most especially beloved by his two most famous pupils - Ben Crenshaw and Tom Kite. However, with regard to top billing for golf instruction, I went with my three favorite "Just the facts ma'am" books that provide a quick reference guide on the fundamentals of grip, set-up, and shot-making.

BEST BOOKS ON GREAT GOLF COURSES

Confidential Guide to Golf Courses Volume 1 Great Britain/Ireland by Tom Doak (2014) - This is the first of a five-volume guide to the world's great courses written by highly acclaimed golf architect Tom Doak (along with co-contributors Ran Morrissett, Masa Nishijima and Darius Oliver). Warning: Given each volume's limited-edition nature, even a preowned version will cost you in the neighborhood of $100. But, what an extraordinary Christmas gift hint to drop on family members! In Volume 1, over 300 courses in Great Britain and Ireland are intelligently reviewed and rated on a 1-10 scale (10 being the best). Doak has an unparalleled ability to put his finger on the essence of a course, both positively and negatively. It is by far the most referenced book in my library as it has proven to be an invaluable resource in helping me determine which, among the many referenced great courses, will best suit my idea of a good walk unspoiled. These include some courses meeting Doak's concept of perfection or near perfection (e.g., St. Andrews/Royal Dornoch – in the 10-9 rating range) as well as those which he considers possessing above average greatness to average greatness (e.g., Doonbeg/Ardglass – in the 7-5 rating range). He finds some redeeming value in nearly all the courses reviewed in the book, though if the rating is below 4 the message is pretty much *caveat emptor*. That is, a 3 rating is equivalent to the average course worldwide, suggesting that one's time and money could be better spent at the many available alternatives that come with a higher rating. Those not as interested in golf travel abroad will find that Volumes 2 and 3 (mainly focusing on the USA) are equally engaging and informative, if only to help you better understand why you may have liked or disliked various courses you have played over the years.

Where Golf is Great – The Finest Courses of Scotland and Ireland by James W. Finegan (2006) - This book is far less expensive than Tom Doak's Guide, referenced above, while still offering an excellent comprehensive introduction to the great courses. It also includes recommendations on sights, attractions, hotels, and restaurants (some dated since the book was published nearly two decades

THE BEST GOLF BOOKS

ago). The book is filled with many large, beautiful color pictures and makes for a perfect coffee table fixture.

Planet Golf (2007) and Planet Golf USA (2009) - Both were written by Darius Oliver, one of the co-contributors in Doak's Confidential Guide series. These works are somewhat of a hybrid of Doak's and Finegan's books. Oliver very adeptly critiques the greatest courses and includes many gorgeous color photos. Like Finegan's book, this tome is large and highly suitable for display.

The Scottish Golf Book by Malcolm Campbell (1999) - For the individual searching for a book devoted exclusively to golf in Scotland, look no further. Campbell introduces the reader to the game's origins and developments, the evolution of golf equipment, the country's greatest stars, its finest courses, and most memorable championships. All of these are illustrated in wonderful, and in some cases rare, photos.

Golf's Finest Par Threes: The Art & Science of the One Shot Hole by Tony Roberts & Michael Bartlett (2011) - I suspect that if you were to assemble a list of your combined favorite/most memorable holes you've played over your lifetime the par threes would dominate. Perhaps this is because so much architectural talent, natural beauty and golf strategy are available for consideration relative to such a compact area. This book offers a comprehensive guide to all things par three and is loaded with terrific photos to reminisce over rounds played at a featured course or to whet your appetite for those yet to be played.

Globetrotter Golfer's Guides to Scotland by David J. Whyte (2000), England/Wales by Mark Rowlinson (2001) and Ireland by Philip Reid (2003). This trilogy of small-size books provides quick reference bottom-line information and splendid maps and pictures covering numerous courses as well as general travel guidance.

World Atlas of Golf (2003) - A true classic co-authored by four of golf's finest writers (Herbert Warren Wind, Pat Ward Thomas, Charles Price, and Peter Thompson). A brief presentation of the world's great courses and how you should play them strategically.

The Golf Course by Geoffrey S. Cornish and Ronald E. Whitten (1981) - Though a little dated, this is a singularly expansive reference guide to virtually all of the world's golf courses and architects. The courses are conveniently grouped by architect. This comes in handy if one plays a course designed by a particular architect and wishes to know what other layouts were designed by him, their comparative quality, and where they are located. The book also provides an excellent outline of the evolution of golf course architecture over the centuries.

BEST BOOKS ON GOLF HISTORY (GENERAL)

Golf History and Tradition by David Stirk (1998) - A Comprehensive and interesting introduction to the game's origins and subsequent developments over several centuries.

Golf in the Making by Ian Henderson and David Stirk (1979) - An excellent companion to Stirk's Golf History and Tradition. It provides a detailed history of the implements of the game, most notably clubs and balls, and the people who made them.

Fifty Years of Golf by Horace G. Hutchinson (1914) - This former golfing great was also an excellent golf historian and writer. His book covers the half-century running roughly 1860-1910, mostly dealing with the sport in Great Britain. It concerns virtually every topic of the game during this remarkable era.

The Story of American Golf by Herbert Warren Wind (1956) - A well-rounded look at the great male and female golfers in the first half of the 20th century.

Golf in America: The First 100 Years by George Peper (1994) - A chronological history of golf in America, from 1887-1988.

BEST BOOKS ON GOLF HISTORY (FOCUSED)

The Greatest Game Ever Played by Mark Frost (2002) - This is the book about which golf's best movie was based. It is the story of the 1913 U.S. Open that pitted the great British professional, Harry Vardon against the young, but fine American amateur, Francis Ouimet. The results of their epic playoff set the world of American golf on fire.

The Match by Mark Frost (2007) - The book tells the absolutely fabulous true story about an impromptu challenge match in 1956 between two of golf's all-time greatest professionals, past their primes but still possessing plenty of game, and two of the then-best young amateurs in the world. The setting is the legendary Cypress Point course. Word leaks out about the match, and thousands flock to the site with barely controllable excitement to witness the event as if it were a major. The back-and-forth slugfest hangs in the balance until the very end. Hollywood couldn't come up with a better story!

Golf's Greatest Championship: The 1960 U.S. Open by Julian I. Graubart (1997) - Talk about drama! This U.S. Open involved a down-to-the-wire finish that included a last major hurrah by Ben Hogan, the coming out party for powerful phenom amateur Jack Nicklaus, and a daring charge by the reigning "King," Arnold Palmer. Fun stuff.

BEST GOLF COMMENTATOR/JOURNALIST BOOKS ON GOLF/GOLF PERSONALITIES

The Darwin Sketchbook by Bernard Darwin (1991) - This book presents portraits of golf's greatest players and other selections from Bernard Darwin's writings. Darwin is the "Godfather" of golf writing; here, one can sample his eloquence.

Following Through by Herbert Warren Wind (1985) - In my opinion, Wind is the GOAT of golf writers. I love anything written by the man, and this book, which includes insightful stories on a few of the world's greatest golf courses and its finest stars, is a splendid introduction to his work.

The Lay of the Land by Pat Ward-Thomas (1990) - The book includes a fine collection of this great golf journalist's stories on players and courses.

The Best of Henry Longhurst by Henry Longhurst (1979) - This book is about golf writing and broadcasting delivered with that unique charming wit that the British are known for. Read all about it!

Down the 19th Fairway: A Golfing Anthology by Peter Dobereiner (1983) - An incredible compendium of stories written by many of the most famous writers and golfers over 100 or so years. In addition, Dobereiner, good with a pen in his own right, gives his views on 18 of the world's greatest courses.

Jenkins at the Majors by Dan Jenkins (2009) - In this book, famed golf writer Dan Jenkins walks you through his coverage of 60 years' worth of majors, from Hogan to Woods. If you love the majors, what better way to get the inside scoop?

Preferred Lies and Other Tales by Jack Whitaker (1998) - Oh, what a voice and a way with words! Anyone who has never watched an episode of Shell's Wonderful World of Golf should do so via YouTube, if only to hear this man wax eloquent about the history of the courses, towns and golfers involved in the featured 18 hole challenge matches. This memoir provides many behind-the-scenes stories about the sports broadcasting world.

Good Bounces and Bad Lies by Ben Wright (1999) - This is a fascinating autobiography by the free-wheeling British golf journalist and commentator.

I Call the Shots by Johnny Miller (1994) - Love him or hate him, he was the voice of televised golf for decades. Worth reading what he candidly has to say about the game.

BEST GOLF BIOGRAPHIES/AUTOBIOGRAPHIES

My Life in Golf by Harry Vardon (1933) - I am fortunate to own book #109 of the 300 limited-edition copies reprinted for the 1981 Memorial Tournament at Muirfield Village (the annual tournament hosted by the course's designer, Jack Nicklaus). For those wishing to read this excellent book but unable to find, and/or unwilling to pay for, an original edition or this limited-edition reprint, there is an alternative. Vardon's daughter-in-law, Audrey Howell, wrote a biography in 1991 titled: "Harry Vardon: The Revealing Story of a Champion Golfer." She relies heavily on Vardon's autobiography but adds information and secrets gleaned from private family history and papers.

Golf is My Game by Robert Tyre (Bobby) Jones, Jr. (1960) - Much has been written about Bobby Jones, but here, one has the opportunity to learn about his life and golf from the man himself. And what an incredible command of the English language he had. If an award was given for the greatest combined golfer/golf writer ever, Bobby would win hands-down. He could arguably win each of the awards on a stand-alone basis!

Tommy's Honor by Kevin Cook (2007) - This is the fascinating story of the life and times of Old Tom Morris and Young Tom Morris. Together, they were Golf's Founding Father and Son. Old Tom was a club and ball maker (transitioning from the feathery ball to the gutta percha), professional (four-time British Open winner), greenskeeper (St. Andrews), and course designer of many of the world's greatest courses. Young Tom was a maverick golf professional who won his first British Open at the age of 17 followed by three more in succession before dying at age 24.

Thirty Years of Championship Golf by Gene Sarazen (1950) - Wonderfully written (no doubt due, in part, that the great Herbert Warren Wind assisted him). It is great fun to read so many fascinating life tales told by this colorful, diminutive Hall of Fame golfer (who essentially invented the sand wedge).

How I Played the Game by Byron Nelson (1993) - This is the autobiography of one of the game's greatest golfers and perhaps its greatest gentleman. "Lord Byron," as he was affectionately known, holds the record for consecutive wins in a single season on the PGA tour (11) and most wins in a single season (18). Trying to match these feats would be similar to a baseball slugger trying to achieve Joe DiMaggio's 56-game hitting streak. His swing was so fluid that the modern mechanical swing simulator is called "Iron Byron." It is a pleasure to walk beside this humble man as he tells of his journey through golf and life.

The Grand Slam: Bobby Jones, America, and the Story of Golf by Mark Frost (2004) - The fact that Frost authored no less than three of the books on my Best Golf Books list reflects my belief in the unique talent he has for providing readers with in-depth and gripping insights into particular persons and events in golf's history. This book is listed in the biography section since Bobby Jones is the primary subject. However, he also describes Jones' life and Grand Slam year experience within the broader context of American golf.

Arnie & Jack: Palmer, Nicklaus, and Golf's Greatest Rivalry by Ian O'Connor (2008) - While Arnold Palmer didn't quite make it to golf's Mount Rushmore of the greatest golfers ever to play the game, he has always been first in the hearts of both fans and players. Meanwhile, even though Jack took the talent scepter from the King, it took decades for him to become loved in a similar, but not quite equal, manner. They were fierce rivals, both on and off the course. And, despite occasional and understandable strains along the way, they maintained mutual respect and friendship. Here is their detailed and moving story.

A.W. Tillinghast: Creator of Golf Courses by Philip Young (2005) - This book presents a definitive examination of the life, times, and philosophies on golf architecture of the creator of famed championship courses such as Winged Foot, Bethpage Black and Baltusrol.

BEST BOOKS ON GOLF ANTIQUES AND THEIR VALUES

Golf Antiques & Other Treasures of the Game by John M. Olman & Morton W. Olman (1992) - The perfect welcome to the world of golf collectibles, suitable for reference by both the novice decorator and the seasoned investor. Before even opening the book, you know you are in for a treat as the jacket cover includes a photo of a centuries-old woodheaded club and feathery golf ball. After reading this book, one will develop a better idea of what manner of collectibles are out there as well their relative age, quality/quantity, and how to recognize a good value when you see them for sale.

The Encyclopedia of Golf Collectibles by John M. Olman and Morton W. Olman (1985) - This is the first book written by the Olmans and is a perfect companion to their later one. It was designed as a more detailed guide to identifying and valuing golf collectibles, from clubs/balls to artwork to statuary to books. It helps one to quickly identify the maker/manufacture date and specific price range of these items. (With the passage of time and increased popularity of golf in general and collecting in particular, the referenced prices will be approximately double now.)

BEST SPECIAL INTEREST GOLF BOOKS

St. Andrews Sojourn: Two Years at Home on the Old Course by George Peper (2006) - What golf addict doesn't dream about St Andrews? I literally have done so many times and am always sad I had to wake up. But, actually having a real-life opportunity to buy and remodel a home overlooking the 18th fairway of the Old Course - now that's a dream come true! Follow George Peper as he shares his experiences living in the "Auld Grey Toon."

Golf is a Funny Game... But it Wasn't Meant to Be by Ken Janke (1992) - A book filled with nothing but the all-time best golf one-liners.

Talking on Tour by Don Wade (2001) - Many have read or come across all or some of the eight "And Then Jack Said to Arnie" etc., books written by Don

Wade, a former senior editor at Golf Digest. This book is a compendium of the best of the best from that series. Insanely funny and intimate vignettes about golf's great players. A must-read.

First off the Tee by Don Van Natta Jr. (2003) - An entertaining summary of the best and worst talents and habits of the golfing Presidents, from Taft to Bush. If I were adding a postscript, I would mention Trump (perhaps the best golfer President, even without taking certain liberties that might cause even Clinton to blush) and his alleged technique for getting listed as the holder, or one-time holder, of the "course record" at the new venues he owned - be the first to play it and shoot the lowest round in your group!

A Good Walk Spoiled: Days and Nights on the PGA Tour by John Feinstein (1995) - For those who wonder what life must really be like on tour, here is the chance to find out from one of golf's ultimate insiders - acclaimed sportswriter John Feinstein.

My Usual Game: Adventures in Golf by David Owen (1995) - A self-described "Golf-Dependent Personality," this former Golf Digest writer humorously shares the ups and downs of his lifetime obsession with golf. I wonder why I liked it so much!

Dream Golf: The Making of Bandon Dunes by Stephen Goodwin (2010) - Hard to believe that a book about building a golf course could be of much interest, but I couldn't put it down even though my addiction to golf was under relative control at the time!

The Spirit of St. Andrews by Alister MacKenzie (1995) - This book, published posthumously, offers the opportunity to learn about the principles of good golf course design from one of the greatest golf architects ever.

The Power of Positive Idiocy: A Collection of Rants and Raves by David Feherty (2010) - This man was a good professional golfer who played on Europe's 1991 Ryder Cup team. However, he is more famous for his incomparable combination of golf wit and humor as a writer, on-course commentator, and stand-up comedian. This book is a collection of his short, insightful commentaries on a wide range of golf subjects.

BEST GOLF INSTRUCTION BOOKS

Master Strokes by Nick Mastroni and Phil Franke' (2003) - This compact book contains over 400 short, easy-to-understand lessons on proper shot techniques. It's a quick refresher course when certain aspects of the game are tanking.

Lesson Tee by Jack Nicklaus (1977) - It never hurts to hear what the GOAT has to say about how to play the game of golf.

Five Lessons: The Modern Fundamentals of Golf by Ben Hogan (1957) - The Grip. Stance and Posture. The First Part of the Swing. The Second Part of the Swing. Summary and Review. These are the items covered in this best-selling golf book of its time. It is the perfect way to start out right in golf (though a few lessons from a professional would also be a thoughtful Christmas present).

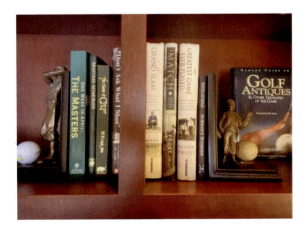

CHAPTER VII

The Best Golf Movies

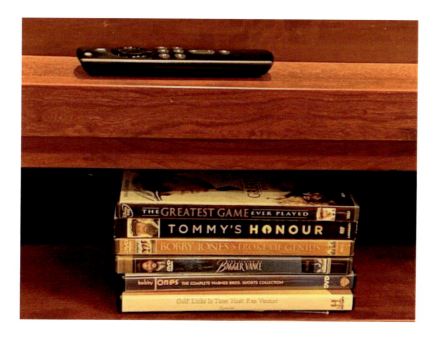

There have been a significant number of movies in which golf has been the exclusive or primary subject. In addition, the game is frequently woven into other film plots, such as the famous match in "Goldfinger" between Sean Connery's James Bond character and his arch nemesis, Goldfinger (shot at Stoke Park Golf Club). Goldfinger's caddy is none other than his trusty sidekick, Odd Job. (Given his "deadly" accuracy with a derby, it is too bad that Odd Job wasn't born a half-century later and brought up with better manners. He almost certainly would have become a world champion disc golfer!) Somehow, Bond again manages to come out on top against all odds. And then there is Michael Douglas' irate character, William Foster, blasting away with a pump-action shotgun at the golf cart of a couple of haughty old golfers after one of them nearly hits Foster with a shot in the movie "Falling Down."

The full-length, golf-themed movies that have been made, both dramatic and comical, generally have been good quality, save for one overwhelmingly bad exception - "CaddyShack II." The five best* golf movies, in my opinion, are:

1. The Greatest Game Ever Played (2005) – The excellent written work by Mark Frost (see Best Books chapter) brought to the big screen. This is a wonderfully filmed period movie with overall historical accuracy (save for a few Hollywood liberties taken to enhance the drama of the epic playoff at the end). Shira LeBeouf does an admirable job playing the part of Francis Ouimet (though he looks nothing like him). I particularly like the acting by Stephen Dillane, who portrays the great and gentlemanly Harry Vardon, though, for some reason, Disney chose to feature him without his traditional mustache!

2. CaddyShack (1980) – The ultimate snobby golf and country club satire, with an all-star cast including Chevy Chase, Rodney Dangerfield, Ted Knight, and Bill Murray. Despite its age, it has a cult-like following among both golfers and non-golfers.

3. Tommy's Honor (2017) – Another critically acclaimed book turned period movie, filmed on location in Scotland with excellent cinematography. The film is a historically accurate story of golf icons Old Tom (Peter Mullan) and Young Tom (Jack Lowden) Morris, including the heartbreaking circumstances surrounding the latter's death at the age of 24.

4. The Legend of Bagger Vance (2000) - Great period film (post WWI American South) featuring Will Smith, Matt Damon, Charlize Theron, and J. Michael Moncrief. While fictional and mystical in nature, some actual historical figures and events are weaved in.

5. Bobby Jones Stroke of Genius (2004) - While some might argue that the film is a bit smarmy at times, it is definitely an inspiring one about the most unique golf career ever. Jim Caviezel portrays the noble character of Bobby Jones, though the tall, lanky, brown-haired Caviezal does not depict Jones' actual physical features - which were short, slightly stout and blond! (And Caviezal's swing does not come close to matching the rounded, smooth-flowing swing of Jones.)

Malcolm McDowell plays the role of Jones' biographer, O.B Keeler. McDowell is a confessed golf addict in real life. What a far cry from the roque youth (Hugo) he portrayed in "A Clockwork Orange!"

* Honorable mention: Happy Gilmore (1996) - The Bob Barker fight scene alone makes the movie worth watching, and Tin Cup (1996) - is an entertaining mix of comedy/light drama.

Aside from movies, there is an excellent variety of very well-made golf documentaries to choose from. Many of these have been produced over the past decade or so. Listed below, in alphabetical order, are what I believe to be the best.

Arnie (2014) - Narrated by Tom Selleck, the viewer gets a thorough look at Arnold Palmer's life and professional career. It explains why his nickname "The King" was earned as much for his charismatic personality and unmatched gestures of kindness toward persons from all walks of life as for his daring prowess and accomplishments on the golf course. Like President John F. Kennedy's treatment by the media during his lifetime (and unlike the scrutiny accorded to Tiger Woods), the documentary gives Arnie a pass relative to his wandering eye with women, instead focusing on his love and "devotion" to his wife, Winnie.

Donald Ross: Discovering the Legend (2015) - This thorough documentary affords the opportunity to examine the great architect's life and work, including commentary from some of golf's great pros, writers, architects, and historians.

Full Swing (2023) - Provides an inside look at life on and off the PGA tour via close-ups of the daily lives of several of its most famous stars, including some controversial defectors to the LIV Tour.

Jack (2017) - An excellent companion to the documentary on Arnold Palmer, Tom Selleck narrates the story of Jack Nicklaus' illustrious life and career. Few realize what a great all-around athlete Jack was: Baseball, football, basketball, fishing, tennis.

St. Andrews: The Greatest Golf Story Ever Told (2021) - Here, one has the opportunity to learn about the origins of the game of golf, its most storied town and course, and the personalities and events that shaped them.

Tiger (2021) - This is an unvarnished look at the rise, fall and comeback of the 21st century's greatest golfer.

CHAPTER VIII

Playing Hickory Golf

The more I learned about the history of beautiful hickory shafted clubs and admired the players who wielded and utilized them as if they were magic wands, the more I desired to try them out myself. When looking online for vintage clubs and other equipment, I came across NorCal Hickory Golf. It describes itself as: "an easygoing group of players who enjoy playing historic golf courses with 100-year-old wooden shafted clubs." The next thing I knew, I entered a three-day match play tournament on the Monterey Peninsula (Monterey Pines, Del Monte and Pacific Grove). It was incredible fun, and the dapper participants excused, without snickers, my naivete in terms of my make-shift plus fours. I had rolled up my standard-length pants to my knees and looked a bit like a circus clown. (After the first round, they taught me the art of adjusting them correctly, with proven fold and tuck techniques.) Later, I bought a pair online and, using it as a sample, took several of my dress pants to a tailor who permanently hemmed them for $20 each.

I subsequently played in tournaments at Harding Park and The Presidio in San Francisco with my son - the youngest and perhaps most enthusiastic participant. Since then, I occasionally play with the hickories on our par 63 executive course. And, lest the retro attire gather dust in the closet, I finally worked up the courage to wear them on occasion at our weekly Men's Group gatherings played on our other, par 72 championship course. They have actually been well received, with one player going so far as to say that I had "raised the bar too high" for golf clothing! So, whether you decide you might like to play with hickory clubs formally (there are societies and tournaments all over the USA and abroad) or just want to knock some balls around your course occasionally, do find a place for hickory in your golf life. If for no other reason, you will appreciate the skill and achievements of those greats from the past who had no other choice but to use them. As a general rule, the balls will travel about 20 yards shorter than with modern equipment, save for the driver, in which case the difference is closer to 40-50 yards. Also, you must take an easier, free-flowing swing with hickories. If you time it well, and hit the ball on the smaller sweet spot on the club face, you can even work the ball better with the older irons.

Below is a rough guide to the names of vintage golf clubs and their modern-day equivalents. (This is a basic list rather than a comprehensive one.) It must be borne in mind that hickory clubs were originally handmade and often customized rather than mass-produced as sets. And, only later were specific numbers assigned to them. As such, there could be significant differences in clubs with the same name.

When examining the hand-forged hickory shaft irons that were in play during the period covering roughly the 1880s-1920s, one will notice distinctive "cleek marks." These were, essentially, trademark calling cards - figures stamped into the surface of the clubhead to identify the maker of the same. Cleek marks continued into the 1930s. However, by then, the marks were primarily decorative - rather than used for identification - as the 1920s-1930s marked the beginning of the age of mass production of matched iron sets by a limited number of large manufacturers. There are about 50 different marks commonly found today. These include, for example, The Tom Stewart of St. Andrews (maker of Bobby Jones' clubs) long pipe; The George Nicoll of Leven, Scotland hand; The Tom Morris of St. Andrews portrait (which came into use after he died in 1908); The Forgan & Son of St. Andrews crown; The MacGregor of Dayton, Ohio shamrock and the Wright & Ditson of Boston Bee Line (bees flying out of bee hive).

Before assembly line production of straight-line grooves on the face of irons became the norm in the 1930s, various combinations of dots, waffle patterns, lines, etc., were used. (Pre-dating the pattern style were smooth-faced irons, which did not impart as much backspin.)

- Driver - Driver.

- Brassie - 2 & 3 Wood. (The term Brassie stems from the fact that brass plates were attached to the sole of the clubhead to avoid causing damage when using it on rough surfaces.)

- Spoon - 4 & 5 Wood. (This name reflects that this wood had, to various degrees, depending on the desired loft, a concave face.)

- Bulldog/Baffy Spoon - 7 Wood. (A utility wood of sorts, particularly when in deeper rough.)

- Cleek/Driving Iron - 1 & 2 Iron.

- Mid Iron - 2-4 Iron.

- Mid Mashie - 3 Iron.

- Mashie Iron - 4 Iron.

- Mashie - 5 Iron.

- Spade Mashie - 6 Iron.

- Mashie Niblick - 7 Iron.

- Pitching Niblick/Lofting Iron - 8 Iron.

- Niblick - 9 Iron.

- Jigger/Chipper - Chipping Wedge. (Generally, this club was short with a low loft, and used for thin trajectory approach shots and chipping around the greens. Some Jiggers were made with much higher lofts for higher pitches around the greens.)

- Putter - Putter.

Before the USGA and R&A limited the maximum number of clubs in the bag to 14 (effective 1938), most players carried about 6-8 clubs in their small, stove pipe-style bags. However, some top golfers were known to have their caddies carry as many as 20 or more clubs, sometimes in their arms! The set that I use in Hickory tournaments is fairly typical - though the better players might prefer to carry a driver (or, more likely, a Brassie for use both off the tee and for long fairway shots). My set (pictured) consists of a Spoon, Mid Mashie, Mashie, Mashie Niblick, Niblick (mine has a decent amount of bounce and a long shaft, making it effective as a combined sand wedge/ 8 iron), Putter, and two utility clubs (Bulldog and Jigger). One can omit the Jigger, if desired, by simply choking down considerably on a Mid Mashie.

Hickory Golf Players at Pacific Grove

CHAPTER IX

The Ultimate Home Golf Retreat – Collecting Golf Antiques, Reproductions & Other Decor

Jack's Library

B uilding an in-home golf retreat is easier and cheaper than you think. And, doing so can be a fun hobby, particularly for golf aficionados whose play on the course is limited during the year's colder months. The same holds true for a golfer who is stymied by an injury, surgery or extended rehab period and wants something to do other than binge-watch another Netflix series.

The obvious question is: "How do I begin?" For me, it was an evolutionary process, initially fueled by sniffing and drooling my way around various golf pro shops and clubhouse locker rooms, lounges, grill rooms, and restaurants. I would say to myself: "Someday I would like to re-create something along these lines." But, I realized it didn't have to happen all at once and found that the means of achieving the goal were often close by. I began making a concerted effort to find beautiful old golf books at used bookstores. I subsequently spent some free time on weekends going to flea markets, thrift stores, antique shops, estate sales, and eBay - typing in words such as "golf antiques," "golf art," "golf statuary,""vintage golf equipment," etc., - where I found all manner of golf related items to decorate my library. Like Rome, my golf room would not be built in a day. Rather, a display shelf became a display case, which led to display walls, which led to a complete golf-themed room - furnishings and all. And then, with the purchase of our new retirement home and the kids out of the nest, I realized that I need not confine my growing golf empire to a single refuge. Instead, I could and did transform a portion of my garage into a locker room/museum by partitioning the space between the two-stall garage and the golf cart garage. I developed the library in a manner that resembled the look and feel of an old Irish/Scottish clubhouse. Even the guest bathroom cried out for participation and was adapted to have an Augusta National shower room theme, enhanced with a bottle of Clubman aftershave on the counter. For an old-school golfer, the smell of Clubman, still available in many traditional clubhouses (and barbershops), evokes the sublimity one feels when entering a bakery and savoring its aroma or sniffing that new-car smell or freshly cut grass on a dewy-morning at the course.

Here are a few places that influenced the design of my rooms: The Tap Room at the Pebble Beach Lodge; The pro shop, pub and lodge rooms at Erin Hills; The Olympic Club's grill room and locker room lounge; The Whistling Straits restaurant, pro shop and locker room and the clubhouses at Royal Troon, Prestwick, Royal Dornoch, North Berwick, Kingsbarns, Doonbeg, and Druids Glen. You don't need to visit these locations; go to the internet and type in, for example, "photos of the inside of _____." Similarly, I frequently went on the internet and looked up things like "traditional libraries," "golf libraries," "golf clubhouses," and "golf club locker rooms" for additional ideas.

I was fortunate to have purchased a new home in one of the last developments in our retirement village, incorporating some custom features into our model during its construction. With specific regard to the library, I had it built in lieu of two small adjoining guest rooms and added a gas fireplace. With my significant amount of unused vacation pay at retirement, I hired a mill worker to build fireplace paneling, bookcases, wainscoting, and an entertainment center.

My next-door neighbor - an excellent amateur carpenter - subsequently assisted me with creating an entrance archway fitted with a 15th-century replica castle door and adding wall shelving and faux ceiling beams (all were researched and ordered online). For these items, I matched the color of the professional millwork myself with stains and varnishes purchased at a local hardware store. Later, I saw beautiful manufactured stonework at an Italian restaurant in Half Moon Bay (on the coast not far south of San Francisco) with an old Tuscan-style look. I researched stonework sites online, found the exact same type as in the restaurant, located a rock nursery that could order it (and who recommended a local installer), and voila, my hundreds of years old looking rock library wall was up and running in a matter of days!

Designing and filling these rooms (along with the backyard tee box and chipping green) took a few years to complete. Still, the journey was quite enjoyable and greatly expanded my knowledge and love of the game's history and implements of play. The costs associated with this type of hobby need not be prohibitive if the items are pursued as outlined above, particularly if one does not feel compelled to own limited-edition originals, entire collections, or pieces in mint condition. Indeed, while searching for golf décor, I also found a couple of thousand dollars worth of new/like new preowned, top brand golf attire for a few hundred dollars. Below are examples of treasured pieces contained in my several rooms, where I found them, how much they cost, and how, in some cases, I modified/utilized them to fit into a desired theme.

The Library. This is my inner sanctum of golf. Admittance generally is by invitation only. However, for impromptu visits, there is a secret password that I will share - but just with you. Simply rattle the Claddagh knocker on the castle entrance door a few times and, when asked for the password, say: "Open the door!" In the meantime, I will serve as your docent, walking you through a few highlights. You can follow along by referencing the photographs of the room.

As you enter, you are fittingly welcomed by a portrait above the fireplace mantel of the Godfather of golf, Old Tom Morris. This was located online after searching "golf art/Old Tom Morris." This new item, including the frame, cost less than $200. On the mantel is a mounted hickory shafted club and vintage golf ball. I built the frame by purchasing some wood trim at the lumber department at Home Depot and cutting it with my trusty miter box, staining it with my favorite Minwax stain, and adding a little satin varnish. The project was completed by attaching a sheet of green felt backing purchased for a couple of dollars at a fabric store. Also on the mantel is a resin model of the 18th hole at St. Andrews. I passed on the opportunity to buy this for $20 at a flea market and immediately regretted that decision. Fortunately, a few months later, I managed to locate another one online, albeit for $60. Next to the fireplace is a set of golf-themed fireplace tools that I purchased at an antique store. A little pricey at around $200, but I couldn't refrain! To the right of the fireplace, standing in the corner, is a reproduction of "Calamity Jane," the putter used by Bobby Jones when he won the Grand Slam. He had a hickory shaft on his version. This one, produced shortly after he retired, has a faux wood shaft look though made of steel. These so-called "transition" clubs were made to appease the old-timers. They were accustomed to the classic look of wood and, therefore, reluctant to convert to the new, shiny steel shafted ones. The shafts were made to look like wood using either pyratone (a plastic-like substance) and/or wood-colored stain. I nearly keeled over when the lady at a flea market said the price for my Calamity Jane was only $5.00! Next to the putter is one of those collapsible metal putting cups that every older golf fanatic practiced with on the living room carpet back in the 1950s-1960s. These can still be found cheaply online.

In the other corner is a circa 1915 stovepipe golf bag I purchased online for $60. It is filled with some of my favorite hickory shafted clubs, including an original Schenectady putter (made famous when Walter Travis used one to win the 1904 British Amateur Open), a so-called "fancy face" Spoon (five wood), a Bulldog (wood headed precursor of the modern utility club), and a variety of irons. The prices paid for these clubs range from $10 - $150. The specialty clubs were located online, and the others were found at flea markets and estate sales. Next to the bag of clubs, I keep a wire basket filled with various low compression reproduction vintage balls for use in Hickory Society golf tournaments. They include mesh, line cut and bramble surface designs. A sleeve of these can be purchased online (e.g., mcintyregolf.com) for $20. Not only do they look great for display purposes, they are also functional. I occasionally invite friends to join me at my course to play a few holes, using hickory clubs and these old-style balls to have a hands-on experience with the type of equipment that Vardon, Jones, et al. were able to master. Above the bag is a copy of the print "The Last Green," by Lawrence Josset. I found this at a garage sale in our neighborhood for $40. Both the print and the frame were in good shape, but I chose to replace the frame and have the print re-matted at a local frame shop for a few hundred dollars.

Moving around the room you see a statuary lamp of a golfer in plus fours and flat cap. I purchased this preowned item online for less than $100. Above the sofa is an almost wall-to-wall shelf that I built to resemble those I saw in Durty Nelly's pub next to Bunratty Castle near Shannon Airport. The supporting corbels were purchased at Lowe's (unfinished) for about $5 each. At the other end of the sofa is a sturdy, larger reproduction vintage golf bag I use for hickory club tournaments. It was purchased online for $200. The bag is filled with an assortment of original vintage clubs, also used in tournaments. Above is a golf-themed clock with a golf ball display rack, which I snapped up for $10 at a Salvation Army thrift store.

The next wall is my pride and joy, as the stonework gives the library an authentic old-world look. On the credenza is a statue of Alister MacKenzie, holding a set of course architectural plans, purchased online for around $200. The large print is a reproduction of "The Society of Coffers at Blackheath" by Lemuel Abbot. I found this at a flea market for $10. I painted the existing inner frame black to add some contrast and had the print triple-matted for $150. The four prints of British Open courses are actually corkboard placemats that I bought as a set for $20 at a flea market. I found some inexpensive matching wood frames and matted the group for about $200. The chess set, featuring vintage-era golfers, located at the base of the credenza, was purchased online for less than $100. Above all this is another shelf I built, upon which rests the only non-golf item, a model of a 17th-century warship. (I know, blasphemy, but I couldn't resist having one, and I wasn't allowed to put it in one of the other rooms in the house!)

Moving to the fourth wall, we see the entertainment center, with bookshelves containing most of my favorite golf books, purchased at bookstores and online for $5-20. On the middle shelf on the right is an original St. Andrews Ginger Beer bottle (circa late 1800s). This cost about $40 online. These were sold by David "Auld Daw" Anderson at the Ginger Beer stall near what is now the 4th hole (formerly 9th hole) of the Old Course, which he set up following his retirement as a senior caddie. Today, the 4th hole is appropriately named "Ginger Beer." Incidentally, his son Jamie was a three-time winner of the British Open. On the left middle shelf is a glass display box containing an original gutta percha ball (circa 1895), an original early rubber core dimple ball (circa 1910), and an original mesh pattern ball (circa 1920). I bought these online for an average of about $40. Between the entertainment center and the door is an original painting (circa 1840) by famous Scottish portrait artist Charles Lees. It depicts a club captain in a traditional red jacket and top hat posing with a long-nosed wooden club. This is the most expensive decorative golf item in my home. The price was reduced from $500 to $350 when the owner of a long-time downtown antique store was retiring. Below, on the floor, is an iron cast doorstop in the form of a vintage golfer in plus fours. The figure is based on a painting of the Prince of Wales, who would briefly serve as King Edward VIII before abdicating the throne. The prince was an avid golfer who enjoyed playing with prominent American pros Walter Hagen and Gene Sarazen. On one occasion, after the three of them had finished a round at Royal St. George's, the prince asked them to join him for a drink in the clubhouse. As they entered, a high-level staff person whispered a reminder to the prince that professional golfers were not permitted inside. The response was that if the club insisted on such silliness, the word "Royal" would be removed, without delay, from the club's name - after which the three enjoyed their libations! Reproductions of this doorstop generally are easy to find online and/or at antique stores for about $20-$40. On the other side of the door are several reproductions of famous prints that were found at an antique store and online for $50-150. Above the door, I placed two inexpensive criss-cross hickory shafted clubs held together with wooden tees.

The Guest Bathroom. Time to move on to the Augusta National shower room. To be honest, I have never seen that room, so I am using a lot of poetic license. I imagine my guest bathroom probably looks closer to the one in the small Crow's Nest quarters (also never seen) on the top floor of the clubhouse, where the amateur players stay. I ordered a print of the famous 12th hole at Augusta for about $60 and took it to a local frame shop for matting. The framed prints "Golf Course" and "Golf Club" were found at an antique store for $20 apiece. The framed photos of Bobby Jones and Jack Nicklaus were purchased online for around $120 each. I looked up "Scottish plaid wallpaper" online and found a pattern that matched the shower curtain, also located online. The wall shelf is of the inexpensive, ready-to-hang variety that can be found in most large home improvement stores.

The Golf Cart Garage. Last stop, the locker room/museum (aka golf cart garage). This room is an eclectic mixture of golf clothing closets and drawers, vintage and modern club storage and display, logo ball exhibit cases (I always purchase a logo ball when I check in at a new course as these provide visible reminders of the experiences there), and a variety of prints, photos, statuary, and other items of interest for which there was insufficient room in the library. I took more than half of the display photos on my phone and framed them, courtesy of the Dollar Store. I removed a number of other pictures from books that I was discarding. These were framed in the same fashion. The plaid chair was purchased at the Salvation Army for $40. Above the chair is a shelf with a few books. They are held up by a couple of bookends, which I made using some scrap wood, a little paint, a sawed-off club head, and a hole drilled into the wood to insert a tee, upon which rests a ball. I made a scale reproduction of the 16th hole at Cypress Point, which can be seen on the bookcase shelf, using supplies from a hobby store. The large reproduction prints of British Isle courses on either side of the mounted semi-circular golf club arrangement were bought at a small family-operated golf equipment and repair shop. They were decorative rather than for sale, but it proved worth making an offer of $75 for each. The hat hangers on the wall are sawed-off golf club heads. I got this idea from the 19th Hole Pub, which overlooks Elie Golf Club in Scotland.

The Tee Box/Chipping Green. Were you hoping there might be another room to peruse? Well then, let's take a look at the one located outdoors. When putting in the landscaping of our home, I decided to pay homage to the wine country by planting 28 grapevines on the little backyard hillside while at the same time fitting in a golf hole to honor the land of my ancestors (as noted in Chapter I, the small harbor town of Glenarm in Antrim County, Ireland). The photo shows the tee box of the par-3 12th hole of the mythical Antrim Glen Golf Club. The custom-made sign and granite shamrock logo tee markers were ordered online through a Florida-based company that makes these things for real golf courses. Balls can be chipped from this area across the "Hogan Bridge" to a small artificial turf green - after first being waved up by the gentleman in the flat cap and plus fours. I built the bridge using the following materials: rocks left over from the home construction and some paver stones, a few bags of cement mix, and rebar purchased from Lowes. Total cost? About $70, 20 hours of labor and a small bottle of Advil. I constructed a larger one (the "Swilcan Burn Bridge") at the other end of the vineyard. Both are fun to look at and provide a safe means to cross the tiny dry creek bed while holding the precious little hands of the grandchildren.

Library

THE ULTIMATE HOME GOLF RETREAT

Library

THE BEST OF ALL THINGS GOLF

Library

THE ULTIMATE HOME GOLF RETREAT

Library

Library

205

THE BEST OF ALL THINGS GOLF

Library

Guest Bathroom

Golf Cart Garage Locker Room/Museum

THE ULTIMATE HOME GOLF RETREAT

Golf Cart Garage

Backyard Tee Box and Chipping Green

CHAPTER X

And for Dessert -
Future Golf Trips & Lessons Learned

I've never been one to put off until tomorrow what I can do ten years in advance - at least when it comes to planning golf travel. However, this can be attributed to something more than just being a Type A personality. As we reach this stage in the book it, hopefully, has become evident that there are an endless number of terrific golf courses out there. Yet, we only have so much time and resources at our disposal. So, priorities must be set to fit in courses that will bring us the greatest amount of pleasure. For some, this might mean sticking to a few local courses and an occasional round while on vacation. Others may wish to tick off all or most of the courses on a particular "Top 100" list in the USA, Europe and/or the world. Still others may determine that, after experiencing an adequate representation of the major course design and philosophy styles, the focus should be on playing those that define their idea of: "The Best." I fall in the latter category. Therefore, the future itineraries set forth below are simply the result of continuing to follow a game plan that has served me well over the years - Do the homework now, and simply push the "Go" button later. It gives ample opportunity to determine golf course/travel possibilities and priorities, and pursue them efficiently. To the extent that my golf experiences have been helpful to the reader in shaping your golf priorities, I feel that I would be remiss if I failed to share these additional possibilities. So, I invite you to join me for an imaginary pint after we've played an imaginary round together at your favorite course described in this book. We can then discuss the list of future trips, the "Lessons Learned" that follow them, or anything else concerning the best of all things golf. Cheers!

TRIP 7 –

Formby GC/Royal Liverpool GC/Royal Birkdale GC/Ganton GC/ Alwoodley GC/Bamburgh Castle GC/Goswick GC (July 2024)

Self-organized. (No golf tour company involved. Tee times and hotels can easily be booked directly via websites, typically up to one year in advance. Hotels can arrange taxis. Travel light with wheeled golf travel bag and carry-on luggage.)

Day 1 - Fly from San Francisco to Manchester via Dublin on Aer Lingus

Day 2 – Arrive in Manchester and take a 35-minute taxi to Chester. Stay at the Grosvenor Hotel. Walk the old streets of Chester.

Day 3 – Take a one-hour train to play Formby, designed by Steel. One mile walk to the clubhouse from Freshfield Golf Road train stop. Dine at Ye Olde King's Head in Chester. Stay at the Grosvenor Hotel.

Day 4 – Take a 40-minute train to play Royal Liverpool (Hoylake), designed by Colt. 3/4 mile walk from the station to the clubhouse. Dine at the clubhouse. Stay at the Grosvenor Hotel.

Day 5 – Take a 45-minute train to Liverpool and visit the Beatles museum. Stay and dine at the Grosvenor Hotel.

Day 6 – Take a 1-hour 20-minute train to play Royal Birkdale, designed by Taylor/Hawtree. 3/4 mile walk from the train station to the clubhouse. Dine at the clubhouse. Stay at the Grosvenor Hotel.

Day 7 – Take a 2-hour 30-minute hour train from Chester to York. Stay at the Grand York Hotel 500 yards from the station and near the city center.

Day 8 – Take a 40-minute taxi to play Ganton, designed by Vardon/MacKenzie & others. Stay at the Grand York Hotel.

Day 9 - Take a 35-minute taxi to play Alwoodley (MacKenzie's first design). Stay at the Grand York Hotel.

Day 10 – Take a 1-hour 40-minute train ride from York to Berwick-upon-Tweed, then take a half-hour taxi to Bamburgh. Dine and stay at the Lord Crewe Hotel.

Day 11 – Take a short walk to visit Bamburgh Castle, then another short walk to play Bamburgh Castle GC (buggies permitted). Stay at the Lord Crewe Hotel.

Day 12 – Take a 20-minute taxi to play Goswick GC, designed by Braid (buggies permitted). Dine at the clubhouse. Stay at the Lord Crewe Hotel.

Day 13 – Take a 30-minute taxi to Berwick-upon-Tweed, then a 3-hour 20-minute train to the Manchester airport. Stay at the Marriott Airport Hotel.

Day 14 – Fly home from Manchester via Dublin on Aer Lingus.

TRIP 8 –
Bandon Dunes Old Macdonald/Bandon Trails/Bandon Dunes (August 2024)

Self-organized. Golf and lodging booked directly with Bandon Dunes via website and phone. Demand is high, so book a year-and-a-half in advance if possible.

Day 1 – Play the Old Macdonald course, designed by Doak. Stay at the Bandon Dunes Resort.

Day 2 – Play the Bandon Trails course, designed by Coore & Crenshaw. Stay at the Bandon Dunes Resort.

Day 3 – Play the Bandon Dunes course, designed by Kidd.

TRIP 9 –

County Louth GC/Royal Dornoch/Brora GC/Nairn GC/Cabot Highlands/ Royal Aberdeen GC/Fraserburgh GC/Cruden Bay GC/Trump Aberdeen (June 2025 - to catch the last of the gorse bloom)

Self-Organized. (Courses and hotels can be booked directly online approximately one year in advance. Hotels will arrange for taxis.)

Day 1 – Fly from San Francisco direct to Dublin via Aer Lingus.

Day 2 – Arrive in Dublin. Short walk to check in at the Radisson Blu Airport Hotel, then take a short bus ride to visit Dublin.

Day 3 – Take a 45-minute taxi to play County Louth, designed by Simpson (or the European Club, designed by Ruddy). Stay at the Radisson Blu Airport Hotel.

Day 4 – Fly Aer Lingus to Inverness, then take a one-hour taxi to Dornoch. Stay at the Links House Hotel (or the new Marine Hotel).

Day 5 – Play Royal Dornoch, designed by Old Tom Morris. Stay at the Links House Hotel.

Day 6 – Take a short taxi to visit Dunrobin Castle, then play nearby Brora Links, designed by Braid (buggies permitted). Stay at the Links House Hotel.

Day 7 – Take 1-hour 15-minute taxi to Nairn. Visit nearby Cawdor Castle and/or Brodie Castle. Stay at the Golf View Hotel.

Day 8 – Play Nairn Golf Club (buggies permitted), then visit the town of Nairn. Stay at the Golf View Hotel.

Day 9 – Play nearby Cabot Highlands (next to Castle Stuart links) - a Doak design opening in 2024. Stay at the Golf View Hotel.

Day 10 – Take a two-hour taxi to Aberdeen. Check in at the Malmaison Hotel, then a 10-minute taxi to play Royal Aberdeen.

Day 11 – Rest day. Visit Balmoral Castle and/or Fraser Castle, then visit the city of Aberdeen. Stay at the Malmaison Hotel.

Day 12 – Take a 50-minute taxi to play Fraserburgh (buggies permitted). Stay at the Malmaison Hotel.

Day 13 – Take a 30-minute taxi to play Cruden Bay. Stay at the Malmaison Hotel.

Day 14 – Take a 15-minute taxi to play Trump International Aberdeen. Stay at the Malmaison Hotel.

Day 15 – Fly from Aberdeen to San Francisco (transfer in London) via British Airways.

TRIP 10 –

Sunningdale GC/Royal St. George's GC/St. Enodoc GC (August 2026 to catch heather bloom)

(Self-organized a la previous trips.)

Day 1 – Fly direct on United from San Francisco to London Heathrow.

Day 2 – Arrive at 11:00 AM and take a 10-minute taxi to Ascot. Stay at the MacDonald Berystede, which is 1.3 miles from the train station. Take a Thames boat tour from Windsor Promenade.

Day 3 – Take a train to London for a double-decker bus tour and a play. Stay at the MacDonald Berystede.

Day 4 – Play Sunningdale (Park) or Swinley Forest (Colt). Stay at the MacDonald Berystede.

Day 5 – Take a 45-minute taxi to St. Pancras International train station, then 1-hour 30-minute train to Sandwich. Visit Deal and White Cliffs of Dover. Stay at the Bell Hotel.

Day 6 – Play Royal St. George's, then take a one-hour train to visit Canterbury. Stay at the Bell Hotel.

Day 7 - Take a 1-hour 30-minute train to visit the seaside town of Rye. Stay at the Mermaid Inn.

Day 8 – Short day trip by train to Hastings to visit town/Norman invasion battlefield & museum. Stay at the Mermaid Inn.

Day 9 – Take a 1-hour 30-minute taxi to Paddington Station and then 1-hour direct train to Oxford. Visit town/university. Stay at the George Street Hotel.

Day 10 – Take a 30-minute train to Moreton-in-Marsh (Cotswolds town) and take a minibus tour of Cotswolds. Stay at the George Street Hotel.

Day 11 – Take a 1-hour 30-minute train to Stratford-upon-Avon (Shakespeare). Stay at the George Street Hotel.

Day 12 – Take a 1-hour 30-minute train to Ascot. Play St. George's Hill, designed by Colt IF couldn't get on either Sunningdale or Swinley the previous Tuesday. Otherwise, visit nearby Hampton Court Palace. Stay at the Royal Berkshire Hotel.

Day 13 – Short train to London to visit Abbey Road studio/Sherlock Holmes Baker Street museum/Charles Dickens home. Stay at the Royal Berkshire Hotel.

Day 14 – Take a 2-hour train to Portsmouth to tour Admiral Nelson's HMS Victory. Stay at the Royal Berkshire Hotel.

Day 15 – Take a 1-hour 30-minute train/short taxi connection to Highclere Castle (Downton Abbey). Stay at the Royal Berkshire Hotel.

Day 16 – Take a 4-hour train to St. Enodoc (change at Reading). Dinner across the inlet at Pastaw fishing village and dine at Rick Stein's fish restaurant. Stay at the St. Enodoc Hotel.

Day 17 – Play St. Enodoc, designed by Braid. Stay at the St. Enodoc Hotel.

Day 18 – Take a 3-hour 30-minute train to Reading. Stay at the Malmaison Hotel, a two-minute walk from the station.

Day 19 – Take a 30-minute taxi to the airport and fly home to San Francisco.

TRIP 11 –
Crail GS/Old Course St. Andrews L/Kingsbarns GL/Muirfield/Gullane GC/North Berwick GC (June 2027)

Arrange through Perry Golf Travel since they have guaranteed tee time privileges at the extremely difficult-to-get-on Old Course and Muirfield. Stay at the Bonnie Badger in Gullane and Rusack's in St. Andrews.

Is That All There Is?

By the time I complete the above-referenced future trips (in the next five years or so, God willing), I will be about 70 years old, having completed my lifetime journey to many of the greatest golf courses in Great Britain, Ireland and the USA. I will then be more than content to play out my final rounds on my home course. However, if I met a leprechaun who said he would grant me three golf course play wishes, I would choose Augusta National Golf Club, National Golf Links of America and The Country Club in Brookline. (If, because of our shared Irish heritage, he tossed in a few bonus wishes, I would go with Oak Hill Country Club, Shinnecock Hills Golf Club and Winged Foot Golf Club. And, if yet another bonus wish was thrown in because our introduction occurred on St. Patrick's Day, I would choose Jack Nicklaus' Muirfield Village Golf Club - but only if the United States Air Force is called in first to drop pesticide to ward off the incessant chant of the cicada bugs - though I could probably overlook having my round bugged if offered an unlimited number of the club's famous milkshakes.) Since a serendipitous encounter of this nature is highly unlikely, I will, in the alternative, make the following offer to any members of these noble clubs - Have me as a guest at your club, and I will see what I can do about getting you on at mine!

LESSONS LEARNED FROM GOLF THAT CAN ALSO KEEP YOU IN THE FAIRWAY OF LIFE (14 "CLUBS," AND A RELIABLE "BAG" TO HOLD THEM IN PLACE)

The 14 Clubs:

1. **Get a Few Professional Lessons.** Do this *before* you jump into the deep waters of golf, or at least refer to a few quality instruction books or videos to establish a good grip, set-up, and knowledge of situational shot-making. Otherwise, you are just reinforcing the same bad habits hour after hour on the range and course. In short, do your homework before taking on a difficult task. If you have no desire for professional lessons or instruction books/videos, then here is a convenient list of my ten favorite reminders/stroke savers:

    A. Grip the club in the left hand diagonally across the finger pads (rather than in the palm) with two and a half knuckles in view and the "V" between the index finger and thumb on the top of both hands, roughly facing your right shoulder. Note that the more knuckles you see, the more prone you will be to hitting a draw/hook, and the fewer knuckles you see will encourage a fade/slice.

    B. Err on the side of using more club than less. Too many people either let their ego get in the way (they don't want to use a longer club than their playing partners) or choose their club based on where it will go if they hit their absolute best golf shot vs. their typical one. Ask the pros who play in the Pro-Ams to identify the biggest mistake they see among their amateur partners, and they will say: "Not using enough club."

C. Bad slicers should not aim further left. You continue to lose valuable yardage. Aim at the target. Close your stance a little, rather than opening it wide, and don't swing over the top and too quickly from the apex of the backswing. Finish the swing (club around your left shoulder, with your belt buckle facing the target at completion). (See also "A." above, as the slice could be the result of an improper (too weak) grip.)

D. Avoid massive body sway in the swing (e.g., reverse pivot) and keep your head relatively level throughout the swing (e.g., to avoid pulling up).

E. Golf is a game of opposites. For example, you have to hit down on the ball to make it go up. Don't try to help it up or you will often hit it fat ("chili dip" it). Let the loft of the club do the work. Think about hitting down on the back of the ball and taking a divot *after* contact, *not* before.

F. If you miss a putt, it is better to miss on the high side ("pro side") rather than the low side. Low-side aim is all or nothing. High-side aim allows the ball to drop in from the front, side or back of the cup.

G. On pitches and chips, don't take a big backswing and then decelerate toward impact out of fear of hitting it too far. Instead, accelerate through impact (a shorter backswing will encourage this) with the belt buckle facing the target at the finish. Also, on chips, take a narrow, slightly open stance with 60-70% of your body weight on the left side, playing the ball off the front of the back (right) foot. And, keep your wrists firm rather than flicking them. This will encourage descending contact on the ball, resulting in the necessary ball flight without any other "help."

H. From a normal lie in a greenside bunker, open the clubface a bit, grip down a couple of inches, open and widen your stance with the ball behind the front (left) foot, crouch down and wiggle your feet into the sand for a firm base, aim a couple inches behind the ball, then swing down the stance line removing a cushion of sand (i.e., no ball contact), finishing high rather than stabbing hard at the sand/ball and leaving the club (and the ball!) in the sand.

- I. From a normal lie in a fairway bunker, play the ball in the middle of your stance and avoid hitting the sand before the ball (i.e., pick it off the sand) by aiming at the front part of the ball and limiting lower body movement. (Offset the resulting decrease in distance by using more club.)
- J. In general, hit the driver with the ball aligned with the back heel of the front foot and then move the ball back a little further in the stance with each subsequent club in the bag, leaving the wedges somewhere towards the middle of the stance. Note that angling the feet in a slight duck-foot fashion at address encourages balance and a fuller turn.

2. **Practice. Practice. Practice.** Few good things in golf and life come easy. As Gary Player said: "The more I practice, the luckier I get." If you don't like driving ranges, simply "practice" by playing more. (I frequently show up at the course an hour or so before darkness and easily squeeze in nine holes as few other golfers are on the course at this time.) If you find that the range better suits your schedule or desired focus, avoid hitting off mats, if possible. That is, a natural turf driving range should be the preferred venue. Otherwise, you will develop a false sense of security - as it is hard to hit a fat shot off a hard mat. At my home course, we have both options, and I am amazed at how many more people opt for the artificial surface - most likely because they don't want to bother making the 250-yard trip to the other end of the range, where an excellent grass facility sits.

3. **Lighten Up!** The game's intent is fun, not agony. Keep the whining to a minimum. Soak in the fresh air, exercise, and camaraderie, and move on to the next shot (or even the next day if the entire round is terrible). I am reminded of this philosophy whenever I

play with my son-in-law, Dan. Upon entering the house after we finish a round, it is hard for family and friends to guess whether he played great or poorly. This reflects good character. You may have read or heard of the following quote by the great 20th century sports writer Grantland Rice: "Eighteen holes of match play will teach you more about your foe or partner than 18 years of dealing with him across a desk." This observation certainly held true concerning my initial and subsequent rounds with Dan. The calm demeanor, integrity and respect he had demonstrated on the course made it a no-brainer decision when he was thoughtful enough to ask me (on a golf course) for permission to marry my beloved daughter.

4. **Play by the Rules**. Yes, technically, we should never deviate from the official USGA rules book. But, unlike the pros, we often don't have the time to warm up for an hour (or even five minutes), and at most public courses, there are many large, unrepaired divots. As such, in some informal competitions among friends (but never in formal contests or tournaments), a best of two drives off the first tee, removal of the ball from an unrepaired divot, or "gimmies" inside the leather, is agreed upon. However, unless this type of limited, upfront arrangement is made among friends or an exception is made by a local rule of the club, do not deviate from the USGA rules. Otherwise, you risk losing trust, respect, and in some cases, even friendships.

5. **Don't Take Yourself Too Seriously**. Unless you are a professional, you are not that good, and there is always somebody better. (Unless your name is Jack Nicklaus!) There is nothing worse than seeing a 24- handicapper throwing tantrums - and clubs! And, play from tees commensurate with your actual handicap, not what you think it could be "If only…" Being able to drive the ball 300 yards (albeit frequently in the woods) does not always equate to playing from the back tees. Irrespective of which tees you choose to play

from, don't hold up others in your group or those behind you. Do unto others…

6. **Root for Your Opponent to Play Their Best** and for you to do the same that day. If you win (whether with handicap strokes or not), so be it. But, if you lose, remember the old adage to be humble in victory and gracious in defeat. (As prime examples of class, recall the "concession" by Jack Nicklaus of Tony Jacklin's short final putt at the Ryder Cup that resulted in a tie for the two teams or Jack's arm around the shoulder of Tom Watson after Tom had just beaten him by a stroke to claim the Claret Jug at the 1977 British Open in golf's greatest major battle ever - the "Dual in the Sun" at Turnberry.) Family "rivalries" can be the worst. But, they can be the best if played in a spirit of healthy competition. One of the most memorable moments of my life (not just in golf) was a long, firm embrace with my son, sharing the humble pride and joy he had after beating his dad for the first time.

7. **Do Not Engage in Gamesmanship!** Friendly banter, yes, but not intentional attempts to disrupt a shot about to be played or in motion. As much as I admired the talents of Seve Ballesteros, I have read many stories about things such as his sudden "need" to clear his throat in the middle of his opponent's putt. As another example, I once was invited to play with two other guests at the private club of someone I'd never met . He was a justifiably proud three-time club champion. Having never played the course, I was performing surprisingly well. On the 17th hole, I was leading by a stroke, and just as I was teeing up my ball, the host offered some "local knowledge." Namely, this seemingly innocent par-3 was one of the most sneaky difficult holes on the course and famous for ruining a player's round. I scored a bogey, and he managed par. So, all tied on the tee box at 18. I needed to sink a downhill curling 10-footer for the win. I was inwardly pleased when it dropped in.

8. **Know Your Limitations**. Sure, everyone wants to improve their game and see how low they can get their handicap, or shoot their

all-time low score. But, at a certain point, enough is enough. For me, it was realizing, after several years of playing a lot during retirement, that my handicap had almost certainly bottomed out. And, that was a good thing. I could relax more and set reasonable goals - like breaking 80 that day. And, if not, there would always be tomorrow. Ultimately, who cares whether your handicap is an 8 (vs. 6) or a 30 (vs. 25). It is a game for goodness sake.

9. **Lower Your Expectations When Playing New Courses.** Shooting five strokes over your customary average is to be expected, especially if you are playing amid the vagaries of links courses. In other words, don't set yourself up for "failure."

10. **Beware of Falling for the Promises of the Latest, Greatest (and Expensive) Equipment.** As with anything else in life, there are few silver bullets. Changing out your equipment every ten years or so is fine for most of us.

11. **Observe and Compliment Your Playing Partners' Accomplishments.** It's not all about you. One of my favorite things is telling someone their shot or putt will make the early edition of the ESPN highlights that night. It always elicits a proud smile. I also enjoy giving them nicknames associated with their name, place of origin or playing style after they hit a beautiful tee shot. I begin with: "THAT'S why they call him..." (and then fill in the blank): "The Buffalo Bomber," "The Sligo Slammer," "The Man With the Southern Draw," "The Drill Bit."

12. **Involve Your Spouse.** If your spouse is a golfer, enjoy a round together whenever possible. (But, do not spend the whole time giving "lessons.") My wife and I do almost everything together, but she does not enjoy playing golf. However, she loves the outdoors and walking - listening to music, books, lectures, etc., on her earpods. So, she often does so while joining me for nine holes. It's great fun having my best friend nearby (and hearing a clap after a birdie or crazy good shot when I didn't even know she was looking).

13. **Don't Offer Unsolicited Advice.** Listening to a 30 handicapper giving constant tips to a 26-36 handicapper is painful. At the same time, helping a person whose game you know well when you see bad habits creeping back in is another sign of good sportsmanship - IF there is a cry for help. As a former elementary school basketball coach of my son's and daughter's teams, I get immense pleasure in being able to help an athlete achieve their potential. As such, I am always thrilled, for example, to observe the joy I see when I can successfully offer a frustrated high handicapper a simple fix for a particular problem that they are seeking to overcome.

14. **Don't Let the Yips Get You Down.** (And you thought I forgot!) In the Preface, I promised to share how I finally came to terms with the off-and-on nightmare of the yips. The bottom line is the need to take the right wrist entirely out of the equation and concentrate on gently rocking the shoulders without moving the head and other body parts. But, how do you control an involuntary jerking of that wrist? Some find they can eliminate the problem with a heavier mallet putter and/or one with a fatter grip. Others address the issue with an arm-lock and/or left-hand low grip. Still others resort to the so-called "claw" hand position. But, what happens when you have tried these fixes and, after working quite well for a while, the yips and the accompanying mental demons suddenly return? The answer? Drum roll, please. Incorporate ALL of them! The thought occurred to me that such a combination would lock that wrist in better than a golf nut in a straight-jacket. Specifically, I inserted a large-size Arm-Lock brand grip on my trusty old Odyssey White Hot Rossie brand mallet putter (with a few lead weight strips on the back to counterbalance the heavier large-size grip), stuck with my left-hand low grip (with the left index finger pointing down the left side of the shaft), and placed my right hand in a moderately angled claw grip position. I know what you are thinking: Overload! Overload! No feel! No feel! But don't give up. You will get used to it. And, in any event, a little less physical

feel will be more than offset by the peace of mind that comes with bombing the yips back to the stone age! (P.S. For really long putts or ones from off the green, I drop the claw grip component without yipping. For most people, the yips are almost always limited to short and medium-short putts.) It's a good idea, whether in golf or life in general, to have "Plan B's." If you suffer from the yips now or sometime in the future, I hope this yip tip gives you an alternative to continued putter's hell.

The Golf Bag – Everyone needs a dependable bag to hold and protect the principles of dedication and altruism reflected in the above-referenced 14 clubs. A bag that will help you to weather all kinds of storms so your clubs can achieve their full potential. For me, that is a higher power that goes by the name of God.

Greywalls Hotel Overlooking Muirfield GC

APPENDIX I

List of All Courses Played by Location According to Star Rating (in alphabetical order) Plus Architect

IRELAND

Carne GL/Hackett & Engh & McIntosh/5.0

Doonbeg/Norman/5.0

Lahinch GC/Old Tom Morris & MacKenzie/5.0

Royal County Down GC/Old Tom Morris & Vardon & Colt/5.0

Ardglass GC/Misc./4.5

Druids Glen/Ruddy/4.5

Enniscrone GC/Hackett/4.5

(The) Island Club/Hackett/4.5

Portsalon/C. Thompson/4.5

Adare Manor Golf Club (Abbey Course)/Hackett/4.0

Adare Golf Club (Manor Course)/Jones Sr. & T. Fazio/4.0

Ballybunion GC (Old Course)/ Misc. Members & Simpson/4.0

Corballis L/Kirby/4.0

Donegal (Murvagh)/GC/Hackett/4.0

Dooks GL/Hackett/4.0

Dromoland Castle/Kirby & JB Carr/4.0

Old Head GL/Misc./4.0

Portstewart GC/Giffin/4.0

Royal Portrush/Colt/4.0

Rosapenna (Old Tom Morris L)/Old Tom & Ruddy/4.0

(County)Sligo/Colt/4.0

Ashford Castle/Hackett/3.5

Ballybunion GC (Cashen Course)/Jones Sr./3.5

(The) K Club/Palmer/3.5

Portmarnock GC/Pickeman/3.5

Portmarnock (Hotel) L/Langer/3.5

Rosapenna (Sandy Hills L)/Ruddy/3.5

Strand Hill GC/McAlister & Hackett/3.5

Tralee GL/Palmer/3.5

SCOTLAND

(St.) Andrews Links (Old Course)/God & Old Tom Morris/5.0+

Cruden Bay GC/Old Tom Morris & Fowler & Simpson/5.0

Gleneagles GC (King's Course)/Braid/5.0

North Berwick GC (West Course)/Strath/5.0

Prestwick GC/Old Tom Morris/5.0

Royal Dornoch/Old Tom Morris/5.0

Turnberry/Fernie/5.0

Carnoustie GL/Old Tom Morris & Braid/4.5

Kingsbarns GL/Steele/4.5

Machrihanish Dunes GC/Kidd/4.5

North Berwick (The Glen Club)/Sayers & Braid/4.5

Castle Stuart/Hanse/4.0

Elie (The Golf House Club)/Old Tom Morris/4.0

Gleneagles GC (Queen's Course)/Braid/4.0

Machrihanish GC/Old Tom Morris/4.0

Musselburgh Links/Unknown/4.0

Panmure GC/Braid/4.0

Royal Troon/Braid/4.0

St. Andrews Links (New Course)/Old Tom Morris/4.0

MEXICO

Cancun Hilton (Now Iberostar)/Dye Jr./4.0

USA

Arizona

Sedona Resort/Panks/4.0

Troon North GC (Pinnacle Course)/Weiskopf & Moorish/ 4.0

We Ko Pa GC/ Coore & Crenshaw/4.0

TPC Scottsdale/Weiskopf & Moorish/3.5

Phantom Horse GC/Richardson/3.5

Tucson CC/W.P. Bell/3.0

California

Pebble Beach Links/Neville & Grant/5.0+

Cypress Point Club/MacKenzie/5.0

Burlingame CC/Jones Sr./4.5

Half Moon Bay GL (Ocean Course)/Hills/4.5

Northwood GC/MacKenzie/4.5

Olympic Club (Lake)/Whiting & W. Watson/4.5

Arrowhead CC/W.P. Bell/4.0

Baylands GL/W.F. Bell & Richardson/4.0

Dragonfly GC/Baird/4.0

Harding Park (TPC) GC/Whiting & W. Watson & Fleming/4.0

Lake Merced GC/W. Locke & MacKenzie/4.0

Lincoln Park GC/Fleming/ 4.0

Monterey Peninsula CC (Shore Course)/ Neville & Strantz/4.0

Oakmont GC (Sugarloaf Course)/Robinson/4.0

Olympic Club (Ocean) /Whiting & W. Watson/4.0

Olympic Club (Cliffs) Course/Weiskopf & Moorish/4.0

Pacific Grove Muni GL/Neville/4.0

Pasatiempo GC/MacKenzie/4.0

Poplar Creek GC/Misc./4.0

Presidio GC/Johnstone & Tillinghast/4.0

Peninsula CC/Ross/4.0

San Francisco GC/Tillinghast/4.0

Schaffer's Mill/Miller & Harbottle/4.0

Sharp Park GC/MacKenzie/4.0

Spanish Bay (Links At)/Tatum & T. Watson & R.T. Jones Jr./4.0

Stanford U/Thomas & W.P. Bell/4.0

Torrey Pines (North & South)/W.P. Bell & W.F. Bell/4.0

Yocha Dehe GC/Brad Bell/4.0

Bayonet GC/McClure & Bates/3.5

Berkeley CC/Hunter & W. Watson/3.5

Bodega Harbour GL/Jones Jr./3.5

California Golf Club/MacKenzie/3.5

Carmel Valley Ranch/Dye/3.5

Chardonnay GC/Pulley/3.5

Cinnabar Hills GC/Harbottle/3.5

Claremont CC/MacKenzie/3.5

Crystal Springs GC/Fowler/3.5

Delta View GC/MacKenzie & Fleming/3.5 (Closed)

Del Paso CC/Black & Phillips/3.5

Eagle Vines GC/Miller/3.5

Eldorado CC/Hughes/3.5

Fleming Course at Harding Park/Fleming/3.5

Fountaingrove CC/Robinson/3.5

Foxtail GC (North Course/Baird/3.5

Gleneagles GC/Fleming/3.5

Golden Gate Park/Fleming/3.5

Green Hills CC/MacKenzie/3.5

Haggin Oaks/MacKenzie/3.5

Half Moon Bay GL (Old Course)/Palmer/3.5

Hiddenbrooke GC/Palmer/3.5

Incline Village/Jones Sr./3.5

Marin CC/Hughes & Harbottle/3.5

Mariners Point GL/Cupp & Fought/3.5

Mayakama/Nicklaus/3.5

Mt. Shasta Resort/Tatum & Summers/3.5

Napa CC/Fream/3.5

Oak Creek GC/Fazio/3.5

Oakmont GC (Valley of the Moon)/Robinson/3.5

Oak Quarry GC/Morgan/3.5

Old Greenwood/Nicklaus/3.5

Orinda CC/W. Watson/3.5

Poppy Hills/R.T.Jones Jr./3.5

Poppy Ridge/Rees Jones/3.5

Redlands CC/MacKenzie/3.5

Saddle Creek Resort/C. Moorish/3.5

San Jose Muni GC/Graves/3.5

San Juan Oaks GC/Couples/3.5

Santa Rosa CC/Fleming/3.5

Seascape GC/Gill Bros./3.5

Silverado (South Course)/Miller/3.5

Stockton CC/Whiting/3.5

Temecula Creek GC/Robinson & Rossen/3.5

Victoria Club/W.P. Bell/3.5

Wente Vineyards/Norman/3.5

Wild Hawk GC/Costello & Moore/3.5

Adobe Creek GC/R.T.Jones Jr./3.0 (Closed)

Aetna Springs GC/Doak/3.0

Bennett Valley GC/Harmon/3.0

Blackhawk CC/Devlin/3.0

Boundary Oak GC/Graves/3.0

Coronado Muni GC/W.F. Bell/3.0

Costa Mesa CC/W.F. Bell/3.0

Coyote Creek GC/Nicklaus/3.0

Cyprus GC/Fleming/3.0

Deep Cliff GC/Glasson/3.0

Del Monte GC/Maud/3.0

Franklin Canyon GC/Graves/3.0

Healdsburg GC/Tayman & MacKenzie/3.0

Hidden Valley Lake CC/W.F. Bell/3.0

Indian Valley GC/Nyberg/3.0

La Quinta Resort (Mountain Course)/Pete Dye/3.0

Little River Inn GC/Hervilla/3.0

Mare Island GC/Nelson/3.0 (Closed)

Mill ValleyGC/Clark/3.0

Monarch Bay GC (Lema Course)/W.F. Bell & Harbottle/3.0

Napa Muni GC/Fleming/3.0

Oak Valley GC/Schmidt & Curley/3.0

Pala Mesa/Rossen/3.0

Paradise Valley GC/Graves/3.0

Peacock Gap GC/W.F. Bell/3.0

PGA Southern CA (Champions Course)/Schmidt & Curley/3.0

Pruneridge GC/Jones Jr./3.0

Rooster Run GC/Bliss/3.0

San Geronimo GC/Graves/3.0

Santa Teresa GC/Santana/3.0

Sea Ranch GL/Graves/3.0

Shoreline GL/Jones Jr./3.0

Skywest GC/Baldock/3.0 (Closed)

Sonoma County Fairgrounds GC/Unknown/3.0

Stonetree GC/Tatum & Summers/3.0

Sunnyvale GC/Glasson/3.0

Tilden Park GC/W.P. Bell/3.0

Vintner's GC/O'Callahan/3.0

Willow Park GC/Baldock/3.0

Windsor GC/Bliss/3.0

Monterey Pines GC/Graves/2.5

Buchanan Fields GC/Graves/2.5

Rancho Solano GC/Baird/2.5

Shelter Cove GL/Hughs/2.5

Spring Valley GC/Anderson/2.5

McGinnis Park/Bliss/2.0

Foxtail GC (South Course)/Baldock/2.0

Pleasant Hill/Unknown/2.0 (Closed)

Colorado

Ballyneal/Doak/4.0

Broadmoor (West Course)/Ross & Jones Sr./3.0

Interlocken GC/Graham & Panks/3.0

Florida

(The) Breakers (Ocean Course)/Findlay, Ross & Rees Jones/4.0

San Jose CC/Ross/4.0

Temecuanna CC/Ross/3.5

Hyde Park GC/Ross/3.0

Pablo Creek C/T. Fazio/3.0

South Hampton GC/McCumber/3.0

TPC Sawgrass/Dye/2.5

West Palm Beach Muni/Unknown/2.5 (Closed 2018/Reopened 2023)

Hawaii

Mauna Lani (South Course)/Nelson & Haworth/5.0

Kaanapali Resort (South Course)/ R.T. Jones Sr./3.5

Princeville Resort (Makai Course)/R.T. Jones Jr./3.0

Indiana

Notre Dame (Burke Course)/Kelly/3.5 (Reduced to 9 holes)

Notre Dame (Warren Course)/Coore & Crenshaw/3.5

Louisiana

GC of New Orleans at Eastover/Lee & Roquemore/3.0

Maryland

Congressional CC (Gold Course)/Emmet, Fazios & Hills/3.5

Marlborough GC/Pulley/3.0

Nevada

LakeRidge/Jones Sr./4.0

Angel Park GC/Palmer/3.5

Red Hawk GC (Lakes Course)/R.T. Jones Jr./3.5

Royal Links GC/Dye Jr./3.5 (Closed)

Wild Creek/Benz/3.5 (Reduced to 9 hole Executive course)

North Carolina

Mid Pines GC/Ross/4.5

Pinehurst (No.3 Course)/Ross/4.0

Asheville GC/Ross/3.5

Duke University GC/Jones Sr./3.5

Grove Park Inn/Ross/3.5

Pinehurst (Cradle Course)/Hanse/3.5

Wolf Laurel CC/Lewis/3.5

Ohio

Brookside CC/Ross/4.0

Glenmoor CC/Nicklaus/4.0

Arrowhead/Unknown/3.5

Clearview GC/Powell/3.5

Congress Lake CC/Ross/3.5

Edgewood/Huntley/3.5

Legends/J. Robinson/3.5

Shady Hollow CC/Mitchell & Force & Huntley/3.5

Tam O'Shanter GC (Hills & Dales Courses)/Paul & Macomber/3.5 (Closed)

Westfield/Cornish/3.5

Wilkshire GC/Easterday/3.5

Chippewa/Harrison & Garbin/3.0

Elms CC/Rottman/3.0

Lyons Den GC/Lyons/3.0

Mayfair/ CCUnknown/3.0

Riceland GC/Unknown/3.0

Sanctuary GC/Huntley/3.0

Zoar GC/Cornish/3.0

Twin Lakes GC/Alves/2.5

Meadows/Staub/2.0 (Closed)

Oregon

Bandon Dunes (Dunes Course)/Kidd/5.0

Bandon Dunes (Pacific Dunes Course)/Doak/5.0

Bandon Dunes (Preserve Course)/Coore & Crenshaw/5.0

Bandon Dunes (Sheep Ranch)/Coore & Crenshaw/4.0

South Carolina

Cobblestone Park GC/Dye Jr./4.0

Palmetto GC/MacKenzie/3.5

Virginia

Greenbrier (The Meadows Course)/Cupp/3.5

Washington DC

East Potomac Park GC/Travis/3.5

West Virginia

Cascades Golf Club/Flynn/3.5

Wisconsin

Erin Hills/Hurdzan & Fry & Whitten/4.5

Whistling Straits/Pete Dye/4.0

APPENDIX II

A Par 72 Dream Course Consisting of the Best 18 Holes From the Best Courses Played List

Hole 1 – Doonbeg Par-5 1st

Hole 2 – Ardglass Par-4 1st

Hole 3 – Bandon Dunes (Pacific Dunes Course) Par-4 4th

Hole 4 – Pebble Beach Par-3 7th

Hole 5 – North Berwick Par-4 13th

Hole 6 – Pebble Beach Par-5 18th

Hole 7 – Old Head Par-4 4th

Hole 8 – Royal County Down Par-4 9th

Hole 9 – Druids Glen Par-3 12th

Hole 10 – Adare Manor Resort – Par- 5 18th

Hole 11 – Mauna Lani Par-4 14th

Hole 12 – Ballybunion Par-4 17th

Hole 13 – Turnberry Par-3 9th

Hole 14 – TPC Scottsdale Par-5 15th

Hole 15 – Carne Par-4 11th

Hole 16 – Machrihanish Dunes Par-4 4th

Hole 17 – Cypress Point Par-3 16th

Hole 18 – St. Andrews Par-4 18th

APPENDIX III

A Par 27 Dream Short Course Consisting of the 9 Best Par-3s From the Best Courses Played List

Hole 1 - Cypress Point 16th

Hole 2 - Pebble Beach 7th

Hole 3 - Druids Glen 12th

Hole 4 - LakeRidge 15th

Hole 5 - Dromoland Castle 7th

Hole 6 - Mauna Lani 15th

Hole 7 - Turnberry 9th

Hole 8 - Royal Troon 8th

Hole 9 - Lahinch 5th

APPENDIX IV

The Hidden Gems List

Elsewhere in this book, I have referenced some courses I consider "Hidden Gems." Several remain almost entirely hidden in the rough, and others are partially obscured, near the fairway of notoriety. A few will never make it anywhere near the top echelons referenced in popular golf magazines and books. But, all meet most of my criteria, outlined in Chapter III, for what qualifies a course for placement among the "Best." (The ultimate factor being fun!) I would go so far as to say that one could play only these Hidden Gems and still experience a well-rounded, relatively inexpensive, and thoroughly enjoyable golf life. And, so, these (all public access) are listed together here to facilitate keeping them on the reader's golf planning radar.

Cruden Bay GC (Scotland)
The Glen Club-North Berwick (Scotland)
Machrihanish Dunes GC (Scotland)
Adare Manor GC-Abbey Course (Ireland)
Ardglass GC (Northern Ireland)
Carne GL (Ireland)
Corballis GC (Ireland)
Dooks GL (Ireland)
Enniscrone GC (Ireland)
Portsalon GC (Ireland)
Rosapenna - Old Tom Morris Course (Ireland)
Sharp Park GC (SF Bay Area, USA)
Lincoln Park GC (SF Bay Area, USA)
Northwood GC (SF Bay Area, USA)
Pacific Grove GL (Monterey Bay Area, USA)
East Potomac Park GC (Washington, D.C. USA)
Asheville Muni Golf Course (NC Mountain Area, USA)
Arrowhead CC (Southern CA, USA)

Honorable Mention

Sonoma County Fairgrounds GC (Santa Rosa, CA USA) - This par 29, nine hole tract is situated entirely within the fairgrounds racetrack. It is a quirky, fun, smaller version of Musselburgh's Old Links Course (which also consists of nine holes inside a racetrack). Like Musselburgh, it is the perfect place to bring the hickory clubs and/or work on the short game, or squeeze in a quick emergency nine. With an average hole length of 167 yards, it is not a pitch and putt course. Greens are small and well-contoured. The bunkers present ample challenges. The overall condition of the layout is very good for a muni. If they added some revetted bunkers, it could be taken to the next level as a Musselburgh-like experience for those unwilling or unable to travel to Scotland. There also is an excellent practice facility on site.

ACKNOWLEDGMENTS

It was easy to remember who to include on this page as the persons to be acknowledged are "All in the Family." Each contributed a unique adroitness to the cause. Endless thanks to: Brother Bruce, a retired sports editor, who contributed seemingly effortless editorial skill; Brother Jerry, for the patient use of his artistic talents as I experimented with various sketch ideas; my dear wife, Kathy, for her willingness to do a watercolor that was outside her comfort zone, and to serve as a sounding board for countless proposed stories and stylistic expressions; Daughter-in-law Sara and son-in-law Dan, for sharing their incredible formatting talents; Son Brian, for his respectful nudges to add a little panache here or a tweak there to make things more interesting and/or clear; and daughter Michelle, for her constant encouragement and support - like an outstanding elementary school teacher - which she happens to be. It was amazing how often I knew modifications were needed in various places and this family team would pinpoint the same, confirming my instincts and helping me address them. And last, a shout out to "The Grid" - Brian's cadre of golf-addicted friends who begged for a work of this nature.

ABOUT THE AUTHOR

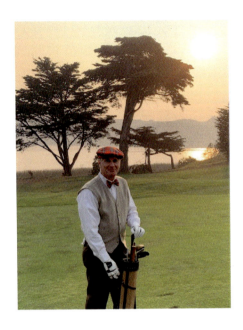

Jack M. Hammel grew up in the small, one-time major steel town of Massillon, Ohio. After graduating Summa Cum Laude from Kent State University with a major in Political Science, he attended the University of Notre Dame, where he received his law degree. For virtually all of his legal career, he served as General Counsel for the Archdiocese of San Francisco. Retired, he lives in California's Sonoma Valley in Oakmont Village, where, as a mid-range single-digit handicapper, he regularly plays golf at its two courses, Valley of the Moon and Sugarloaf. Jack and his wife, Kathy, are the proud parents of two children and grandparents of three.